QUEER THEORY

QUEER THEORY

The French Response

BRUNO PERREAU

STANFORD UNIVERSITY PRESS • STANFORD, CALIFORNIA

Stanford University Press
Stanford, California

Printed in the United States of America on acid-free, archival-quality paper

Library of Congress Cataloging-in-Publication Data

Names: Perreau, Bruno, author.
Title: Queer theory : the French response / Bruno Perreau.
Description: Stanford, California : Stanford University Press, 2016. |
   Includes bibliographical references and index. | Description based on
   print version record and CIP data provided by publisher; resource not
   viewed.
Identifiers: LCCN 2016021434 (print) | LCCN 2016020134 (ebook) |
   ISBN 9781503600461 (electronic) | ISBN 9780804798860 (cloth : alk. paper) |
   ISBN 9781503600447 (pbk. : alk. paper)
Subjects: LCSH: Queer theory—France. | Homosexuality—Political
   aspects—France. | Same-sex marriage—Political aspects—France. | Group
   identity—Political aspects—France. | Nationalism—France.
Classification: LCC HQ76.3.F8 (print) | LCC HQ76.3.F8 P47 2016 (ebook) | DDC
   306.7601—dc23
LC record available at https://lccn.loc.gov/2016021434

Typeset by Bruce Lundquist in 10/14 Minion Pro

CONTENTS

Acknowledgments   vii

Introduction   1

1 Who's Afraid of "Gender Theory"?   17

2 The Many Meanings of Queer   75

3 Transatlantic Homecomings   113

4 The Specter of Queer Politics   145

   Conclusion   183

   Notes   191

   Index   243

ACKNOWLEDGMENTS

This book is a direct response to the many questions I was asked by my American friends and colleagues about public demonstrations against the so-called marriage for all law in France. Its roots nevertheless extend further back, to the days when I was a young scholar in political science at the Sorbonne, carrying out my early research into how legal theory was being used to further a reactionary agenda. Several leading intellectuals such as jurist Pierre Legendre had condemned the idea of civil union in very harsh terms—they were predicting the end of civilization and a return to barbarity, so concerned were they to preserve a timeless anthropological order inscribed in the law. Their protests greatly influenced political decision making, for example, elimination of joint parental status for homosexual couples from the new law. Thus, right before my eyes, just as I was beginning my academic career, I had a striking example of the political impact of theory—or, more exactly, of the idea of theory. In addition, from 1999 to 2004 I had followed a seminar on "The Sociology of Homosexualities" run by Françoise Gaspard and Didier Eribon at the École des Hautes Études en Sciences Sociales (EHESS). This seminar was one of the main places where queer theory was being discussed in France. The course not only sparked concern on the part of EHESS management, but its legitimacy was even challenged in the Assemblée Nationale. I was therefore hardly surprised when, nearly fifteen years later, the people demonstrating against gay marriage denounced the collapse of the natural order of the family as a result of "gender theory," by which they meant American queer theory. The recent history recounted in this book is thus closely interwoven with my own career—when I analyze the fantasies triggered by queer theory, I am simultaneously interrogating the imaginative construct that informs (and probably conditions) my current presence in the United States. In that respect, the book reflects a certain dislocation: it offers an analysis of French theory's return to France by an author who traveled in the opposite direction—wherein also lies, perhaps, its appeal.

While it is hard to list everyone who contributes to the writing of a book, this one is clearly indebted to six years of unflagging support from the Massachusetts Institute of Technology, in particular the Global Studies and Languages Section of the School of Humanities, Arts, and Social Sciences, as well as the French Initiatives Endowment Fund. I am particularly grateful to Cynthia Reed, John Reed, Melissa Nobles, Deborah Fitzgerald, Jeffrey Ravel, Ian Condry, Emma Teng, Jing Wang, William Uricchio, Elizabeth Wood, Elizabeth Garrels, Shigeru Miyagawa, Paloma Duong, Bettina Stoetzer, Sally Haslanger, Edward Schiappa, Edward B. Turk, Isabelle de Courtivron, Marie-Hélène Huet, Catherine Clark, Sabine Levet, Cathy Culot, Leanna Rezvani, Gilberte Furstenberg, Jane Dunphy, Ellen Crocker, Elouise Evee-Jones, Lisa Hickler, Kevin McLellan, Jeffrey Pearlin, Andrew McPherson, and Andrea Wirth.

The book was written during a year at the Stanford Humanities Center, where I was warmly received. My thanks go to the center's team, especially Caroline Winterer, Roland Hsu, and Robert Barrick. My ideas were also greatly enriched by conversations with other fellows, to whom I am equally grateful.

I also express my gratitude to Jesus College, Cambridge, which regularly welcomed me as a research associate over a three-year period. Special thanks go to Véronique Mottier and James Clackson. My presence at Cambridge was made possible by the award of a Newton Fellowship from the British Academy, whose personnel also merit my warm thanks.

The Center for European Studies at Harvard, where I am a member of the Non-Resident Faculty, is a highly valued focus of critical discussion, and I am particularly grateful to Laura Frader and Hilary Silver.

Beyond my own institutions, I have been lucky to work regularly with remarkable colleagues whose astute comments during our discussions have provided the starting point for many of the questions I address. I first thank Natacha Chetcuti, who worked with me on conducting interviews and assembling archive material. Our intellectual partnership has been extremely valuable to me. Special thanks also go to David Paternotte, Joan W. Scott, Françoise Gaspard, Claude Servan-Schreiber, Judith Butler, George Chauncey, Hélène Périvier, Jean Zaganiaris, Daniel Borrillo, Marianne Blidon, Camille Robcis, Sandrine Sanos, Todd Shepard, and Judith Surkis.

Some of the arguments developed in Chapter 1 were partly inspired by my article "The Power of Theory: Same-Sex Marriage, Education, and Gender Panic in France," in *After Marriage Equality*, ed. Carlos A. Ball (NYU Press, 2016). I am grateful to the editor for supporting development of the project I had begun to study under his auspices.

The writing of this book was substantially enriched by its meticulous translation into English by Deke Dusinberre. His patience and grasp of language have enabled me to explore transatlantic resonances I had not initially imagined.

Special thanks also go to my editor at Stanford University Press, Emily-Jane Cohen. Her sharp yet benevolent perspective helped me situate my work in the long history of critical thought in France and the United States.

My family and friends have provided precious support, and as I have, they have had to deal with the many cultural adjustments required by my move to far-off America. I particularly acknowledge Michèle Perreau-Bonnet, Jean-Baptiste Perrin, Franck Delaire, Marie Donzel, and Olympio Perrimond.

Either Natacha Chetcuti or I conducted the semiguided interviews for this book in the physical presence of the interviewees or via Skype. These interviews enabled me to flesh out my knowledge of queer movements, media, and studies in France. Based on this same material, Natacha Chetcuti is currently preparing a different study on the role of the "queer signifier" on approaches to self-labeling and on personal careers. My warm thanks therefore go to all those people who answered our questions and/or made their archived documentation available to us, in particular Stéphanie Kunert, Vincent He-Say, Pascale Molinier, Rosa Deluxe, Paola Bacchetta, Nelly Quemener, Marion Perrin, Maxime Cervulle, Marie (Marche des Tordu[e]s), Marco Dell'Omodarme, Luca Greco, Maxime Cervulle, Arnaud Alessandrin, Bronwyn Winter, Judith Butler, Christine Delphy, Emilie Jouvet, Elisabeth Lebovici, Éric Fassin, Françoise Picq, Jean-Yves Le Talec, Gianfranco Rebucini, Jean Jean (La Croisère), João Gabriell, Karine Espineira, Liliane Kandel, Lucas Morin, Clément Lacoin, Lolla Zappi, Jean Allouch, Vincent Bourseul, Sandra Boehringer, Romain Seuzaret, Ghislain de Salins, Laurie Laufer, Michel Feher, Gerard Koskovich, Christian de Leusse, and Aurélien Davennes.

Finally, this book would never have been written had I not come across, in 1999, Didier Eribon's *Insult and the Making of the Gay Self*, a book that I have not only never closed but that has prompted me to open numerous others. Many of the arguments I develop here are, I trust, a tribute to the pioneering work done by Eribon in all his publications. It is therefore fitting that these pages are dedicated to him.

QUEER THEORY

INTRODUCTION

IN THE WINTER OF 2012–13, hundreds of thousands of people marched in the streets of Paris to protest the legal extension of marriage and adoption to same-sex couples. The scope of the demonstrations surprised foreign observers: How could France, perceived as extremely liberal in regard to sexual mores, display such hostility to the rights of gays and lesbians?[1]

Public demonstrations by reactionary groups are not unusual in European democracies, and France is no exception. It witnessed mass marches when the legislature debated bills on abortion (1975), state supervision of Catholic schools (1984), and civil unions (1999). The media response to the demonstrations against gay marriage was nevertheless unparalleled; the socialist government even backtracked on several occasions, ultimately withdrawing measures related to equality at school and the legal status of stepparents in order to "appease" the demonstrators. Despite passage of the so-called marriage for all law—the Taubira Act (named after French minister of justice Christiane Taubira, who sponsored the bill)—demonstrations against gay marriage continue to be organized even today on a regular basis in Paris and other large cities in France.[2]

On the other side of the Atlantic, one key aspect of the anti-gay-marriage movement in France went almost unnoticed. The demonstrators were not merely denouncing the potentially damaging effect of the law on marriage; they were also claiming that its origin was to be found in "gender theory," an ideology imported from America. By gender theory they mean queer theory in general and, more specifically, the work of philosopher Judith Butler, whose publications were translated into French throughout the first decade of the new millennium. French opponents of gay marriage, supported by the Vatican, are now attacking school curricula that explore male/female equality, which they claim is further proof of the growing empire of gender theory. They see it as queer propaganda that will not only pervert young people but also destroy the French nation itself. Whether through marriage, parenthood, or school, they dread the possibility that lesbians and gay men may find a way to literally reproduce themselves.

This book discusses various facets of the French response to queer theory, from the mobilization of activists and the seminars of scholars to the emergence of queer media and the decision to translate this or that kind of work. It sheds new light on recent events around gay marriage—perceiving queer theory as a threat to France means overlooking the fact that queer theory itself has been largely inspired by French writers and thinkers. To a certain extent, the book examines the return of French theory to France from the perspective of queer theory and the polemics over marriage and kinship, thereby exploring how France conceptualizes America. By examining mutual influences across the Atlantic, my work analyzes changes in the idea of national identity in France and the United States, offering insight into recent attempts to theorize the notion of "community."

I demonstrate that the French notion of an American invasion is a fantasy expressing the fear of the propagation of homosexuality.[3] This fear has two interlinked dimensions, which might be described as vertical and horizontal: the first concerns an obsession with passing homosexuality on to children; the second, a refusal to conceptualize "the community" through a critical reexamination of the identities generated by sexual minorities. From this standpoint, gay marriage ushered in a new legal era but did not alter the immunological impetus behind the way French national identity has been forged. The national body remains defined by its effort to "immunize" itself against minority cultures, in particular homosexuals. Rejecting both cosmopolitanism and culturalism, I offer a theory of minority politics that considers an ongoing critique of norms as the foundation of citizenship, in which a feeling of belonging arises from regular reexamination of it.

Gay Marriage in France: A Question of Gender

After the Assemblée Nationale passed the Taubira Act on April 23, 2013, the act was examined by the Conseil Constitutionnel, which judged the new law to be in keeping with the French constitution.[4] It was thus proclaimed law by the president of the French Republic on May 17, 2013. Just two days later, the press announced the celebration of the "first" gay marriage in France.[5] It was not, however, the first gay wedding. On June 5, 2004, the green-party mayor of Bègles, Noël Mamère, officiated over the marriage of two men. This wedding arose from a petition launched by sociologists Didier Eribon and Françoise Gaspard, lawyer Caroline Mécary, and legal scholar Daniel Borrillo subsequent to a session of the seminar "The Sociology of Homosexualities" run by Eribon and Gaspard at the École des Hautes Études en Sciences Sociales (EHESS) and led by Borrillo. In a context marked by San Francisco mayor Gavin Newsom's performance of gay weddings and by a violent homophobic assault in northern France (where a man was seriously burned by his attackers), this petition, dubbed "A Manifesto for Equal Rights," called on mayors in France to react by performing gay marriages. Published in *Le Monde* on March 17, 2004, the manifesto garnered the support of many intellectuals and artists, including Jacques Derrida, Paul Veyne, and Jane Birkin, as well as politicians such as Mamère. It was therefore logical that Mamère would perform a marriage when two men presented themselves at his town hall. The conservative government's minister of the interior, Dominique de Villepin, suspended Mamère from his mayoral office for one month. As the case made its way through the courts, the marriage was annulled by the Tribunal de Grande Instance (county court) in Bordeaux on July 24, 2004, a ruling upheld by the Cour d'Appel on April 19, 2005, and confirmed by the highest appellate court, the Cour de Cassation, on March 13, 2007. The courts held that only a man and a woman could contract a marriage. Since the appeal process had the effect of suspending the initial ruling, the marriage performed in Bègles remained valid for nearly a year. The Socialist Party criticized Mamère's initiative because of the need to respect existing law, but for the first time the party committed itself to a policy of extending marriage to same-sex couples, at a time when other socialist parties in Europe (for example, those in Belgium and Spain) were preparing to reform—or already had reformed—marriage laws.[6] The position adopted by the Socialist Party's steering committee on May 11, 2004, nevertheless consigned the issue of homosexual parenthood to later debate, repeating the party's highly cautious approach to this issue during the earlier debate on civil unions.[7]

Public debate on marriage, previously focused on sexual orientation, swiftly extended to the additional dimension of gender. In 2005, Camille Barré and Monica Leon, two transsexual women (male to female), only one of whom had had her legal status altered, went to their local mayor to be married. Since the decision of the Tribunal de Grande Instance in Bordeaux had stipulated that marriage was open only to couples composed of a legally recognized male and female, Barré and Leon believed they were within their rights. Their local mayor, the conservative politician Patrick Ollier, nevertheless refused to publish the banns, thereby preventing the marriage from taking place. The couple appealed this decision, but the Tribunal de Grande Instance in Nanterre found that Barré and Leon were outside the law because they wished to marry "as women." The district attorney, Bernard Pagès, even argued that "their main goal was not really marriage in the usual sense, because it was alien to the goal of behaving like husband and wife."[8] This decision was confirmed by an appellate court in Versailles, which on July 8, 2005, held that Barré and Leon were trying to twist the law purely for "activist" reasons and the law should not yield to this type of suit.[9] The affair revealed the extent to which, in France, the issue of marriage immediately became cast in terms of gender ("as women," "behaving like"). If, several years later, opponents of gay marriage accused gender theory of being the origin of the Taubira Act, they were themselves just echoing a gendered view of marriage already part of public debate.

The incident of the marriage performed in Bègles, like the decision handed down by the county court in Nanterre, revealed that equal rights between homosexuals and heterosexuals were advancing at a snail's pace in France. Legal recognition of lesbians and gays through the Taubira Act both maintained and created new inequalities between married heterosexual and married homosexual couples. For example, there is no automatic presumption of a parental tie within married homosexual couples, requiring that a spouse's biological child must be adopted. When that biological child is the product of medically assisted procreation (MAP) effected abroad, some French courts have refused to grant adoption, arguing that a 1994 law on bioethics has been violated.[10] (The law made MAP legal in France only for heterosexual couples with medically proven cases of infertility.) The nation's highest appeals court had to intervene, declaring that MAP conducted outside French borders should not be an obstacle to adoption.[11] It nevertheless remains the case that should the biological parent die before adoption is granted, the child becomes an orphan, a situation that does not arise within a heterosexual couple.

Another ruling by the Cour de Cassation struck down an order preventing a Moroccan national residing in France from marrying his partner, a French citizen.[12] France had signed bilateral conventions with eleven countries stipulating that marriage laws in the country of origin would apply to respective foreign nationals living in France (from Morocco, Tunisia, Algeria, Bosnia-Herzegovina, Serbia, Montenegro, Kosovo, Slovenia, Poland, Laos, or Cambodia).[13] A ministerial directive dated May 29, 2013, stated that application of the Taubira Act would confirm those conventions, thereby outlawing marriages between certain binational homosexual couples. In its ruling, however, the Cour de Cassation pointed out that the convention signed by France and Morocco on August 10, 1981, included a reserve clause stating that the convention would not apply if the legal dispositions of one state threatened public order in the other. In this instance, the judges decided that implementation of the Taubira Act would be seriously affected by application of the Franco-Moroccan agreement; they therefore struck down the restrictive interpretation of homosexual marriage that the French administration had issued in its directive of May 2013. The judges nevertheless set two conditions on the application of their ruling: the foreign nationals in question had to be residents of France; and their home country, if not recognizing homosexual marriage, must not have a law explicitly prohibiting it.

In addition to marriage-related inequality, other types of discrimination could have been eliminated through reform but were maintained in the new law: prohibiting MAP for single women and lesbian couples, outlawing surrogate pregnancies (which more particularly affect gays), and medicalizing a change in the legal status of transsexual individuals. Thanks only to a legislative amendment passed on July 12, 2016, has change of biological sex ceased to be a precondition for a change of legal status. Change of gender marker must nevertheless be pronounced by a judge on the basis of sufficient evidence. Placing marriage on the political agenda therefore shut down what jurisprudence was having difficulty containing, the linkage of sex and gender produced by the institution of marriage.[14] Interestingly, the preamble to the bill on "marriage for all" argued for the extension of marriage to homosexual couples in the name of a historic process and to match more advanced legislation in other countries, yet it made no mention of the principles of equality, liberty, and dignity.[15] The marriage-for-all law did not therefore constitute a complete success for sexual minorities but was a kind of concession to their struggle, just as civil unions had been in the past, legalized by the legislature only after many years of lobbying by organizations that defended homosexuals and spearheaded the fight against AIDS.

From this standpoint, France has experienced no clear "before-and-after" watershed with regard to gay marriage. The study I am undertaking therefore involves a critical analysis of the history of the present, too often understood solely from its legal aspect. The temporal perspective is in fact itself the object of major normative conflicts—whereas opponents to marriage for all see the reform as a dangerous departure, proponents of equal rights view it as part of an ongoing process. The more conservative liberals, meanwhile, hope that the new law will satisfy gay and lesbian demands once and for all. Conceptually grasping this temporal perspective, and thereby transcending the mythology of victorious struggle, can thus have political significance. Such a critique strikes me as all the more important insofar as lesbian, gay, bisexual, and transgender (LGBT) cultures themselves exist in a queer time.[16] The law, of course, provides an analytical structure: it has recognized and provided security to many gay and lesbian families with respect to their names, financial estates, health, and so on. Its impact is therefore real and significant. The relationship of LGBT individuals to the law has itself changed, especially in terms of their more frequent recourse to jurisprudence. Yet has there been any profound change in the modes of thought that shape sexuality and citizenship? I argue that, despite legal reforms, the "straight mind"—that is, a mode of thought based on a reification of the difference between the sexes[17]—continues to function as a political totem in France and that the majority conceptualization of citizenship is as operative today as it was prior to marriage for all. Preventing any change to that conceptualization caused opponents of the law to pour into the streets—and they continue to do so. Ultimately, performing homosexual marriages is not the key issue behind their struggle. Even the staunchest opponents have never tried to disrupt a wedding ceremony. Their activism targets above all the idea of marriage as a vector of meaning and moral values.

Since the student uprisings of May 1968, French conservatives have criticized the moral relativism of postmodern society. Contemporary society is purportedly undermined by its nihilism and rejection of tradition. Conservatism is not restricted to one political party but cuts across the political spectrum as well as social, professional, geographic, and other categories. In fact, it is the expression of commonplaces largely reflected in the French media where many commentators complain about how shallow the educational system is,[18] how impolite young people are, and even how uncivil laughter can be.[19] Sexuality is one of the mainsprings of this moral reaction, as also witnessed in October 2014 by the destruction of an artwork by Paul McCarthy by anti-gay-marriage activists: unable to bear the idea that the middle of Place Vendôme in Paris could host a work of art in the form of a green tree suggestive of a sex toy, they laid waste to the art and physically attacked the artist.[20] While these activists thought they were invested with the role of saving a society corrupted by its leaders and subjected to influential minorities, their crusade also revealed a form of fascination with sexuality itself, a fascination more broadly typical of an attachment to order.[21]

It is therefore no coincidence that the legal recognition of homosexuality is the focus of numerous fantasies and moral tensions. Conservatives argue that heterosexuality and homosexuality are not morally equivalent behaviors, hence should not be considered as such by the law. Believing that their convictions have been aggrieved, conservatives now position themselves as the "underdog" and demand that their vision of the world be recognized in turn. In other words, they appropriate the idea of moral relativism to their own benefit even as they criticize it when applied to LGBT cultures. They see themselves as majority victims of a system henceforth devised to benefit minorities. Today they invoke neutrality of treatment toward all citizens in order to pitch their struggle as an equivalent of the struggle for LGBT rights. That sheds light on why it is so important to opponents of gay marriage to credit the idea that LGBT rights are the product of a "theory." By proceeding in this way, they seek to legitimize their own doctrine. References to the United States become all the more potent, allowing them to think that there exists an organized effort to sabotage the foundations of French identity: criticism of gay marriage is strengthened by being bound to nearly two centuries of French fascination with, and wariness of, the United States.[22]

Queer Echoes

In looking back at the American shore, I adopt the notion of "fantasy echo" developed by historian Joan W. Scott to explore the construction of tradition. Scott shows that fantasies of the past help establish categories used in the present. By introducing the idea of echo, she argues that this relationship to transhistorical identity is illusory because it overlooks not only swings in meaning that categories can assume over time but also the complex, unstable mechanism of identification with those categories. Starting from Scott's notion, I intend to show that transatlantic exchanges are the product of cultural fantasies whose effect, if not function, is to mask their original source. Thus, "French theory" becomes American when it returns home to France.[23] This book strives to recontextualize and repoliticize these mutual exchanges. What is being analyzed here is the transnational construction of the very idea of queer theory. By what mechanisms do highly disparate theses and methods become united into a single theoretical category? How does this operation occur, and who participates in it? When I use the term "queer theory," I am referring to an intellectual approach with multifarious, variable meanings. The use of "theory" in the singular does not mean I adhere to the idea of a coherent corpus of theory; it would be particularly ironic to suggest that publications and research demonstrating the uncertainty inherent in any process of definition should be brought together under one label. The same comment applies to my use of "French theory." Many French intellectuals became leading figures in critical philosophy in the United States in the 1970s and 1980s because they provided theoretical resistance to the neoliberal dogma then sweeping across academic America. These intellectuals, who deconstructed the social norms inscribed in language itself, soon became identified as the representatives of French theory; they included Michel Foucault, Jacques Derrida, Hélène Cixous, Gilles Deleuze, Jacques Lacan, Julia Kristeva, and Jean Baudrillard. The label "French theory," however, masks major differences between them (as well as differences in the quality of their work). The term "French theory" became so widespread because it generated a national identity: by lumping all writers of French nationality under one label, French theory enabled American academics to fuel critical analysis of American culture itself.

And it was precisely to interrogate analytical categories that Scott suggested conceiving fantasy and echo in the formation of cultural identities:

> The term signifies the repetition of something imagined or an imagined repetition. In either case the repetition is not exact since an echo is an imperfect return of sound. Fantasy, as noun or adjective, refers to plays of the mind that are creative and not always rational. For thinking the problem of retrospective identification it may not matter which is the noun and which the adjective. Retrospective identifications, after all, are imagined repetitions and repetitions of imagined resemblances.[24]

Scott underscores the immanence of the making of identities—the fantasy echo is not an imaginative construct exterior to the individual; it is the very setting in which identity manufactures itself (through empathy, analogy, opposition, and so on). In other words, cultural fantasy invents a point of reference (here, American queer theory), clings to it, and by force of repeated telling, effaces the very traces of its making. This is the echo in the fantasy; like a sound diffracted many times, it becomes hard to pinpoint it with any accuracy. The original can of electoral accession to power in the 1970s by accepting the rules of the game, to the extent of feeling a need to intensify some of the republic's principles and symbols. This phenomenon became more marked with the rise of the far right in the 1980s. To distinguish itself from the clientelism of conservative politicians who blithely flirted with the extreme right, France's Socialist Party developed an "anticommunitarian" discourse that recognized minority groups only on the condition that they shed their specific identity and history. A paradigmatic example was the debate over whether women should be allowed to wear the Islamic headscarf, which began in 1989 during celebrations for the two hundredth anniversary of the French Revolution. Some nonconformist voices within the party, often shaped by local experiences, found themselves sidelined at that point.

But one question still remains unanswered: If the forces of reaction *and* left-wing republicanism both display the same wariness of minorities, shouldn't they welcome a queer critique of established identities? I show that queer theory also presents them with a problem because it undermines the two mechanisms sustaining the French fantasy of the body politic: the transfiguration of the difference between the sexes and the creation of an immunologically based definition of the nation. Indeed, fear of the contagiousness of homosexuality was not only at the heart of the movement opposing gay marriage but also a structural feature of various types of psychoanalytical and literary discourse in France. Homosexuality allegedly sought just one thing: the infinite extension of immediate pleasure. In this respect homosexuality was perceived as a "death drive" (as allegedly demonstrated by the AIDS epidemic) since it not only rejected sexual alterity but projected the future as nothing but more of the same, that is, more homosexuals. Gays and lesbians were thus simultaneously stigmatized for *not* having children and for *having* them, for rejecting the national genealogy while proposing a competing one.

Given this situation, might "a sense of belonging" be conceptualized differently? Several philosophers now associated with "new French theory" on American campuses—particularly Maurice Blanchot and Jean-Luc Nancy—have strived to rethink the notion of "common" following the collapse of the communist bloc. They argue that a community is always unattainable, unavowable, negative, that it escapes all attempts to grasp it. I argue that their theories are valid only in the case of majority cultures; minorities do not have the luxury of disavowing, once and for all, their sense of belonging. In contrast, what Didier Eribon calls "avowed communities" are able to transform themselves and consequently transform the norm. This could be the basis of critical alliances between queer theory, class analysis, and liberal thought in the context of post–marriage equality. These alliances could be forged on the argument that community is not a constantly receding horizon but a critical return to an experienced event, what Michel Foucault would have described as "a lover leav[ing] in a taxi."[36]

of information and monitoring on research into gender ever since the Fourth World Conference on Women, held in Beijing in September 1995.

In 1962, Pope John XXIII opened the Second Vatican Council to reconsider Church doctrine in a contemporary world marked by major social and technological changes. Vatican II (as the council was known) ended in 1965 under the new pope, Paul VI. The council promoted Christian humanism, a philosophy—inspired by secular humanism—that recognized certain inalienable human rights. These rights, however, were not the consequence of life in society but of human "nature." Susan A. Ross has shown that this nature is simultaneously physical and spiritual in the tradition of pre–Vatican II discussion of marriage and sexuality, which focused on a woman's "docility" and natural "receptivity" for children.[16] Three years later, the encyclical *Humanae Vitae* condemned birth-control pills in the name of this "natural law."[17] The theology of Pope John Paul II derived straight from this natural law while placing particular stress on the complementarity of the sexes,[18] as he did in his 1979 *Theology of the Body* and his 1995 "Letter to Women,"[19] the latter published to make an impact on the Beijing conference. Above all, however, John Paul II founded several institutions charged with monitoring changes in the family, method of reproduction, and sexuality, such as the Pontifical Council for the Family (1981) and the Pontifical Academy for Life (1994). Opus Dei, an institution founded in 1928 to evangelize people through education and local charities—thereby setting everyone on the path to sainthood—promoted the complementarity of a man's and a woman's contribution to the family. In 1982 Opus Dei became a personal prelature, that is, an institution with no territorial boundaries, placed directly in the service of the pope.

Benedict XVI continued his predecessor's work while setting natural law against what he called "moral relativism" in a speech to members of the International Theological Commission in 2007.[20] Before the UN General Assembly in 2008, Benedict argued that human rights "are based on the natural law inscribed on human hearts and present in different cultures and civilizations. Removing human rights from this context would mean restricting their range and yielding to a relativistic conception." According to the pope, the primary relativistic problem is the challenge to the complementarity of the sexes within the family, the family being the fruit of the laws of the "Creator."[21] In other words, as sociologist Éric Fassin has shown, the Vatican's natural law is nothing other than the "law of nature."[22] Human rights are conditioned by a biological determinism willed by God: "In order to avoid the domination of one sex or the other, their differences tend to be denied, viewed as mere effects of historical and cultural conditioning. In this perspective, physical difference, termed *sex*, is minimized, while the purely cultural element, termed *gender*, is emphasized to the maximum and held to be primary." Benedict XVI denounced "ideologies, which, for example, call into question the family, in its natural two-parent structure of mother and father, and make homosexuality and heterosexuality virtually equivalent, in a new model of polymorphous sexuality."[23]

A year later, the Vatican's Pontifical Council for the Family published a manual, *Lexicon: Ambiguous and Debatable Terms regarding Family Life and Ethical Questions*, to help the faithful understand misuse of gender, sexuality, and the body.[24] All these efforts sought to defend human ecology and mobilize an entire semantic arsenal that echoed a notion of "risk" already current in European democracies when discussing issues of climate, security, and health.[25] This new packaging also served theological tradition as established by Saint Thomas Aquinas to oppose "unnatural" acts.[26] When Pope Francis asked in 2013, "If a person is gay and seeks God and has good will, who am I to judge?," a swarm of commentators spoke of the Church's new openness to the question of homosexuality.[27] From the standpoint of forgiveness, however, tolerance toward homosexuals is hardly new—but that tolerance is possible only if their behavior has already been condemned. Thus, in January 2015 Francis declared that homosexual marriage was a threat to the family that "disfigure[d] God's plan for creation."[28] And in February he argued that gender theory was ideological colonization: "It colonizes the people with an idea that changes, or wants to change, a mentality or a structure."[29] The pope thereby conveyed the idea of twin dangers, territorial invasion (of the human body as sacred ground) and conversion of minds and institutions. This latter process he could all the more easily ascribe to gender studies, since he was a product of the order founded by Ignatius of Loyola, the Company of Jesus, one of whose main missions is evangelization. Finally, Francis compared gender theory to nuclear weapons, their potential for the destruction of nature allegedly being the same. He thus remained totally in line with his predecessors and their theology of natural law.

How was this theology disseminated in Europe, and how did it evolve into opposition to the teaching of gender theory in France? The process entailed three components: Vatican monitoring of international authorities and their programs of "gender equality"; disinformation on research into gender, notably queer theory; and the use of intermediaries close to the Vatican who

Traditional Street Marches

Opposition to marriage for all arose from these religious networks. Contrary to a common belief that Catholics are little inclined to demonstrate, they proved to be highly organized and viewed street demonstrations as a kind of "public-inspired referendum."[50] On August 14, 2012, the archbishop of Lyon, Cardinal Philippe Barbarin, declared, "Parliament isn't God the Father!,"[51] calling for further action. The organization Manif pour Tous was swiftly formed to oppose marriage for all. On September 5, fifty leading members of French Catholic networks secretly met in premises on Place Saint-Sulpice in Paris. Those present included Karine Le Mené, daughter of Dr. Jérôme Lejeune (of the foundation of the same name), and Ludovine de la Rochère, public relations officer for the Lejeune foundation and the Conference of Bishops of France. Also in attendance were Antoine Renard, president of the joint Catholic family associations; Vincent Terrenoir, president of the Movement for World Unity through the Catholic Church; Tugdual Derville; Marie-José Thollot, president of an association of large families; Élisabeth Montfort, a former member of the European parliament (for a party led by the ultraconservative Catholic politician Philippe de Villiers); and Béatrice Bourges, a lawyer and active opponent of homosexual parenthood. Also present was Alain Escada, representing Civitas (a far-right group linked to the Confraternity of Saint Pius X, which was founded in the 1970s and had already made a name for itself by organizing street prayers against artworks considered blasphemous, notably Andres Serrano's *Piss Christ*). A few days later, however, the new group chose Frigide Barjot (whose real name is Virginie Tellenne), a devout Catholic formerly associated with gay Paris nightlife, as its spokesperson, with the idea of projecting a softer image of their opposition to the proposed new marriage bill. Indeed, Civitas had already begun to organize street prayers, and it was feared this might discredit the movement in the eyes of the general public during this period of controversies over secularism.[52]

Barjot, who became very devout following a pilgrimage to Lourdes in 2004 and was a great admirer of Pope Benedict XVI, projected a completely different image. She was known above all as a former television celebrity and extravagant reveler surrounded by gay friends. Given the failure of the movement opposing legalization of civil unions led by Boutin, Barjot's leadership was designed to "modernize" opposition to the Taubira bill—Manif pour Tous presented itself as having no religious affiliation. In the same spirit, several ad hoc groups were

FIGURE 2. Civitas: Prayers against "marriage for all" in front of the Sénat, April 4, 2013. Source: © Christian Hartmann / Reuters. Reprinted with permission.

created within Manif pour Tous itself. Although they had almost no members, these subgroups were supposed to demonstrate that the organization had support extending beyond its traditional backers: for example, La Gauche pour le Mariage Républicain (Liberals for Republican Marriage), led by Laurence Tcheng (a former student of François Hollande at Sciences Po);[53] and Plus Gay sans Mariage (Gayer without Marriage), headed by Xavier Bongibault, himself homosexual yet hostile to the proposed new bill.[54] This discourse, viewed as positive by the leaders of Manif pour Tous, also influenced the recruitment of activists themselves. Sociologist Sophie Rétif has demonstrated how the concern to create a positive image of the faith was central to Catholic mobilization, as was perhaps a sense of a certain stigmatization in a society where the Church's positions are often mocked.[55]

Barjot's leadership and the organization's heavily mediatized approach nevertheless created internal tensions from the beginning. Although formed around a shared goal, the group was composed of highly varied schools of thought. Activists' relationship to their religion had a direct impact on public statements—some treated their faith as a purely personal matter; others, as a revelation that called for the evangelization of all. As Manif pour Tous devel-

FIGURE 5. Les Antigones. Source: http://lesantigones.fr/the-antigones-send-a-message -to-the-femen/, posted June 4, 2013.

marriage for all by Femen, a feminist group originally from Ukraine that specialized in shock street tactics. The white-garbed Antigones claimed they were restoring women's freedom to be feminine rather than feminist: "We do not recognize ourselves in the image imposed on us by an ultra-minority ideology that dominates the political sphere and the media: gender theory and sextremism. . . . We, Antigones, advocate femininity for women—it is our profound, integral nature." Les Antigones associated fertility with social asset: "Women have a different sensibility, different attitudes, and different methods of action from men. These differences represent an asset to be cultivated, an otherness that is fertile on every level."[77]

Finally, like Antigone opposing Creon, they said they were fighting in the name of a transcendental principle of justice that trumped statute law: "We, Antigones, favor legitimacy over legality. When man-made laws overstep natural laws—that is, the unwritten norms that are the foundation of human experience—it is our duty to rebel."[78] Les Antigones said they were rebelling against the dominant, lax values of post-1968 society. They presented themselves as resistance fighters, as did the Hommen, who depicted the current political establishment as Nazi or Stalinist and called for the restoration of French masculinity (which they felt had been demeaned), as had previously been done when France was liberated from German occupation.

FIGURE 6. Hommen: Recuperation of the image of Resistance hero Jean Moulin with the message, "No to gay marriage." Source: http://hommen-officiel.tumblr.com/.

The Hommen group emphasized the "protection of children." By stressing masculine strength—which they felt had been warped through exhibitionist female nudity in the public sphere, as epitomized by Femen[79]—they sought to remind people that a man's role was to defend his family.[80] They exemplify what Pierre Bourdieu called "masculinity as nobility."[81] Masked, bare-chested, these men displayed slim, young, white bodies, very similar to one another, distinguished only by pants of different colors. They thus militated for a society in which men controlled the public sphere through a kind of solidarity among heterosexual men, defined by a taboo against homosexuality yet also, and paradoxically, characterized by a pronounced homoeroticism,[82] a phenomenon equally present, if less pronounced, among Manif pour Tous.[83]

A number of small far-right groups joined the Manif pour Tous demonstrations, where they created disturbances from the fall of 2013 onward, including Jeunesses Nationalistes (Nationalist Youth), Groupe Union Défense (Union Defense Group), and Hommage National (National Tribute). Their behavior

FIGURE 7. Les Hommen: Demonstration against gay marriage. Toulouse, April 17, 2013. Source: © Éric Cabanis/ AFP. Reprinted with permission.

FIGURE 8. Young men demonstrating against same-sex marriage. Paris, April 24, 2013. Source: © Antoine Antoniol / Getty Image Europe / AFP. Reprinted with permission.

was designed to trigger public disorder through vandalism or commando raids against symbolic sites and sometimes individuals. What seemed new was these groups' active use of the Internet to recruit new members—yet their use of social networks left them more exposed than in the past, when their meetings and actions were cloaked somewhat in secrecy.[84] In a way, their mobilization against the Taubira Act transformed these far-right groups' strategies; Bloc Identitaire (Identity Block) even formed an "identity and kinship" committee to theorize its participation in the demonstrations. Defense of the traditional family hinged on a defense of Europe's Christian roots. While it would be an exaggeration to suggest that these far-right groups shared an organized network with Catholic associations opposing the Taubira Act, their strategies clearly converged in 2013–14, as well as their fear of decadence through the spread of homosexuality.

Finally, demonstrations to block the Taubira Act were joined by the monarchist movement Action Française.[85] Its presence was played down because Manif pour Tous feared that the monarchists' rejection of the republic would discredit opposition to the bill. Networks overlapped between Manif pour Tous and Restauration Nationale, a legitimist branch of Charles Maurras's royalist movement.[86] In early 2014 the reactionary blogosphere frequently drew

FIGURE 9. Civitas: "France needs children, no need of homosexuals." Paris, November 18, 2012. Source: © Kenzo Tribouillard / AFP. Reprinted with permission.

comparisons with the riot of February 6, 1934, a far-right antiparliamentarian incident orchestrated by Action Française and Les Camelots du Roi.[87] Nearly ninety years later, however, the parallels were spurious.[88] The riot of 1934 was sparked by a banking scandal known as the Stavisky Affair, leading to the fall of Édouard Daladier's cabinet and the formation of a government of national union. The motivation for the demonstrations was very different in relation to the Taubira Act, and in 2014 the left-wing response seemed poorly organized and even largely demobilized, whereas after 1934 the French left became highly coordinated (leading in 1936 to the election of a Popular Front government).[89] Manif pour Tous was not a classic mobilization of French right-wing forces but was primarily based on religious convictions.[90]

Moved by Religious Convictions

Although opposition to gay marriage and gender theory cannot be reduced to religion, that aspect has remained central. Political scientist Gaël Brustier states that Manif pour Tous was not "'a French-style' Tea Party,"[91] yet all components of French opposition to gay marriage have very strong religious roots and ties to anti-abortion networks. They develop a discourse that targets "the elites," in which minorities, the media, and the political establishment are designated enemies of the people. While Manif pour Tous claimed that protesting high taxes was not a priority, the organization could rally its troops when tax reform affected heterosexual families with numerous children.[92] According to Brustier, the American and French movements are not comparable given France's "different social, political, and religious history."[93] France's "secular democracy" can nevertheless include highly ambivalent political behavior toward religion: for example, while attending a canonization ceremony at the Vatican, French prime minister Manuel Valls chose to repeat his opposition to the extension of MAP to lesbian couples and single women. France is hardly alone in vaunting separation of Church and State as part of its national identity. What differs between France and the United States, however, is religious observance itself— according to the Sociovision Institute, only 10 percent of the French population practices any religion, and fully 53 percent claim to be nonbelievers.[94] Unlike in the United States, opposition to gay marriage in France is almost never expressed in terms of religious freedom, which would oblige Catholic movements to recognize the legitimacy of *all* religions. And Catholic activists rely on secular democracy to stave off competition from other religions, particularly Islam.

Opposition to gay marriage was therefore expressed in the name of the collective good and of society's underlying anthropological structures, not in the name of freedom of religion. This was another reason why opposition to gay marriage was pitched in terms of gender theory.

Catholic authorities played a key role in triggering the movement. Not only did Church leadership issue a call in the summer of 2012 for opposition to any new bill that would threaten the traditional family, but those same leaders promoted the demonstrations throughout the fall of that year. The archbishop of Paris, Cardinal André Vingt-Trois, advocated dissent against the bill on several occasions. He met with François Hollande on July 17, 2012, and during a mass at Lourdes on August 15, Assumption Day, he asked the faithful to pray that children would "cease being the object of adult desires and conflicts" and also urged elected officials to follow "the inclination of their consciences." The cardinal added that "the objectively confused propensity [to homosexuality] is experienced by most of them [i.e., homosexuals] as an ordeal." Homosexuals must therefore "be welcomed with respect, compassion, and sensitivity."[95] Cardinal Vingt-Trois went further, however, because he sought to influence public debate—throughout the fall of 2012 he instructed the bishops under his authority to support the demonstrators.[96] Interviewed on Radio Notre-Dame on February 2, 2013, he asserted that "you don't ask for freedom of conscience; you take it!"[97] In so doing, the Catholic authorities sought to forge a common front with other monotheistic religions. Céline Béraud commented that "while there has been no joint, simultaneous statement, . . . the great similarity of official religious positions against extending marriage to homosexual couples is striking, in both form and content."[98]

On October 2, 2012, Orthodox Christian bishops, via the Assemblée des Évêques Orthodoxes (Assembly of Orthodox Bishops), published a press release showing their disapproval of the proposed bill, as did Protestants on the Conseil de la Fédération Protestante de France (Council of the French Protestant Federation).[99] On October 18, Gilles Bernheim, a conservative Jew and the grand rabbi of France, sent an essay in the form of questions and answers to François Hollande that expressed disapproval of the bill.[100] On November 6, Mohammed Moussaoui, president of the Conseil Français du Culte Musulman (French Council of Muslim Cult; CFCM) published a press release objecting to the legalization of marriage for same-sex couples.[101] Another, more radical, Islamic organization, the Union des Organisations Islamiques de France (Union of French Islamic Organizations; UOIF), issued a statement on November 13,

Their shared opposition to the Taubira Act drew Manif pour Tous activists, Les Veilleurs, and elected officials into the same "partisan milieu."[138] Several new executive members of the Parti Chrétien Démocrate founded by Christine Boutin in 2001 came from the ranks of Les Veilleurs, such as Xavier Lenormand (public relations officer for Les Veilleurs), Mathieu Colombani (a chief representative for the party), and Jean Roucher (president of the party's youth group). Several Manif pour Tous activists were also the founders of Sens Commun (Common Sense), an association whose spokesperson was Madeleine Bazin de Jessey, an early supporter of Manif pour Tous and Les Veilleurs. Sens Commun was designed to be a platform for turning social energy into political power:

> There was the period of indignation and mobilization, which, despite its scope, was not enough to influence the political and legislative process. . . . If we continue to shun the political arena, politics will continue to dominate us. Political commitment is no longer an option; it has become a necessity. Having noted the efforts of several leaders of the UMP to oppose the Taubira Act and its purported "reform of civilization," Sens Commun has decided to join the UMP in order to share, consolidate, and constantly spur those bold efforts.[139]

In December 2014, Bazin de Jessey was named national secretary of the UMP.[140] In June 2015, Anne Lorne, the regional coordinator for Sens Commun, became national secretary for children's matters in the same party (henceforth called Les Républicains, the UMP having changed its name in May 2015). Similarly Force Vive (Vital Force), the party headed by Christine Boutin for the European elections in June 2014, included members of Manif pour Tous and Les Veilleurs, such as Bénédicte de Dinechin in the greater Paris region and Samuel Lafont in southeastern France (Lafont was the cofounder of an association called Camping pour Tous (Camping for All).[141] While participation in the social movement against the Taubira Act was acknowledged, these candidates were running without a distinct political label. Thus, Manif pour Tous illustrated a kind of politicization characterized by the paradoxical claim that it was remaining aloof from politics. The paradox became acute when Manif pour Tous became a political party itself, as attested by a ruling published in the *Journal Officiel* on April 24, 2015. Eleven days earlier the national campaign financing commission (Commission Nationale des Comptes de Campagne et des Financements Politiques) announced that the "funding body of the political grouping known as Manif pour Tous . . . has been certified as the financing organ of the Manif pour Tous political party for its activities throughout France

(continental and abroad)."[142] This change in strategy, although a logical consequence of the partisan atmosphere in which Manif pour Tous is steeped, was
not officially announced by the organization's members. This ambiguous political move could create a tactical problem for the left, which is more accustomed
to direct partisan confrontation.

The Majority's Universal Aspirations

Throughout debate on the Taubira bill, the socialist government followed
the line laid down by President Hollande: avoid dividing the country.[143] That
explains why the administration decided to label the reform "marriage for
all" and why both supporters and opponents of the extension of marriage
and joint adoption to homosexual couples were largely consulted throughout
the fall and winter via legislative hearings and meetings with the president.[144]
Briefly galvanized by this increase in visibility and recognition,[145] the leaders
of the anti-gay-marriage movement nevertheless had to admit that the bill
would inevitably become law once the Sénat passed it on terms very similar
to those of the Assemblée. However, the desire of the legislative majority and
the administration to remain united behind the bill had another motive—to
get it over with as quickly as possible. The polemic triggered by marriage for
all was too troublesome for politicians unconvinced of the need for reform.
Ségolène Royal, who had backed calls for the legalization of marriage for homosexual couples when she was a presidential candidate in 2007, now declared that she had never really been favorable to it and would have preferred
a form of civil union "that would not have led to confrontations like this."[146]
Christophe Caresche, a legislator from Paris, stated that "it was time to end it;
we want to move on to other things."[147] The mayoral candidate in Marseille,
Patrick Mennucci, ascribed his defeat in the 2014 municipal elections to the
passage of the marriage for all act.[148]

Discussing the rights of a minority from a majority perspective is one
thing, but seeing minority issues dominate public debate for months on end
is quite another. This panic in the face of an "inversion" of norms can also be
explained by the Socialist Party's attachment to the ideal of a French Republic
that is "one and indivisible,"[149] as previously expressed in numerous debates on
social issues such as prostitution and wearing the Islamic headscarf. The very
expression "marriage for all," adopted by the government to win support for
the bill through an abstract, universalizing ideal, proved to be double-edged.

The official explanation for the need for a new law was unambiguous: "The purpose of this bill is to extend the right of matrimony to individuals of the same sex and consequently to accord parenthood to these couples through the mechanism of adoption."[150] The government therefore decided to introduce a bill clearly designed for homosexual couples while presenting it to the media in a euphemistic manner. Thus, the administration left itself open to criticism by giving concrete form to its own confusion—some members of the legislative opposition easily alleged that marriage for all could be literally for "all," hence incestuous, polygamous, or zoophiliac. The official justification for the bill was equally revealing, for although it referred to the need to catch up with other European countries that already permitted lesbians and gays to marry, it never mentioned the principle of equality.

Equality was nevertheless at the heart of a May 20, 2013, administrative decree explaining how the newly passed law was to be implemented. Active opposition to the bill thus ultimately altered governmental rhetoric in a paradoxical way. Another key factor had been the sponsorship of the bill by Minister of Justice Christiane Taubira. A black woman originally from French Guiana and a member of the Parti Radical de Gauche (a liberal party independent of the Socialist Party), Taubira had been behind a law passed in 2001 that recognized slavery as a crime against humanity. She therefore defended her new bill by linking it to the principle of equality for minority cultures. Invoking post-colonial writers such as Aimé Césaire and Léon-Gontran Damas, she spoke of the contribution of minorities to the collective good and of the need to assert, rather than disguise, identity. She thereby diverged from the universalist discourse that predominated within the Socialist Party.[151]

In the spring of 2013 there were thus two types of reaction within the government's socialist majority with regard to the Taubira bill—a desire to be finished with an awkward bill as soon as possible and a defense of the principle of equality subsequent to the euphemisms and hesitations of the fall of 2012. While the administration ultimately clearly asserted the principle of equality, the final bill maintained differences in treatment between heterosexuals and homosexuals.[152] The extension of MAP to homosexuals was postponed, subject to a favorable future opinion from the Comité Consultatif National d'Éthique (National Ethics Commission),[153] so MAP remained legally available to heterosexuals only; the presumption of paternity was neither abolished nor transformed into a presumption of parenthood applicable to all (a child born to a married homosexual couple must be adopted by the partner of its biological parent); and the concept of "legal parent," which was initially supposed to replace "legal father" and "legal mother," was ultimately dropped. Thus, from the start marriage for all was placed under the aegis of the Socialist Party's universalist rhetoric but without the advocated rights being truly universal, as several left-wing legislators were quick to complain.[154]

The Political Economy of Marriage for All

Another striking feature of the debate within the left was the absence of economic and social arguments.[155] Two days after final passage of the law extending marriage and joint adoption to homosexual couples, Prime Minister Jean-Marc Ayrault declared to the newspaper *20 Minutes*, "We are not going to launch a new debate every day. Each reform has its own pace. I don't want to forcefully push through reforms. More than ever I want to unite the French people in the battle for employment."[156] Philippe Doucet, a legislator from Val d'Oise, was even more explicit:

> We've won the contest for the world's longest marriage for all. No less than eight months of parliamentary debate, as against twenty-four hours in New Zealand. It all went on much too long. We need to return to the real social and economic issues. . . . It's very well to have new rights, but they don't reflect the real worries of the French people. We have to tell it like it is: this marriage for all, no one gives a damn.[157]

The call to a return to "real issues"—in this case, economic ones—simply reproduces, in the realm of public discussion, the hierarchy of sexuality that the marriage for all bill was designed to fight. It supposes not only that marriage is not an economic issue but also that lesbians and gays are apparently not concerned by social-welfare questions and, more broadly, the employment crisis. In fact, lesbians and gays, confronted with a social stigma, face greater problems of poverty than the average population. They are far from the stereotype of a high-income, white, urban, homosexual male put forth by the UMP legislator from the Rhône, Philippe Meunier, in September 2012 when he described—in the far-right newspaper *Minute*—homosexual marriage as a "whim of egocentric middle-class bohemians."[158] Several reports have revealed a very large percentage of young gays among the homeless; more generally, salaries and level of social welfare are higher among heterosexuals than homosexuals, especially lesbians.[159] The authors of these reports also note that marriage reduces the negative impact of poverty for married couples and their children. In France,

being married means joint tax returns, easier inheritance procedures, rever-
sion of state pension following a spouse's death, and financial solidarity among
several generations of the family. Extending legal marriage to same-sex couples
is therefore not only an economic issue but one that calls for reconsideration
of social benefits, retirement, children's education, the management of working
hours, vacation times, and so on, according to criteria that are no longer strictly
anchored to the criterion of gender.[160]

The refusal to consider marriage a "real issue"—and, more broadly, the almost total absence of any economic analysis during the debate over marriage—
was rooted in a mythological vision of "the people." When Doucet called for
a return to "the French people," as though the bill on marriage and adoption
did not concern them, he was tacitly embracing the idea that the new law was
designed for a separate category—gays and lesbians. The same rhetoric of "real
people" was extensively used by Manif pour Tous, which sought to play on the
same patriotic heartstrings: in order to show that the movement was speaking
in the name of France, it conspicuously wielded the image of Marianne—the
emblem of the French Republic—at every demonstration. Marianne also reinforces the traditional division of gender roles in politics: the women act as
symbols, while the men make the decisions.

FIGURE 11. Manif pour Tous: Mariannes and Gavroches. Paris, February 3, 2014.
Source: © Christophe Becker. Reprinted with permission.

Lack of any argument demonstrating the positive economic impact of marriage for all made it easy for opponents of the bill to claim they were defending the underprivileged. In so doing, they borrowed imagery directly drawn from workers' and union struggles. Manif pour Tous posters included raised fists (patriotically colored red, white, and blue) with the slogan, "Hands off marriage; it's jobs you should encourage." A drawing of a factory was labeled, "A job that pays, not marriage for gays," while another poster—alluding to the imminent closure of a car factory in Aulnay—proclaimed, "What counts is Aulnay, not weddings all gay."

FIGURE 12. Manif pour Tous poster: "What counts is Aulnay, not weddings all gay." Source: http://www.lamanifpourtous.fr/.

During the marches many kids were dressed like Gavroche, the street urchin made famous in Victor Hugo's *Les Misérables*, a symbol of abandoned, wretched childhood. Unloved by his parents, Gavroche was thrust into the street on his own. In the French collective imagination this character has come to symbolize poverty in nineteenth-century Paris. But Gavroche's story was also marked by the secret of his background: his two biological brothers, given up at birth but adopted, also find themselves in the street when their adoptive mother is arrested. Without knowing they are his brothers, Gavroche takes them in for a day. Finally, Gavroche becomes a powerful symbol of liberal republicanism when he dies on the barricades during the 1832 uprising against the royalist regime. By appropriating this image of the street urchin, Manif pour Tous sought to present itself as a bulwark against homoparenthood and the accompanying risk of love-starved children ignorant of their roots. That argument might seem surprising given that the Gavroche of Hugo's novel did indeed have a mother and a father who abandoned him. *Les Misérables* is also the tale of a successful "adoption" by a single man: little Cosette is placed by her single, ostracized mother in a family that treats her like a slave (and who turn out to be Gavroche's parents), whereas Jean Valjean,

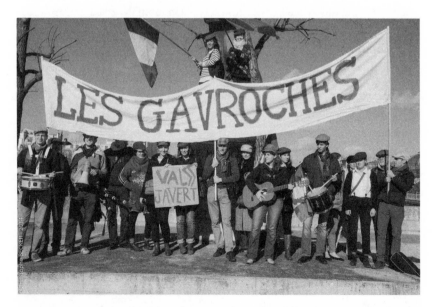

FIGURE 13. Manif pour Tous: The Gavroches. Paris, February 3, 2014. Source: © Christophe Becker. Reprinted with permission.

who had promised Cosette's mother he would look after her daughter, rescues the girl and brings her up alone. The Manif pour Tous demonstrators did not bother with such details, however. What mattered to them was above all the symbol and the possibility of snatching from the left this image of the afflicted people. For this reason a group of adult demonstrators also dubbed themselves Les Gavroches when protesting the policing efforts of Manuel Valls, then minister of the interior, during the marches—their signs spelled his name ValSS and compared him to Javert, the police inspector who hunts down Jean Valjean in *Les Misérables*.[161]

Childhood and the Sacredness of the Body

The presence of children in the marches was heavily emphasized. Demonstrators did not hesitate to use their own children to symbolize their resistance to the Taubira Act, sometimes going to questionable lengths such as gagging children to protest the arrest of an activist or placing "children up front" to use them as a shield when the police sought to disperse a demonstration.[162] The idea of protecting children rests on the observation that gay marriage makes joint adoption possible, so a child's civil record will indicate two parents while ignoring any distinction of "the difference between the sexes." Children deprived of this fundamental equilibrium between a mother and a father would allegedly be hostages to homosexuals' desire to have children. Like a chick that has fallen from its nest and needs two wings to fly, a child purportedly finds its equilibrium through the complementarity of paternal and maternal roles. That is what the early public events staged by Manif pour Tous sought to demonstrate in October 2012.

In *The Politics of Adoption* I showed that this notion of sexual difference as a condition of parenthood was rooted in the bioethical reforms of the 1980s and 1990s (backed by both conservative and liberal governments in France). The difference between the sexes became a condition for access to MAP once the gendered body was conceived as a "national asset" to be protected from abuse by (globalized) technology as well as from attitudes toward the body arising from cultures deemed too "alien" to French tradition (a classic example is outlawing wearing the Islamic headscarf). The making of future citizens within the traditional family cell, marked by the dissymmetry of gender roles, has been increasingly justified from the standpoint of a biological need to "start a family."[163] The philosophy of natural law, straight from the Vatican, found a perfect sounding board in today's context of the increasingly biological basis for establishing legal kinship. The rhetoric employed by Manif pour Tous was so audible in a country where religious observance is very low because it rested on a discursive and institutional reasoning that turns the body into a sanctuary, as earlier expressed in debate over civil unions.[164]

In this instance Manif pour Tous also played more explicitly on confusion between an adult "desire for parenthood" and a "desire for children" than had been the case in earlier opposition to civil unions. The subtext associating homosexuality with pedophilia made it easier to erect traditional gender roles as a rampart against decadence and perversion.[165] It stems from a subtle se-

FIGURE 14. Manif pour Tous poster: "And you? What do you prefer?" Source: http://www.lamanifpourtous.fr/.

mantic slippage between being a "minor" and being a "minority" and thereby becomes linked to the idea of the contagion of homosexual practices (minors exposed to minority sexuality), which find a means of reproduction—in the literal sense of the term—in kinship. In a certain way, the movements opposing marriage for all and gender theory adopted homoparenthood as a symbol of dangerous changes in the mode of child rearing itself, stigmatizing minorities while playing on the fantasy of the "corruption" of minors.

Finally, Manif pour Tous pinned its argument on the difference between the sexes to another on the commodification of the body, an unnatural practice par excellence. The organization denounced the Taubira Act as the first step toward making MAP available to single women and lesbian couples, and above all it opposed legalization of surrogate pregnancies. The polemic grew louder when an administrative directive signed by Taubira on January 25, 2013, authorized the delivery of certificates of French nationality to infants born of surrogate pregnancy abroad if at least one of the parents is French.[166] This directive did not legalize surrogate pregnancy in France but simply applied French nationality law, which stipulates that any child born of a French citizen, whether in France or abroad, is entitled to French citizenship. The directive, challenged by Les Juristes pour l'Enfance (Jurists for Childhood, an ad hoc group close

FIGURE 15. Manif pour Tous: "Today gender theory, tomorrow the benefits of pedophilia." Lyon, February 2, 2014. Source: © Christian Hartmann / Reuters. Reprinted with permission.

to Manif pour Tous), was upheld by the Conseil d'État (Council of State) on December 12, 2014, which argued that

> the sole fact that the birth of a child abroad is the result of a contract that is not valid under French law cannot lead—without disproportionately infringing, in terms of nationality, the child's right to respect for its private life as guaranteed by Article 8 of the European Convention for the Protection of Human Rights and Fundamental Freedoms—to the denial of the French nationality to which that child has a right by virtue of Article 18 of the Civil Code as monitored by the legal authorities, once the child's filiation with a French national has been established."[167]

FIGURE 16. Manif pour Tous poster: "Neither for rent nor for sale." Source: http://www.lamanifpourtous.fr/.

In a press release reacting to this decision by the Conseil d'État, Ludovine de la Rochère asserted that "the child's main interest is to have its father and mother. The issue of nationality is secondary and is being used here as an excuse. Surrogate pregnancy cannot be regulated; it must be abolished!" Deprived of documents confirming its nationality, a child would find itself in an illegal situation in its own country, running immediate risks that far exceed the question of parental roles, such as legal residence, access to health care, and so on. De la Rochère nevertheless believed that "the direct result of this directive . . . will be increased commodification of *the* child and injurious abuse of *the* woman."[168] In a ruling handed down on July 3, 2015, France's highest appeal court (Cour de Cassation) stated that French law and the European Convention on Human Rights both supported the right of a child born abroad of surrogate pregnancy to be registered as French if one parent is a French national.[169] Socialist prime minister Manuel Valls "took note" of the ruling but pointed out that "surrogate pregnancy was strictly forbidden in France."[170]

The argument invoking the marketing of the body of *the* woman and the commodification of *the* child is not expressed in the name of the freedom of *women* to dispose of their own bodies—a principle rejected by the main groups within Manif pour Tous (starting with the staunch anti-abortion lobby, Alliance Vita)—or of the autonomy of *children*. The principle implicitly underpinning the position of Manif pour Tous is the sacredness of the body as a gift of God. The Vatican describes *woman* as she who is with *child*. She is therefore invested with a mission that transcends her and thus cannot freely decide to use her body to bear other people's children. Calls within the Catholic community to join Manif pour Tous leave no doubt about what lies behind the argument of the marketing of the human body. For strategic reasons, however, the public position adopted by Manif pour Tous stressed the threat of slavery,[171] an argument that converged with the anticapitalist critique of surrogate pregnancy adopted by almost all the French left (except the Green Party and some members of the Parti Radical de Gauche).

Fantasies over the "Theory"

The reform of marriage and adoption laws sparked a revealing debate in French society, because it provided both backers and opponents an opportunity to assert certain moral values in a context heavily colored by the issue of identity (immigration, religion, bioethics). Compared to the pragmatism of debates in

Belgium, Spain, the United Kingdom, and Portugal, discussion in France focused on theoretical considerations of the idea of civilization, anthropological precedents, and French national identity. This approach stems from a strong belief in the power of abstract notions of citizenship that purportedly shape, indeed condition, individual behavior. It was therefore hardly surprising that opponents of marriage for all in France, much more than elsewhere, situated the origin of this reform in what they call "gender theory." While similar polemics over gender theory exist in other European countries, notably Belgium, Italy, and—more recently—Germany and Poland,[172] French protests were unprecedented in scope and have therefore served as a model even if local discourses circulate via other channels not directly involving France.[173] David Paternotte noted that reactionary opposition to homosexual rights had flourished in Spain and Italy even prior to the debate in France: "One should not wonder why such a movement erupted in France in [recent] years, but rather why it has been more successful there."[174] The scope of opposition to gender theory throughout Europe has been facilitated by new tools of communication. La Manif pour Tous not only exported its operating methods and public-relations techniques abroad (notably Italy),[175] but its leaders were also invited to speak in other countries, as was recently the case in Germany.[176] However, the spread of Manif pour Tous and other groups such as Les Veilleurs has not led to uniformity throughout Europe. Debate in each country is carried out on its own terms—in France, the school issue and anti-Americanism come to the fore, whereas opposition to LGBT rights in other countries also concerns national identity but is more likely to be expressed as a rejection of the European Union and transnational alliances among LGBT militants.[177] Manif pour Tous has also turned toward Russia. A delegation associated with the organization visited the Patriarchate in Moscow.[178] De La Rochère explained that the delegation's members were not, strictly speaking, leaders of Manif and that Manif pour Tous was nondenominational.[179] In July 2015, the Moscow branch of United Russia, the largest political party in Russia, adopted Manif pour Tous's imagery when designing a "flag for straights" in opposition to "gay fever."[180] The goal of the Moscow branch's battle flag is to adopt an affirmative, rather than defensive, stance while recruiting support for the traditional family.

Criticism of the theory in France often retains the English term "gender" as a way of stressing its foreignness. Its detractors claim that "gender theory" was invented in the United States, a society built on a consumerist, communitarian, and politically correct model, hence fundamentally incompatible with France's own traditions of intercourse between the sexes. This approach raises suspicions of a foreign plot against the nation's interests, a plot in which sexual minorities are accused of complicity.[181] This fantasy of betrayal by a "sexualist international" has very deep roots in conservative and ultraconservative thinking in France.[182] Caricatures and articles in the press in the 1930s showed "perverts" as feminized, subject to their irresistible attraction to the triumphant masculinity of enemy forces, ever ready to inform, corrupt, and, of course, betray. Perverts belonged simultaneously to an inferior race and an international plot. As Proust described in his passage on the "accursed race" in *Contre Sainte Beuve*, they are the enemy within, like the stateless Jew. Left-wing leaders of the day, such as Léon Blum, were often caricatured as perverts.[183] Jewish women, meanwhile, were often pictured as brutish, dangerous, youth-corrupting viragos. Their gender deviance was at odds with the "national ideal of femininity, which confirmed the dominance of masculinity."[184]

Some attacks on gender theory use the same tactics today. Judith Butler, the only queer writer to be widely known in France (others have been only partially translated and have not had the same media impact),[185] has been attacked by opponents of gender theory for being a woman, a lesbian, American, intellectual, Jewish, and liberal.[186] She is depicted as a veritable Antichrist, reviving all the stereotypes of the virago and the Jewish female. Rejection of gender

FIGURE 17. "Gender theory, here we come!" Source: Facebook page of "The whole truth about the inventor of Gender Studies." Source: https://www.facebook.com/343324779126 723/photos/pb.343324779126723.-2207520000.1461200575./481978061928060 /?type=3&theater.

theory can also take the form of a true crusade in which France, as "the church's eldest daughter," has a special moral responsibility. During a speech to the National Organization for Marriage in Washington, D.C., on June 19, 2014, de la Rochère stressed the fact that France was raising its voice in support of efforts in the United States to promote a universal definition of parenthood based on a heterosexual couple united in matrimony.[187]

Finally, it is important to note that the fight against the alleged invasion of gender theory converged with even more explicitly nationalist and anti-Semitic demonstrations. An event dubbed "The Day of Wrath" was organized in Paris on January 26, 2014, bringing together a loose coalition of far-right and populist groups (including Civitas and Hommen) ostensibly to attack the government's tax policies but resulting in a raw public expression of anti-Semitism.[188] Fascist-style groups (such as Bloc Identitaire) marched to shouts of "Out, out, Jew! France is not for you!" Lists of public figures from Jewish backgrounds were plastered on bus shelters. Many sympathizers of the former stand-up comic Dieudonné, convicted several times of anti-Semitic libel, used the occasion to perform a salute that Dieudonné calls the *quenelle*, a cross between an inverted Nazi salute and the traditional "up yours" gesture implying humiliation via sexual penetration, ultimately meaning "screw the system."[189] A few participants at Manif pour Tous events did the same, playing on the "oppose-the-system" effect.[190] A few days after the Day of Wrath demonstration, the walls of an LGBT center in Toulouse were covered in swastikas and homophobic, anti-Semitic, sexist graffiti. The idea of invasion and betrayal creates unlikely alliances between some groups that demand freedom of conscience and expression from a democratic government they consider corrupted by internationalist minorities and others that denounce the emasculation of France the better to condemn immigration. These alliances are made possible by a shared rhetorical impulse, despite profound internal contradictions.[191]

The Monstrous Minority

While debate over marriage and parenthood consistently links homophobia to anti-Semitism via the figure of the enemy within, it also invokes imaginative notions of freakishness and radical foreignness (the latter rooted in racial stereotypes). Early on Manif pour Tous made a special point of targeting Christiane Taubira, depicting her as a powerful, castrating black woman who used the law to strike at children, who could uproot an entire forest (the tree being simultaneous symbols of genealogy and humankind's roots in nature).[192] She was pictured as a half-human, half-Godzilla figure, a monstrous emblem of the destruction of the French family.

In 2001 Taubira was also the sponsor of a French law making slavery a crime against humanity. Her opponents employed the issue of sexuality to avenge what they saw as another insult to national honor, a law that obliged France to display what they felt was pointless "repentance." The Civitas organization marched to chants of "Banania so good, Taubira no good" (Banania was a brand of chocolate whose advertising mascot was a good—because submissive and uneducated—Negro).[193] It thereby established a direct link between colonialism and marriage for all. Reform of marriage laws was equated with a new "demolition" of French identity, an identity based on the white patriarchal family. Opposition to gay marriage thus offered an opportunity to challenge the anti-racial-discrimination measures of the Taubira bill of 2001: via the image of a freak, sexuality resignified the excessive nature of all minority identities, simultaneously ostentatious and corrupting. The racialized mon-

FIGURE 18. Manif pour Tous poster: "May 26 in Paris. Mammoth Demo." Source: http://www.lamanifpourtous.fr/.

ster expressed a fear of a devouring, egotistical sexuality, itself sparking fear of a race of brutal, disloyal citizens who could never become part of the "real" France, characterized by the moderateness of its universalist philosophy. The fear of repentance and debt toward minorities masked, however, the real stakes behind both Taubira bills: it is not a mere question of reparation for discriminations past and present nor of simple recognition (which would merely incorporate excluded peoples into the community of citizens without redefining that community) but of reconceiving the national community by instituting a critical perspective on collective memory. As Melissa Nobles has stressed,

FIGURE 19. Manif pour Tous poster: "Where Taubira slithers, roots wither." Source: http://www.lamanifpourtous.fr/.

"Apologies are desired, offered, and given in order to change the terms and meanings of membership in a political community."[194]

The symbol of a freak could also be used to condemn gender theory from the perspective of creationism. According to Manif pour Tous posters, androgynous animals (such as snails) were ready to devour children; primitive animals like mammoths—symbolizing the "theory" of evolution—would reduce France's youngest citizens to their basest instincts. Thus, certain elected officials and far-right groups such as Jeunesses Nationalistes were able to assert that marriage for all opened the way to zoophile weddings, since the concept

FIGURE 20. Manif pour Tous poster: "Save our children—from the Taubira Act." Source: http://www.lamanifpourtous.fr/.

was already, in itself, a form of bestiality.[195] In a rearguard action, Christian parthenogenesis suddenly became the paragon of civilization.[196]

The allusions to animality peaked when Taubira visited the city of Angers in her capacity as minister of justice and was greeted by children in a protest group who made monkeylike cries. They waved bananas as they shouted, "Have a banana, you old monkey."[197] On November 13, 2013, punning on banana in an expression that means "back to form," the cover of the far-right weekly *Minute* read, "Cunning Monkey: Taubira Back on the Banana." These racist slurs appeared just days after a Front National candidate, Anne-Sophie

FIGURE 21. Manif pour Tous poster: "Sex 'education' in primary school—hands off our kids." Source: http://www.lamanifpourtous.fr/.

Leclère—convicted of racial insults in July 2014 (a decision overturned in June 2015 for procedural irregularities)[198]—published two photos on her Facebook page comparing Taubira to a monkey; one photo was widely disseminated by neo-Nazi groups such as Boulevard Hitler, which offered apologies to the monkey for being compared to Taubira. Leclère was expelled from the Front National on December 1, 2013, but the party backed her appeal against her conviction.

Also the object of attack was Najat Vallaud-Belkacem, the minister for women's rights who backed the implementation of a male/female equality

FIGURE 22. Manif pour Tous poster: "Stop gender theory at school." Source: http://www.lamanifpourtous.fr/.

curriculum in schools. Her promotion to the post of minister of education on August 26, 2014, was felt to be a provocation by opponents of marriage for all. De la Rochère declared,

> Through the ministry of education, the government can indoctrinate children under the guise of equality, treating students as neutered, undifferentiated beings. Najat Vallaud-Belkacem believes in the anthropological utopia of sex struggle the way some people used to believe in class struggle. This is serious. We wonder what François Hollande is trying to do by making such a controversial appointment—it's shocking and absurd.[199]

A few days later, on September 4, the Catholic magazine *Valeurs Actuelles* ran the headline, "The Ayatollah: Investigation into the Minister of Reeducation." It thereby associated the minister's Moroccan background with religious fanaticism even as, in veiled terms (*reeducation*), it alluded to the brainwashing of children via gender theory.[200] The previous day the cover of *Minute* read: "A Moroccan Muslim at National Education: The Vallaud-Belkacem Controversy." The magazine refused to acknowledge the minister's French citizenship and deliberately played on Islamophobic prejudices. This series of racial slurs shed indirect light on one of the implicit goals of Manif pour Tous and Printemps Français: the demand for a racially, religiously, and sexually pure France.

However, there was a paradox at the heart of this fantasy of purity. The image of the freak or monster, by definition bestial and impure, establishes the symbolic frontiers of civilized humanity.[201] A monster is dangerous because it embodies a brutal, destructive force. As is paradoxically recognized, it has superhuman powers, exercising simultaneously a power of fascination and repulsion. From this viewpoint, casting Taubira and Vallaud-Belkacem as "two powerful women" directly echoes the character of the queer child (and also reinforces the idea of a conspiracy). Adversaries of gender theory criticized its supposed danger to children; by disturbing their frames of reference, such theory threatens to make those children sexually undifferentiated. Katherine Bond Stockton has shown how movies and literature have used the figure of the queer child for its oneiric power:[202] simultaneously feared and admired, such children offer a glimpse of other worlds because their very existence shows that the insistence on a predetermined model does not stem from any social necessity (whereas conservative groups view affirmation of the heterosexual model a necessity for reproduction itself). One of the favorite targets of Manif pour Tous and Printemps Français was Céline Sciamma's film *Tomboy*, released in 2011. The plot involves a ten-year-old girl who, following a move, is willingly taken for a boy by her new friends. That very indeterminateness was the target of attacks, which suggested that the film was a foretaste of what awaited French society: any social legitimization of homosexuality would inevitably lead to a confusion of identities and consequently generated widespread transsexuality and trans identities. The fantasy of the queer child is the flip side of the figure of the infantile adult homosexual. In Chapter 4 I return to the connection between the idea of the future and the many theories that describe homosexuality as halted sexual development and as fixation at an infantile stage. In this respect, it is particularly significant that opponents of gender theory focused primarily on schools.

The Focus on Schools

Signs at the march on October 5, 2014, announced: "We won't let schools bring our children up—child rearing is the parents' role." Why such mistrust of schools, and why did schools become central to public debate? The first reason is that many opponents came from federations of Catholic parent-teacher associations.[203] The second is that there is residual wariness of secular schools among Catholic activists, a mistrust dating back to the late nineteenth century and expressed on numerous occasions, as in 1984 during demonstrations for private education (in opposition to a bill that would change the regulations for private schools, many of which are parochial). Historian Grégoire Kauffmann refers to "nostalgia" for "the preindustrial world" when the Catholic religion still largely dictated values.[204]

Wariness toward gender theory therefore reflected wariness toward today's schools. Several high-profile writers such as Michel Onfray contributed to the fight against "phony gender theory" in schools in the name of preserving traditional academic skills in the face of the "craziness" of postmodern education.[205] In recent years Farida Belghoul has also been organizing opposition via the Internet and public meetings. This vocational high school teacher was an active communist in the 1970s, became involved in the antiracism movement in the 1980s, and has lately moved close to Dieudonné and the far right.[206] She now denounces "LGBT propaganda" and children being corrupted. Playing up rumors, she even claimed that gender theory led to teaching masturbation in kindergarten.[207] In particular, Belghoul targeted the pilot program featuring a "primer on equality" (Les ABCD de l'Égalité). It was launched in nearly six hundred classrooms in the fall of 2013 and comprised texts and exercises

FIGURE 23. Manif pour Tous: "No to gender theory." Paris, February 3, 2014. © Christophe Becker. Reprinted with permission.

designed to prompt students to think about inequalities between men and women; it stemmed from an educational reform bill passed in July 2013, which included the goal of "teaching values of respect and equality among boys and girls, men and women." To counter the program, in December 2013 Belghoul organized a "no-school-today" movement that urged parents not to send their children to school one day per month.[208] The first day was scheduled for January 24, 2014. Exploiting local networks through e-mail and text messaging, Belghoul solicited support from parents who had themselves developed a certain fear or mistrust of schools, often being socially powerless or excluded. Her efforts thus paralleled the work of Catholic family associations, which, being richer in cultural and economic capital, stressed changes in teaching methods themselves. This could be seen in a network called Vigi Gender,[209] in the attempt by the Associations Familiales Catholiques (AFC) to challenge the new education law in the Conseil d'État,[210] and in the pressure applied to several municipal libraries targeted by activists affiliated with Printemps Français as "ideological libraries."[211]

These same groups objected to the action of high school boys in Nantes who decided to wear skirts to school as a sign of protest against sexual prejudice. The one-day event, which took place on May 16, 2014, was criticized by Manif pour Tous, which argued that "skirt day" was the logical outcome of gender theory in a morally derelict society.[212] Skirt day thus became a symbol of resistance to the reactionary trend. However, this elevation of skirts to the level of symbol did not originally stem from debate over gender theory but from the controversy over multiculturalism and the wearing of Islamic headscarves at school, a controversy that began in 1989 when France was celebrating the bicentenary of its revolution. The significance of wearing a skirt was therefore much more ambiguous than the context of debate over marriage for all and gender theory would suggest. For nearly a decade skirts had become a symbol of women's freedom of choice as promoted by several feminist groups close to the Socialist Party, notably Osez le Féminisme! (Dare to Be Feminist!) and Ni Putes ni Soumises (Neither Whores nor Doormats). Yet skirts were also a device through which headscarves were perceived, in contrast, as inevitably worn only by constraint.

These ambiguities were reflected in a film by Jean-Paul Lilienfeld released in March 2009, *La Journée de la jupe* (Skirt Day).[213] In the movie, a high school teacher fed up with her students' aggressiveness takes her whole class hostage after finding a gun a student had brought to school. The film shows how schools are "disarmed" in the face of students from largely immigrant backgrounds, students who do not accept the school's authority or its values, particularly male/female equality. The teacher, whom we ultimately learn has North African roots, is shot by the police. As a sign of tribute, some of her female students finally begin wearing skirts again, something her colleagues and students no longer dared to do. The focus on skirts is particularly interesting given that wearing pants was long identified with the women's liberation movement.[214] A French dress regulation dated November 17, 1800, forbade women to wear pants as a way of limiting their access to certain professions. The regulation was slightly relaxed in 1892 and 1909 but only on one of two conditions: "if the woman has the handles of a bicycle or the reins of a horse in her hands"(!). Although it had fallen out of use, this regulation was formally rescinded by ministerial decree only on January 13, 2013, in the heat of the debate over gender theory.

Opposition to skirt day by Manif pour Tous can also be understood as a rejection of the alleged feminization of French social values. Such feminization was seen as desanctifying male virility, thereby making heterosexual relationships more complicated, indeed difficult. This argument was frequently developed in the mass media by far-right pundits like Éric Zemmour and Alain

Soral, who accused feminism of having destroyed romantic relationships based on male/female dissymmetry. The argument was also advanced in the more filtered form of "life counseling" promoted by an entire psychosocial doxa conveyed through magazines and television programs devoted to health, leisure, and beauty.[215] The phenomenon therefore extends beyond reactionary movements alone: what is at stake is not so much practices as the values associated with them. In the eyes of reactionaries, what queer theory corrupts through its analyses of processes of repetition is the very idea of an educational model. Thibaud Collin, a professor of philosophy linked to Manif pour Tous and the Fondation de Service Politique (Foundation for Political Service, an organization that stresses Europe's Christian roots) thus expressed anxiety that queer theory would turn schools into a "site of confrontation" between the sexes, preventing the natural "imitation" that is "at the heart of any learning process."[216] Butler's argument that gender is a copy without an original leads to a process of subjectification that Collin thinks frustrates any conceptualization of the unity and aim of the individual. He believes that "critical queer theory [is] a kind of anthropological remedy for sexuality's loss of purpose. In a society that considers homosexuality a sexual lifestyle as legitimate as the male/female relationship, this postulate will have an impact on the way people understand the difference between the sexes and their specificities."[217] He proposes a didactic practice of meditation on those specificities, which he draws from the anthropology of Karol Wojtyla, a meditation that progressively leads to the unification of the individual. In other words, if God made *man* in his image, arguing that the image of man is based not on a model but on constant reinvention means tampering with the divine model itself. Queer theory thereby challenges the patrilogical tradition of Catholicism and, more broadly, all monotheistic religions. It also explains why the school issue became the focus of debate over gender theory, because that is where one learns not sexuality itself but the logos. Collin added:

> The curricula in the national education program designed to counter various discriminations, notably homophobia, create an increasing blurring of an understanding of sexual difference. . . . Which raises the question of "purpose" within the education system. . . . Being secular, the state must slowly disengage itself from any ethical or anthropological choices. . . . So [there is] no word, of course, on the purpose of sexuality in terms of the communion of individuals or of fecundity.[218]

School is a particularly powerful locus of identity fantasies because it is perceived as the place where children are literally manufactured. Students themselves largely draw their discourse from the way school is described in the media and public debate in general.[219] Political controversies on gay marriage thus help disseminate the idea that school is not a place of learning but of reeducation.

Political Emotions: A Double-Edged Sword

Campaigns against teaching so-called gender theory thus function on two levels: by insinuating that sex and sexuality can be learned, they place the debate on irrational foundations; and by stressing the idea of a plot, they seek to win support by spurring fears of the commodification of children. Christine Boutin's strategy during her 2012 campaign for president was emblematic of the myth of "reeducation." Through twisted appropriation of fragments of classic Western culture (including a famous quotation by Simone de Beauvoir, considered seminal by many feminist movements) and popular culture (such as bearded drag queen Conchita Wurst's winning of the 2014 Eurovision Song Contest), she presented herself as the sole rampart against the reification of children. While playing on fear is an effective way to get voters' attention, it is not sufficient to guarantee support if unaccompanied by a concrete platform that reflects well-established electoral sociology.[220] Boutin's campaigns were thus double-edged swords. Because she did not start from realistic premises, she became the butt of satirical TV shows and numerous Internet sites.[221] Several spoof posters circulated on the web, mocking not only Christine Boutin as the guardian of youth but also Manif pour Tous as the promoter of a model of society that was outmoded and silly.[222]

Confronted with opposition to marriage reform and joint adoption by homosexual couples, LGBT associations moved into action on several occasions. The two main demonstrations took place in Paris on December 16, 2012, and January 27, 2013.[223] They drew roughly 150,000 participants according to the organizers, 60,000 according to the police. In attendance were not only artists (including Orlan and Jane Birkin) but also local officials (Jean-Paul Huchon, the socialist president of the Ile-de-France region, and Bertrand Delanoë, the socialist mayor of Paris and one of the few openly gay politicians), a government minister (Cécile Duflot, the green minister of housing), as well as LGBT activists. Many participants decided to respond to Manif pour Tous in an ironic tone, as witnessed by the slogans on a number of signs: "We promise, Christine, to keep our hands off our cousins" (Christine Boutin was married to her first cousin); "Even with two papas, the same UMP" (the UMP was riven by a leadership crisis that resulted in two co-presidents, Jean-François Copé and François Fillon); "François, don't be so frigid" (double mockery of President François Hollande and Frigide Barjot).

Other demonstrators attacked the Socialist Party directly for its indecision over several clauses of the bill, especially the presumption of parenthood

FIGURE 24. Christine Boutin's poster for her 2012 presidential campaign: "You will be a woman, my son! (almost) Rudyard Kipling. Sign the petition against teaching gender theory in high school science classes." Source: http://franceculture.fr/.

and the absence of legal clauses on MAP. One sign read, "The PS retreats, the fascists advance." The party's failure to employ economic arguments was also targeted: "Wedding lists for gays will kick-start the economy." One mixed feminist collective asserted its demands not only for marriage and adoption reform but also MAP and surrogate pregnancy with three shouts of "Yes, yes, yes!"[224] Following two women's flagrant kiss right before the eyes of Manif pour Tous in Marseille,[225] regular "kiss-ins" were held,[226] even after the Taubira bill was passed, in reaction to new demonstrations or threats to the law[227]—in November 2014 a kiss-in was held in front of the headquarters of Nicolas Sarkozy's campaign for the presidency of the UMP after he announced that he was in favor of repealing the Taubira Act.

While these efforts displayed real creativity,[228] they were insufficient to counteract the high media profile of demonstrations against the bill.[229] Thus, they contrast with the extensive media coverage given to the marriage ceremony in Bègles in 2004. Putting marriage for all on the parliamentary agenda was in fact the product—as it is for other gender-related issues—of complex "multilevel governance."[230] It operated simultaneously on the European level (both European Union legislation and jurisprudence established by the European Court of Human Rights, which increasingly influences national laws),[231] the national level (the development of "expertise" in family law),[232] and the local level (as early as 1995, campaigns for marriage reforms were led by many LGBT associations, spearheaded by AIDES, a community-based organization against HIV founded after Michel Foucault's death).[233] This phenomenon was not exclusively French, because marriage for all was being placed on the legislative agenda throughout Europe.[234] In the case of France, the extension of marriage to same-sex couples by socialist governments in Belgium and Spain put considerable pressure on the Socialist Party to join the movement. Finally, the emergence of the idea of marriage for homosexual couples was promoted by communication across well-established personal networks at the intersection of the political, activist, and academic spheres.[235] It was therefore somewhat harder for the media spotlight to pick out promoters of the political implementation of marriage for all.

Meanwhile, Manif pour Tous, although riddled by internal tensions, made it a point of honor to present a fairly unified front (as witnessed by its work on its logo and imagery, adopted in identical form throughout the country).[236] Although LGBT associations had united for a while over the battle for civil unions, they had largely fragmented since that time,[237] not because the demand for marriage reform was less popular than civil unions—only a few dissenting voices were heard, such as that of Marie-Jo Bonnet, a former activist in the Front Homosexuel d'Action Révolutionnaire and the Gouines Rouges (Red Dykes), who opposed gay marriage, MAP, and surrogate pregnancy[238]—but mainly because individual LGBT associations' relationships to the establishment varied considerably. While some groups remained close to political parties (Homosexualité et Socialisme, Gaylib, Inter-LGBT, among others), many groups refused to take action in a political sphere whose legitimacy they contested. Such was the case with women-only lesbian groups (La Barbare), social networks and blogs (*Le Blog de João*),[239] and certain queer and feminist associations (Queer Food for Love and Les Panthères Roses [Pink Panthers], respectively). The fantasy of a unified theory triumphed over the reality of fragmented social movements.

CHAPTER 1 has shown that the fantasy of an invasion of French society via gender theory preceded legislative debate over extending marriage and joint adoption to same-sex couples. The fear of reeducating children fueled the notion that gender trouble could be taught and that heterosexual marriage was one of the last ramparts against this minority pressure. There was a direct link between dread of an American invasion and fear of contagion by a minority culture, that is, the propagation of its erotic, political, and social practices. Debate over marriage and adoption was so shaped by this scenario that the very terms of debate were imposed on advocates of reform, who were obliged to reply point by point. As a direct consequence, it became impossible to propose new ways of envisaging the couple and the family,[240] of carefully studying the relevant reforms. Such was notably the case with MAP (which was postponed for an indefinite period),[241] the presumption of parenthood, restrictions on homosexual marriage for nationals of certain foreign countries, self-determination for transgender persons, and so on. Therefore, in coming years sexual minorities might have to take the jurisprudential route again (as they did in the past in regard to civil unions and adoption by single parents) rather than the legislative one to change the law and limit the scope of the discrimination they suffer.[242] The Cour de Cassation, France's highest appeals court, has already decreed that the adoption of the biological child of a partner conceived abroad through MAP is not a violation of law. It also validated the marriage of a Franco-Moroccan homosexual couple despite a convention between the two countries that stipulates application of marriage laws in the country of origin, except where public order may be affected. Fantasies over theory are therefore not inert—they directly affect people's lives. By asserting new ways of thinking, they force people to adapt their relationship to the public sphere and the law. This constant shift cannot be grasped by the catch-all term "gender theory." Chapter 2 explains that the notion of gender theory is merely a synecdoche for "queer theory" and discusses its impact in France.

CHAPTER 2

THE MANY MEANINGS OF QUEER

WHAT DO FRENCH OPPONENTS of queer theory mean when they talk of an "American" theory? Why do they turn Judith Butler into the symbol of a theory they claim to oppose? A study of the many books and articles on the subject leaves no doubt that what they call gender theory refers to a set of American publications on sex and sexuality, which allegedly culminated in queer theory. Essayist Alain de Benoist, founder of Groupement de Recherche et d'Études pour la Civilisation Européenne (Research and Study Group for European Civilization, GRECE), a pagan, neoconservative think tank, explains:

> The notion of "gender" as used in the theory of the same name appeared in the 1950s and 1960s in clinical studies of pathological categories such as hermaph-rodism, intersexuality, and transsexuality. In the United States, gender theory then became popular among feminist movements, followed by the major uni-versities, where "gender studies" soon displaced the earlier "feminist studies" and "women's studies." In 1990, Judith Butler provided the canonical form of the theory in a book that enjoyed nearly worldwide success.[1]

The notion of gender is criticized for denying physical determinism and ben-efiting an ideology of pure subjectivity. "Judith Butler, for example, feels that the body is originally a 'neutral surface.'"[2] Benoist argues that Butler's neu-tered vision is a kind of "death wish," while essayist Bérénice Levet calls it a form of "puerility."[3] While gender theory works as a catch-all concept that ranges from the work of American psychologist John Money in the 1950s to recent teaching material on male/female equality in French public schools, it tends to result in a denunciation of any denial of biological sexes or any deconstruction of the symbolic primacy of fecund heterosexuality and in the assertion of the infantilism or death drive of its academic advocates. These are the same arguments traditionally mobilized against homosexuality itself. Marguerite Peeters is very clear about what is at stake: she claims that the theory embodies a shift from a "feminist interpretation" to a "homosexual interpretation" of gender.[4] Many online comments share this vision and directly evoke the sexual orientation of the academics themselves. The Catholic blog *Le Salon Beige* states, "This type of book is a product of theories developed by lesbian academics in California."[5]

While the notion of gender theory covers a wide range of research, it functions—through a double fantasy of the foreign and the foreigner—in a context in which power relationships are undergoing partial redistribution due to reforms in civil law. More specifically, the anxiety involves fear of epistemological castration. Gender theory's crime is not only the deconstruction of relations between the sexes but also an attack on the linkage of male/masculinity/knowledge. Levet refers to a "vanished phallus," citing such emblematic examples as Gayle Rubin, Paul B. Preciado, Joan Scott, and Céline Sciamma (in addition to Judith Butler, on whom Levet focused most of her attention). All are placed in the lineage of Simone de Beauvoir and the question of "becoming" a woman.[6] In the end, the issue raised by public opponents of gender theory is one of a ramifying process of "becoming," not restricted by a gendered definition of the production of knowledge. The focus on certain female academics can also be explained by how they are perceived from the standpoint of *their* gender. Butler has explained that whenever her work is attacked, the attack also targets what she exemplifies as an individual.[7] She can even make fun of the situation: when she was inducted as a knight into the Ordre des Arts et des Lettres at the French consulate in San Francisco on January 26, 2015, she joked, "I've been wondering how to get used to the idea of being dubbed a knight. Becoming a knight is very queer!"[8]

THIS CHAPTER on the presence of queer theory in France does not seek to map out various spheres of French "reception" of queer theory—such an approach is doomed to failure due to the great plasticity of the way queer theory is used and to the mosaic-like nature of queer theory itself. Such mapping would tend to fossilize the meaning of practices that are both mobile and polysemic. What interests me is an analysis of the complex relationship to identity and the fantasies that arise from the idea of American culture, on the basis of which interpretive communities are constituted.[9] Didier Eribon has supplied a perfect example of this complexity.[10] In 1997, Eve Sedgwick participated in the first major symposium on gay and lesbian studies to be hosted in France. Organized by Eribon at the Pompidou Center in Paris, it was attended by most of the writers associated with the idea of queer theory in the United States. Sedgwick's paper was titled "Making Queer Meanings." However, given the difficulty of translating the word "queer" for a French audience, she decided—in consultation with Eribon—to use the term "gay": "Construire des significations gay." By the time the proceedings of the symposium were about to be published, a debate had arisen over the terms "gay" and "queer" themselves, so Sedgwick and Eribon decided to return to the original English word: "Construire des significations queer."[11] Oblivious of that history, a recent anthology of essays by Sedgwick not previously published in English, *The Weather in Proust*, included the paper under the title used at the symposium itself: "Making Gay Meanings."[12] The translation thus carried out a rearguard action: The term "queer," associated with a certain critique of the word "gay" in the United States, was used in the published French title of Sedgwick's paper, whereas the term "gay," which seemed more acceptable to a French audience in the late 1990s, was used for the English title. In other words, the "source" was so marked by its echo that it was itself thereby transformed. Thus, this chapter studies fluid cultural meanings without seeking to pinpoint their exact point of origin or arrival.

First I discuss the context of the emergence of queer theory in the United States in the early 1990s and why that phenomenon was relatively unnoticed in France. Only a few activist LGBT movements adopted this new tool as part of their operative arsenal—such as Les Soeurs de la Perpétuelle Indulgence and ACT UP Paris—without, however, particularly emphasizing the word "queer." So the emergence of queer theory in France as a movement, indeed a "corpus," dates to the latter half of the 1990s, when several academic workshops and seminars began analyzing writings on queer theory, sometimes engaging in dialogue with the authors. Didier Eribon, Éric Fassin, Françoise Gaspard, Michel Feher, Jean Allouch, Paul B. Preciado, and Marie-Hélène/Sam Bourcier all played important roles in this pioneering work. The early 2000s were marked by a new phenomenon, the use of the word "queer" in the mass media (especially television) in both commercials and entertainment programs. The use of an English term directed to a non-English audience reflected a strategy of orchestrating a new approach to diversity without actually naming what was really involved. Finally, I describe the rise of a new, activist generation that labeled itself "queer," using the term either to critique forms of exclusion and mercantilism that govern traditional LGBT organizations or to broaden gay and lesbian movements to other struggles. In so doing, I present two movements: Les Tordu(e)s, a group that arose in opposition to the Paris Pride March; and Queer Week at the elite college Sciences Po, a week of events, debates, and workshops on gender and sexuality organized by the students. The chapter concludes by linking the multiple meanings of "queer" to an analysis of the effects of its reiterated use in the public sphere.

Queer Theory's Wrong Gender

Since the fantasy of a queer conspiracy underpins denunciations of gender theory, I first briefly describe the emergence of queer theory. In the United States, queer theory initially arose as a critique of the essentialist tendency of certain schools of gender studies in the 1980s. The notion of gender appeared in American academia in the mid-1950s when John Money studied the behavior of hermaphroditic patients whom he encountered in the Johns Hopkins University endocrinology department.[13] This notion was not an invention of clinical psychology or of psychoanalytical theory. It was simply a semantic coinage that served Money's desire to describe the roles and identities associated or dissociated with each sex.[14] The term "gender" became more widespread thanks to books by psychoanalyst Robert Stoller and sociologist Ann Oakley.[15] Very quickly, however, gender as a system of classification tended to give way to analyses of gender as a set of qualities associated with the two sexes. This approach tended to remove sex itself from the analysis, as though the biological status of man and woman went without saying. This phenomenon was particularly marked among theorists of maternalist philosophy (such as Nancy Chodorow and Carol Gilligan), who sought to valorize moral qualities specific to women. The idea of female writing also occasionally took an essentialist drift, guided by a need to forge a group of women into an interpretive community. Queer theory arose in opposition to this drift.[16]

The first main push toward queer theory came in the 1980s from American historian Joan W. Scott and philosopher and poet Denise Riley.[17] Both demonstrated that gender is a critical category from which the notion of sex itself

must be questioned. Scott and Riley showed that individual and collective relationships to the notion of gender fluctuate historically, even as the meanings
of the term "gender" itself simultaneously shift. Gender, as a critical tool, thus
led to a double deconstruction of the processes of identification and categorization, which then effectively paved the way for queer theory.[18] Another impetus
came from Chicana studies[19]—Gloria Anzaldúa was one of the first academics to use the term "queer" to describe herself, referring to the strangeness of
categorical shifts triggered by her multiple identities; as a lesbian born in Texas
to Mexican parents, she had to deal with sexism, racism, homophobia, and
class racism. Anzaldúa thus adopted the term "queer" in her 1987 book, Borderlands—La Frontera: The New Mestiza.[20] The third push came from the new
attention brought to bear on materialist analyses by Gayle Rubin and Monique
Wittig. Both of them addressed, if in very different ways, the heterosexist assumptions of Western knowledge, especially how hierarchical systems are
based on the notion of difference. The fourth factor influencing the emergence
of queer theory was the growth of critical analysis of identities in the wake of
the Birmingham school of cultural studies, which explored the field of popular
cultures and minority literatures and served to introduce into the United States
poststructuralist texts devoted to the proliferation of discourses on humanity.
Finally, perhaps the most decisive influence came from activist efforts themselves, particularly the inclusion of trans people and the fight against AIDS, as
epitomized by ACT UP New York, founded in 1987. During the late 1980s, future queer theorists witnessed street actions of a new type, which were crucial
to a rethinking of performativity, as illustrated by David Halperin's work on the
influence of Foucault via queer theory:

> Foucault's approach also opens up, correspondingly, the possibility of a *queer*
> *politics* defined not by the struggle to liberate a common, repressed, preexisting
> nature but by an on-going process of self-constitution and self-transformation—
> a queer politics anchored in the perilous and shifting sands of non-identity, po-
> sitionality, discursive reversibility, and collective self-invention. In that sense
> perhaps it is not too much to say that Foucault produced the non-theory of
> which ACT UP is the practice.[21]

While the pertinence of the notion of non-identity might be questioned—a
notion that Halperin himself tended to moderate in later work where he explored the potential conditions for a gay culture and subjectivity[22]—queer theory does indeed link an analysis of performativity of identities to a critique of

difference as a system of thought. Noting that sexual categories, in particular the homosexual/heterosexual dichotomy, have structured Western ways of categorizing and behaving throughout the twentieth century, Butler, Sedgwick, and Teresa de Lauretis began deconstructing the performative power of categories of gender and sexuality.[23] All three, in highly different spheres—philosophy, literature, and media studies, respectively—undertook a critique of the hegemony of heterosexual representations of society and its impact on subjectivity, the body, and the naming of self. Queer not only is a reappropriation of an epithet (meaning strange, bizarre, warped, or, at the level of insult, a fag)—a reappropriation that makes it possible to shift categories, methods, and fields of legitimate knowledge—but also indicates that a queer analysis will be attentive to the crossing of categorical, national, racial, and other boundaries. In fact, "queer" derives etymologically from the Indo-European root -twerkw, which means "across." Queer theory shows that sexual categories and behaviors never perfectly coincide, that subjects constitute themselves across the gaps. Queer theory is therefore not built around an object or an anti-object but stems more from a critique or strategic approach attentive to displacements, zones of friction, and lapses in norms.[24] It covers highly diverse studies whose fields and references often have little in common except a shared reference to the critical watershed of the performative aspect of identities, which acquired greater visibility in the early 1990s.[25]

Queer theory quickly became a key academic movement at a time when neoliberal economics were triumphing. It offers a way to challenge policies of sexual identity that perceive the subject as having political and economic unity.[26] Furthermore, queer theory promotes new perspectives on gender studies themselves by reconceptualizing variations in gender and transgender practices. Leslie Feinberg shows, for example, that transgender experiences are not always troubling but might also be experienced as a doubling or multiplying of identities or as a dissolution or side-stepping of identity.[27] Jack Halberstam's *Female Masculinity* also represents a watershed in queer theory by demonstrating the existence of many forms of masculinity, which can be conceptualized and expressed outside the framework of the male body, as witnessed by lesbians, butches, and trans dykes, as well as heterosexual women who do not adhere to forms of femininity associated with passivity and dependence.[28] These studies and others have revitalized the way that subjectification is conceptualized. Queer theory nevertheless encounters its limits if it fails to pay attention to the role of institutions. When it becomes a simple hermeneutic exercise centered on subjectification, it runs the risk of settling into predetermined territories and loses the capacity to counter the very categories it engenders. [29]

Queer yet Unknowing

I challenge the term "reception" when conceptualizing queer theory in France not only because queer theory makes many references to French sources from the 1960s–1980s but also because the activist environment that inspired queer theory in the United States was already a transatlantic phenomenon, even before the first translations and conferences had been held in France. [30] Sociologist Jean-Yves Le Talec, a member of the French Soeurs de la Perpétuelle Indulgence, has described spending the summer of 1991 in Los Angeles. [31] The Californian convent of Sisters of Perpetual Indulgence was in regular contact with the Queer Nation organization at that time, although the term "queer" was not very popular among the sisters, who already had their own linguistic arsenal, including "gender fuck" and "radical faeries." The word "queer" nevertheless spread among LGBT spheres in the early 1990s, referring not so much to queer theory as to an antinormative activism that promoted multiple sexual identities, cultures, and practices. The term "queer" was subsequently adopted by e-mail lists such as the France Queer Resource Directory, the French branch of a European database that has been online since 1994 and regularly posts announcements of queer events. Such was the case with the International Queer Liberation Tour, a queer performance festival organized in Utrecht, Netherlands, that toured Europe in the summer of 1995. Gay anarchist networks affiliated with *Androzine*, a magazine edited by Bruno Peuportier, were also directly aware of initiatives by North American queer groups, such as Queers United in Support of Political Prisoners. [32] In a post dated March 7, 1995, Peuportier described various alternative queer fanzines, making the following comment on the Québécois fanzine *Queer Terrorist/Queer Tapette*: "With a title like that, it must be a Canadian gay fanzine." [33] Clearly, here queer does not refer to queer theory but to antinormative sexual minorities from the LGBT ranks, to the extent of becoming interchangeable with the word "gay."

It was only after queer theory acquired greater visibility in France—that is, after the first academic seminars were organized, the first translations were published, and the term reached the media—that the use of queer would become distinct from use of the acronym LGBT. The queer and LGBT activist movements nevertheless remained connected, if only through the lives of their advocates. Such was the case of Jean-Jean, who authored the fanzine *Star* in Lyon in the 1990s and participated in La Croisière (The Cruise, a gay anarchist event launched in Toulouse in 1998, modeled on the Berlin organization Homoland but ended in 2003).[34] La Croisière published a fanzine, *Bangbang*, and participated in several Gay Pride parades in Toulouse. The idea of a venue where gay anarchists could meet, socialize, and debate was thus linked to the promotion of greater visibility for the LGBT community. In the wake of La Croisière, several gay squats were opened in Toulouse, usually surviving for only a few months, such as Le Sissies; sometimes these squats, such as Sextoy, reopened as queer squats. However, some activists, including Jean-Jean himself, rejected the term "queer" because they felt it did not have the same power to overturn homegrown labels of discrimination and offense in French, such as *pédé* (fag), *gouine* (dyke), *travelo* (drag), *tapette* (pansy), *camioneuse* (butch), and *goudou* (lezzy). Jean-Jean claimed that "a queer celebration is a closet celebration!"[35] In practice, the ways that French activists label themselves were fairly fluid, combining old categories and references to "queer." The latter term lent global legitimacy to organizations that were part of a local web of associations and made it possible to establish international connections. The Croisière event was thus also organized in Belgium and Switzerland. The *pédé* identity was considered a unifying link by participants even as their discourse referred to "queerness and identities."[36] Similarly, a group called Queermunard—punning on Communard—which organized parties and events in Toulouse in the early 2010s, brandished the epithets *trans*, *pédé*, and *gouine*.

The work of circumscribing the term "queer" in French was partly carried out when the idea of queer theory was introduced into activist circles. This introduction was accompanied by the reading of a few classic texts on queer theory. Symptomatic of this phenomenon were the regular summer seminars on homosexuality known as the Universités d'Été Euroméditerranéennes sur les Homosexualités (Euromediterranean Summer University on Homosexualities, UEEH). Launched in 1979 by Groupe de Libération Homosexuelle (Homosexual Liberation Group) in Marseille, these seminars drew LGBT activists and scholars together to explore new forms of knowledge based on shared social experiences in a self-managed environment. The UEEH seminars ceased for nearly ten years when the activist world was dealing with most difficult period of the AIDS epidemic and then recommenced in 1999, when the seminars were relabeled Rencontres Lesbigaytransqueerintersexeféministes. At the 1999 session, media sociologist Marie-Hélène/Sam Bourcier ran an introductory workshop on the notion of queer titled "Screw Your Gender." In 2002, a paper was presented on queer movements on American campuses. That same year, Queer Factory, an artistic collective founded by writers Erik Rémès and Cy Jung with cabaret performer Madame H, proposed a theatrical workshop titled "Queer Academy." The protagonists recounted their sexual and political experiences, raising the notion of "queer" for discussion. "Queer" was defined as a subversion of norms and a rejection of assigned identity, but the finer points and arguments of queer theory were not addressed.[37] Similarly, queer workshops that advocated sexual experimentation with no presumptions about the individual's sex or gender gradually disappeared. Vincent Bourseul, then treasurer of ACT UP Paris and present at UEEH several years running, noted that in regard to speaking out, the domination of academic knowledge was not always easy to curb.[38] Furthermore, the idea of pansexual workshops raised various issues of consent, which resulted in numerous regulations. In the end, these initiatives gave way to the inscription of each individual's desire within the lesbian, gay, or trans subculture in which the participants had been socialized (cruising venues, language, relationship to the body, division of roles, and so on).

The term "queer" is the locus of numerous divergences over the way individuals establish themselves in activist communities. These tensions lend the word both its polysemic nature and great mobility. Thus, ACT UP Paris has always been attuned to the queer register (itself inspired by camp humor and the world of drag performance), although the organization did not necessarily adopt it as an underlying principle of action.[39] Philippe Mangeot, a former president of ACT UP Paris, explained as much when Emmanuelle Cosse (also former leader of the ecology party, and now minister for housing and sustainable habitat) became the association's first heterosexual president.

> It is impossible to overstate the fact that the French language lacks a suitable translation of "queer." At ACT UP we have sufficiently perverted the meaning of the word *pédé* to make it a potential equivalent of queer. I would like to point out, for those who don't know it, that Emmanuelle Cosse, who is currently assuming the presidency of ACT UP, is perhaps less homosexual than Rémès, Pouliquen, and le Bitoux [Jan-Paul Pouliquen and Jean le Bitoux were two gay activists], but she is infinitely more *pédée* than they are.[40]

While the link between ACT UP's methods and queer theory is obvious (through zaps, manifestos, and joint actions with other minorities such as undocumented workers and prostitutes' associations),[41] queer theory was not necessarily backed up by all members. The founding president of ACT UP, Didier Lestrade, argued that queer theory's focus on gender performances would overshadow the health emergency created by the AIDS epidemic: "The queer movement sprang up in order to escape from the distress of AIDS. Queer theorists addressed that issue in order to avoid addressing AIDS. It's a deformation—the idea of survival doesn't even enter into the queer world." Lestrade's comment was not just an accusation of elitism: "The only thing really holding back the adaptation of queer philosophy in France is the lack of academic structures and publishing outlets that would nourish debate." He stressed that queer theory lacked urgency, indeed led to a position that undermined collective responsibility in the name of individual freedom: "It is well known that the paradigm of the queer spirit, that quest for total liberty, has led to relapses and bareback sex. Let's look this straight in the face. If I'm queer, if I view myself as a totally unique individual in society, then my sense of freedom inevitably pushes me toward unrestricted sexuality."[42] This idea of unbridled freedom is a commonplace regarding queer theory and reflects neither the content nor the history of that theory. Lestrade's comments should nevertheless be understood in light of the fact that several advocates of bareback sex, such as Guillaume Dustan and Erik Rémès, used the label "queer" in the media when justifying their position.[43] The slipperiness of the term "queer" in French also stems from a process of depoliticization: If every sexual experience can be given a queer gloss, then what political meaning does the term retain? That was the subject addressed by several academic seminars keen to return to the critical significance of the thrust of queer theory as it emerged in the United States in 1990.

Intellectual Cleavages

In 1996, sociologist Éric Fassin and philosopher Michel Feher organized a seminar at the exclusive École Normale Supérieure (ENS) in Paris. Initially titled "Sexual Discordances and Romantic Tales," the seminar later became "Current Sexual Affairs: The Politics of Gender, Sexuality, and Kinship" when the pair was joined by psychoanalyst Michel Tort. Feher, although Belgian, had obtained his master's degree from Columbia University in New York and then wrote his doctoral thesis, "The Betwixt: An Outline for a Theory of Influence," at the Université de Paris I (Panthéon-Sorbonne) under the supervision of Michel Serres, defended in 1985 before a jury chaired by Gilles Deleuze. Back in

New York, Feher became the editor of *Zone Books* magazine and then founded and codirected the publishing house of the same name. He served as the campaign director for the "Sarajevo" party led by Bernard-Henri Lévy and André Glucksmann in the 1994 European parliamentary elections and wrote on multiculturalism for *Esprit* magazine.[44] Key influences were the question of eroticism (in 1989 Feher coedited *Fragments for a History of the Human Body*) and his encounter with Éric Fassin, then assistant director of the Institute of French Studies at New York University. After having read Fassin's article on Clarence Thomas, also published in *Esprit*,[45] Feher and Fassin undertook a deconstruction of the rhetoric of the segment of French left-wing thought that was increasingly aligning itself with strict right-wing American arguments against "politically correct" multiculturalism.[46] Fassin and Feher thereby explored a position counter to the philosophy of *Esprit*. Their seminar at the ENS, headed by Fassin, was one tool of this critical undertaking. The seminar, serving as an interface between France and the United States, was more than just a field of translation (Fassin orchestrated publication of the French translation, by philosopher Cynthia Kraus, of Butler's *Gender Trouble*),[47] because it created the space for a contextualization of the political stakes of sexuality even as it played a significant role in training younger scholars. For example, historian Camille Robcis, a regular participant in the seminar, devoted her early research to the role of psychoanalytical and anthropological networks in the elaboration of sexual policies in France.[48] Also in the wake of the ENS seminar on sexual politics there emerged a critique of contemporary expertise on the family and the law in France. In 1999, Fassin and legal experts Marcela Iacub and Daniel Borrillo edited a book on these issues.[49]

Media sociologist Marie-Hélène/Sam Bourcier launched a different initiative in 1996 when he founded Zoo, a working group that addressed the issue of queerness. It organized a day-long seminar in June of that year at the Centre Gai et Lesbien de Paris, which raised the question, "When will gay, lesbian, and queer studies arrive in France?"[50] In 1997 Zoo met and held several seminars, which included, alongside Bourcier, Marco Dell'Omodarme (a student of philosophy), Claudie Lesselier (a feminist activist), Catherine Deschamps (a PhD candidate in social anthropology studying bisexuality), Georges Sidéris (a doctoral student in Byzantine studies), Olivier Jablonski (a member of ACT UP Paris and moderator of the online archive *Le Séminaire gai*), and Karine Espineira and Maud-Yeuse Thomas (who would later jointly found the Observatoire des Transidentités). In 1996 Zoo drew a distinction between "queer culture" and "lesbian and gay culture" but did not initially view them as antagonistic. The introduction to the group's first seminar stated that "when we, at Zoo, refer to gays, bis, trans, lesbians, or dykes, we are not speaking of rigid categories, hermetically sealed from each other." It went on to declare: "Let's be clear: at Zoo we want 'gay studies' and 'queer studies' to develop."[51] The introduction to the Zoo seminar avoided defining queer and queer studies, preferring instead to employ queer as a tool to which all could impart their own meaning. "So I don't want to say much about what queer is, if only because we don't all have the same vision of queerness. I will only say that queer is nonassimilationist and nonessentialist. That's all I'll say. We didn't want to do an educational rap on what queerness is."[52]

Zoo advocated nonconformism (and a certain anti-academicism) in terms of form, combined with direct links to the world of activism—it sought to be a site of open debate, even welcoming a certain cacophony.[53] The term "queer" was perceived as a symbol of this teeming discourse on gender and as a pioneering act of transformation of relationships of power and knowledge. Zoo also promoted the translation of key texts from English. In its wake the Balland publishing house issued French editions under an imprint headed by Guillaume Dustan, of Bourcier's *Queer Zones*, Monique Wittig's *La Pensée straight*, and Paul B. Preciado's *Le Manifeste contra-sexuel*. Preciado, a former student of Derrida, scorned phallocentric academic performance and proposed a different approach in which "the dildo precedes the penis."[54] Preciado's work is directly inspired by Teresa de Lauretis's exploration of the technologies of gender. Bourcier also translated three articles by de Lauretis, anthologized as *Théorie queer et Cultures populaires: de Foucault à Cronenberg*. The volume included an introduction by social psychologist Pascale Molinier, who herself oversaw publication of an article by Butler on the bodies of athletes.[55] Also in the wake of Zoo there emerged the group ArchiQ—Marco Dell'Omodarme, thanks to his experience as a salaried employee of ACT UP Paris, worked with Bourcier to establish an LGBT archive that created a conflict with another project backed by the Paris city hall,[56] but with no result so far.[57] This archival work represents an extension of reflection on queer time frames and the question of collective memory.[58] The Zoo seminars adopted an nonassimilationist stance.[59] They conveyed a real fascination with a "different world" where all norms could be eliminated by the collective act of speaking out and creating subcultures. Yet any nonassimilationist exercise tends to resignify (if only through opposition) the very norms it contests.[60]

Eribon, as a sociologist, has instead demonstrated how subjectification has always been informed by norms, even ones that are not desired.[61] Eribon is Michel Foucault's biographer and was also close to Georges Dumézil and Claude Lévi-Strauss. He taught for several years as a visiting scholar at the University of California, Berkeley, taking an active part in the emergence of queer theory. In June 1997 he invited important specialists in the field to a symposium at the Pompidou Center in Paris.[62] The press labeled him a dangerous agent of the Americanization of French universities. *Le Monde* published a front-page article by Frédéric Martel (a former adviser to socialist cabinet minister Martine Aubry as well as the author of *Le Rose et le Noir*) that described the Pompidou event as a threat to French culture.[63] Repeating the main thesis of his book, the "ghettoization" of homosexuals, Martel leveled accusations against, pell-mell, the establishment of "gay libraries," the symposium being held at the Pompidou Center, attendees Pierre Bourdieu and Monique Wittig (without explicitly naming the latter), the allegedly "identity-based" interpretation of Foucault's work, and American-style communitarianism:

> While we might be pleased that the Pompidou Center is hosting a series of lectures on homosexuality—that is its role—we are soon disillusioned. By claiming that the concept of gay and lesbian studies is self-evident, all debate is squelched. By including analyses solely from communitarian thinkers and American academics with a propagandist outlook, the project is reduced to an activist event. . . . By claiming to find consolation in the glorification of their own culture, some gay activists explicitly challenge all value judgments. Whether academic or artistic, such judgments are purportedly based on criteria that are imposed (by, implicitly, the "heterosexual establishment") and then reinforced in the final analysis by establishment structures. . . . Could a heterosexual student enroll in a department of gay and lesbian studies and feel comfortable there? Could gay students in that department free themselves from the political pressures of that community, avoid becoming the mouthpiece of their own kind?[64]

Martel argued that unhappy gays and lesbians found consolation in a communitarian activism that excluded them from the universality of knowledge and representation (since they could henceforth represent only their own group). By critiquing power relationships, gays and lesbians even threatened heterosexual sociability. Gay and lesbian studies were denounced for being American, which meant associating the United States with a culture that criticized norms, whereas France represented the maintenance of tradition. Pierre Bourdieu then wrote to *Le Monde* in response to Martel's article, which "contained a series of untruths and absurdities," and attacked him personally: "It is most unfortunate that French intellectual life is so closed that issues being discussed in universities through Europe and the world can still be presented, in your publication, as the expression of a 'homosexual conspiracy' against philosophy and culture."[65] Bourcier and Zoo, however, quickly accused Bourdieu of appropriating minority discourse to his own ends. Bourcier referred to him on several occasions as a "dominator" since he dared to point out that relationships of domination cannot be eliminated through the magic of performance.[66]

In the fall of 1997 Françoise Gaspard, a professor at EHESS, launched a seminar, "The Sociology of Homosexualities." She involved Eribon, who was then writing his *Réflexions sur la question gay*. The seminar, which ran until 2004, sparked controversy about Gaspard and Eribon; communist legislator Maxime Gremetz even queried minister of education Claude Allègre about why Eribon was allowed to teach even though he had no post at EHESS.[67] Each year focused on a different theme: in 1998–99, "The State of Gay and Lesbian Studies"; in 1999–2000, "Questioning the Difference between the Sexes"; in 2000–1, "Writing the History of Homosexualities"; in 2001–2, "Gay and Lesbian Literature"; and, after a one-year hiatus, "News from the 1970s: Homosexual Politics" in 2003–4.

Numerous American academics participated in the seminar on the sociology of homosexualities, including Michael Lucey, David Halperin, Judith Butler, Leo Bersani, Carolyn Dean, Elizabeth Ladenson, and George Chauncey. Queer theory was discussed without, however, focusing on the label "queer" itself or on the idea of a corpus. All kinds of cultural practices that influenced individual relationships to the body, to a sense of belonging, language, and law were dissected, the better to analyze how they shaped and cut across categories. For example, in January 2003 Anne F. Garréta presented her novel *Pas un Jour* (Not a Single Day), in which each chapter described the life of a female lover through a narrative of sexuality that did not hinge on a first-person viewpoint (which would have implied the classic approach to narrative as self-confession).[68] Similarly, in 2004 filmmaker Lionel Soukaz showed his films *Race d'Ep* (1979) and *Ire* (1980), which superimposed images of emblematic venues of homosexual culture with pictures of current events, sexual intercourse, and so on. Soukaz also discussed difficulties with the police during various screenings. Rather than seeking to retrospectively "queer" an artwork that in fact had not been conceived as such, the seminar undertook an analysis of the way collage practices made it possible to rethink how norms and identities are interwoven and the resulting effects on institutions. A similar motive induced Eribon and the Fayard publishing house to issue French translations of George Chauncey's *Gay New York, 1840–1940* and, later, Michael Lucey's *The Misfits of the Family: Balzac and the Social Forms of Sexuality*.[69] Gaspard and Eribon's seminar was also aimed at training a new generation of scholars. Doctoral students regularly presented their research there, where they might be able to meet the French and American academics who had inspired it. The seminar paved the way for numerous studies, notably in the field of cultural history (having been regularly attended by historians Sandrine Sanos, Sandra Boehringer, Florence Tamagne, Laure Murat, and Hélène Fleckinger) as well as sociology (Arnaud Lerch, Natacha Chetcuti, Sébastien Chauvin, Etienne Ollion), geography (Marianne Blidon), law (Daniel Borrillo, Caroline Mécary), art (Elisabeth Lebovici), and political science (myself). Participants also included key members of LGBT movements, such as bookseller Chantal Bigot, American archivist Gerard Koskovich, and feminist leader Anne Le Gall. Following the seminar, a symposium was organized in 2004 to discuss the work of these young academics.[70]

Bourcier attended the first meeting of the "Sociology of Homosexualities" seminar, seeking to make his mark on it. He attacked Gaspard and Eribon for organizing their seminar in an academic context. He also criticized Gaspard's satisfaction with the fact that the seminar was being jointly run by a man and a woman (Gaspard was promoting the idea of "parity," or equality of numbers of men and women, in political institutions). Marco Dell'Omodarme, who also attended that first session, explained: "We soon left. We had already moved well beyond such categories."[71] Other tensions regularly arose as symposia and translations followed one another. A notable case was the presentation at the ENS of Fassin's translation of Butler's *Gender Trouble*. Bourcier accused Fassin of seeking to appropriate and dilute Butler's main arguments, thus incorporating her work into the academic fields of paternalistic philosophy and psychoanalysis (Bourcier cited Catherine Malabou's and Étienne Balibar's critical analyses of Butler's work).[72] With a few of his friends, Bourcier mounted a zap against the seminar in the name of an ad hoc group, Panik Qulture. The group's leaflet stated that "the way *Gender Trouble* is penetrating France excludes too many sexual-political players and seeks to clean up the effects of queer philosophy and policies by straightening and depoliticizing them. Even though it happens to be the private dream of the queens of American theory, we have no need of intellectual audiences—they're the ones who hijack public discussion in France." The leaflet went on to add, in English: "Judith, don't get hegemonic on our backs! Stop betraying your people!"[73] Bourcier pursued her protests by placing responsibility more directly on Butler, who made increasingly frequent visits to France after 2005. According to Bourcier, the "second Butler" (the author of *Undoing Gender*), reintroduced a pathological element into sexuality in general and transgender identities in particular.[74] This thesis was the central theme of a seminar Bourcier launched at EHESS in 2008. Titled "Fuck My Brain," it was hosted by the same academic unit where the seminar on the sociology of homosexualities had been held (Centre d'Analyse et d'Intervention Sociologiques [CADIS]). Les Éditions Amsterdam, which had published translations of most of Butler's books, backed Bourcier's argument.[75] In 2011 it published *Queer Zones 3*, which made a frontal attack on Butler's theses. With a certain irony, the translator of Butler's *Undoing Gender* was none other than Maxime Cervulle, who was close to Bourcier and had been the spokesperson (under the pseudonym Marcela Moustache) for the Panik Qulture zap against Butler in 2005 but met Butler after that event.[76] On May 22–23, 2009, Bourcier organized another symposium, "Transgenders: New Identities and Visibilities," in conjunction with Chantal Zabus and David Coad. It was largely hailed by trans organizations, even if several trans activists thought that Bourcier's accusations during the symposium could be harmful to the trans movement.[77]

What were the stakes in this intellectual battle over the presence of queer theory in France? This question was at the heart of a special issue of *Paragraph* magazine, published by the University of Edinburgh Press as part of a research project carried out in the United Kingdom by Oliver Davis and Hector Kollias.[78] In that issue, Bourcier published an English-language translation of the chapter in his *Queer Zones 3* in which he attacked the "second Butler";[79] Régis Révenin offered a historical assessment of the field yet overlooked two key paths through which queer theory had been introduced into France: the seminar run by Fassin, Feher, and Tort and the one run by Eribon and Gaspard.[80] Adrian Rifkin, meanwhile, argued that the 1997 symposium at the Pompidou Center focused on an already canonical queer corpus and left little room for innovation.[81] In other words, this special issue of *Paragraph* basically adopted Bourcier's interpretation of queerness as a nonassimilationist tactic, as presented in her three-volume *Queer Zones*. Conversely, the places where queer theory was conceptualized without necessarily lionizing the term itself tended to be dismissed as conformist or were simply overlooked. Any ambivalent relationships to the norm (simultaneously incorporating and challenging it) were subsumed by the oppositional attitude (the only exceptions to this tendency were the countervailing articles by Claire Boyle and Lisa Downing).[82]

In a special issue of *French Cultural Studies* that followed a symposium on Eribon's work held on April 23, 2011, Oliver Davis situated the clash between Bourcier and Eribon at the level of stylistic approach:

> Eribon's work as a gay activist and theorist has always been problematically bourgeois. Bourgeois not just in its increasingly obsessive focus on equality of access to the respectable social institution of marriage, about which more in a moment, but also in the very manner in which it has been articulated: by contrast with Bourcier's lively interventions, Eribon's blend of sober Sartreanism and overzealous Bourdieusian sociology sometimes leaves the reader wondering why any individual, or society, would even want to embrace, or even reflect upon, deviance from the sexual norm.[83]

Yet is such an explanation sufficient, reducing as it does spontaneity to the form of public verbal expression, confusing spontaneity with innovation? The personal histories of Bourcier and Eribon reveal far more complex social relationships underlying the way they express themselves.[84] Furthermore, Bourcier and Eribon share, if on different registers, a sharply critical perspective on the role of psychoanalysis in the public sphere. Yet while most schools of psychoanalysis in France are indeed dens of conservatism with respect to sexual minorities,[85] a few of them have also displayed interest in queer theory. Because of the attention to the question of eroticism paid by the Lacanian school of psychoanalysis,[86] Éditions et Publications de l'École Lacanienne (EPEL), spearheaded by Jean Allouch,[87] became interested in publishing gay and lesbian studies and queer theory. Claude Calame, a historian of ancient Greece, presented a paper that discussed the work of David Halperin, particularly "Why Is Diotima a Woman?" Halperin, as the author of numerous articles on eroticism in Plato, as well as on AIDS and the politics of the body in Foucault's work, was a guest of EPEL in April 1999, not long after the publication of a French translation of *Is the Rectum a Grave?* by Leo Bersani. Bersani had expressed major reservations over queer theory, which meant that the debate with David Halperin continued via EPEL, which published French translations in 2000 of *One Hundred Years of Homosexuality and Other Essays on Greek Love* and *Saint Foucault.* Also through Halperin, EPEL came in closer contact with Gayle Rubin, whose 1994 interview with Judith Butler ("Sexual Traffic," published as "Marché au sexe") was followed by French translations of essays by Butler ("Imitation and

Gender Insubordination") and Rubin ("Thinking Sex"). In 2003, EPEL published a translation of Butler's *Antigone's Claim* as *Antigone: la parenté entre vie and mort.* EPEL's publishing efforts have continued unflaggingly into the present—recent titles include translations of Halperin's *How to Be Gay* (2015), David Caron's *My Father and I: The Marais and the Queerness of Community* (2015), and a selection of essays by Lee Edelman under the French title, *L'Impossible Homosexuel: huit essais de théorie queer* (2013). Among the chorus of psychoanalysts objecting first to civil unions and then to gay marriage and adoption by homosexual couples, EPEL sang a different tune. As Allouch pointed out, "Psychoanalysis is not a science in whose name some public expertise can be invoked; it is above all erotology."[88] Nor should it be forgotten that Butler was initially invited to France by the Collège International de Philosophie to speak about Heidegger, with no connection to her work on gender. Later the Espace Analytique, reestablished in 1994 on the model of the Centre Freudien de Formation et de Recherches Psychanalytiques, invited Butler to speak on the question of gender.[89] Very few places in France were receptive to queer theory. The Lacanian school and the Espace Analytique were exceptions.[90] Rarer still were any attempts by the psychoanalytical sector in France not just to host but to generate queer analyses—from that standpoint, Vincent Bourseul's work represents another exception.[91]

More recently, other queer initiatives have emerged. In 2013, Amélie Le Renard, Delphine Naudier, and Geneviève Pruvost organized a seminar at EHESS, "The Uses of Queer Theories: Norms, Sexualities, Power." At this seminar conceptual appropriations have been analyzed by the likes of Pascale Molinier, Charlotte Prieur, and Rachele Borghi.[92] In the realm of linguistics, Luca Greco has studied drag king performance and methods of "rewriting" the body.[93] Other research into trans identities is now more directly aligned with queer theory than previously—Jean Zaganiaris, for example, is working on forms of cultural hybridity in Moroccan literature from the perspective of its interface with France.[94] Zaganiaris presented his work at the Queer Days held in Bordeaux on February 7–8, 2013, alongside Arnaud Alessandrin, Karine Espineira, and Maude-Yeuse Thomas, who presented their *Trans-yclopédie.* Rachele Borghi delivered a paper on the notion of "performance" from the analytical perspective of post-pornography—as her presentation progressed, Borghi removed her clothes, revealing how our view of the individual who is speaking is affected by appearance. Her presentation, like her teaching appointment at the Université de Paris IV, was the object of a campaign on social networks by people associated with Manif pour Tous, denouncing queer decadence.[95] The mobilization of opponents to marriage for all was made possible by the fact that the word "queer" had appeared in the French mass media from 2000 onward, reinforcing the idea that, following the inception of civil unions, a more insidious transformation was occurring on the level of image.

Mass Entertainment: Queer as Euphemism

The media spotlight focused on the notion of queerness in 2004 when mainstream television station TF1 aired a makeover program that featured five gay men whose mission involved imparting some dynamism to a "tacky" straight guy. Whereas the homosexual dimension was explicit in the American original—*Queer Eye for the Straight Guy*—the title of the French adaptation remained euphemistic: *Queer, cinq experts dans le vent* (Queer: Five Cool Experts). Not only did "queer" not have any pejorative connotation in French; in fact, it was totally unknown to most viewers (only the show *Queer as Folk* had been previously aired in France, starting in 1999, but under its English title and only on a cable channel, Canal+).[96] The word "queer" was used by TF1 to avoid referring to homosexuality even while playing on the comic effects of its overwhelming presence. The French entertainment industry could thus target a new gay audience without the risk of "shocking" the general public. This approach also allowed the channel to flaunt its "open-mindedness" and concern for social diversity. The American show featured five gay men, all experts in their respective fields—cuisine, interior design, fashion, cosmetics, and psychology—who were summoned by a heterosexual woman to make over her partner, change his everyday habits, and renovate their shared home. Although the show was aimed toward the straight man, it functioned to restore the heterosexual relationship itself. In fact, it was based on the principle that a straight woman's idea of the perfect couple would involve a relationship with a gay man.[97] However, the absence of sexual attraction forces the woman to accept reality, which means a romantic relationship with straight men. The only way to make the situation workable, then, would be to act as though this romantic partner resembled the "impossible"—because gay—lover. In the American program, the play on sexual stereotypes was reinforced by a play on class stereotypes: "refined" homosexual tastes were associated with luxury, while straight tastes were considered vulgar, associated with lower-class culture. The gay experts would empty the house of its junk. They thereby demonstrated the existence of a "straight closet" full of items in "poor taste." Paradoxically, by showing that certain attributes of male heterosexuality are "in the closet," the experts reinforced the impression that heterosexuality itself did not reside there—it was a question of objects, not people. The show simultaneously reinforced the idea that homosexuality is primarily of interest when it makes heterosexuality possible. But at least the US version used the word "queer" to make the homosexuality of the five advisers more explicit, whereas in France the term was used to mask what lay behind the presence of the five "cool" experts.[98] The word "queer" did engage the norm from a critical angle but perverted normal roles, although the perversion was purely superficial, because opening the "straight closet" meant keeping the "gay closet" tightly closed: compared to the straight couples, the gay advisers had no family, no love life. They popped up from nowhere and existed only through the job they did. In other words, the French show used the word "queer" to capitalize on a very traditional division of sexual roles, in which the gay individuals were not labeled, had no independent existence. The entertainment industry thereby invented the spectacle of "the spectacle of the closet."[99]

So in the French media, the word "queer" became a promotional device (displaying open-mindedness) within a programming strategy that remained governed by the usual majority norms.[100] Thierry Ardisson, a TV host, producer, and former advertising consultant, realized this as early as 1999, when he petitioned the Institut National de la Propriété Industrielle (National Institute of Industrial Property) to register the word "queer" as a trademark for a line of clothing.[101] During those years, the term continued to be used in the French entertainment media but then went out of fashion and faded.[102] That trend was contemporary with the launching of a gay cable TV channel, Pink TV, by producer Pascal Houzelot, with Canal+ and TF1 as the main shareholders. The channel broadcast on cable and satellite channels from 2004 to 2007, then drastically reduced its programming and finally folded due to lack of financial resources. Pink TV was the first to broadcast the series The L Word in 2004. Several media celebrities participated in the show, including TF1's prime-time news anchorwoman, Claire Chazal, and the author and future minister of culture, Frédéric Mitterrand. So did Bourcier, who was a commentator on a show called Le Set and co-hosted a talk program with journalist Alex Taylor from 2004 to 2006.

The early 2000s were thus marked by a double strategy, which involved launching new shows for a gay audience while displaying diversity in programs aimed at a wider audience, with the term "queer" as the operative pivot of that strategy. The press interviewed TV audiences about this emerging phenomenon and their acceptance of shows "on gays"—journalists stressed that the period was notable for its open-mindedness on the condition that a separate category, or community, was not created.[103] The "queer moment" in French media thus corresponded to a wish to refurbish the image of the press and TV through the concept of "diversity," which was a buzzword in the spheres of politics and media in the mid-2000s. This concept made it possible to recognize certain minorities by awarding them positions of responsibility or places in the media spotlight without questioning the very principle of how they were depicted. This rejuvenated image of the media sought above all to create new markets. The regular presence of gays in the media, especially advertising, dated from the early 1990s. At the time that presence served largely as a foil, via the new angle that gay individuals offered. Only in the late 1990s, during debate over the legalization of civil unions, did attention to gay consumers also emerge.[104] The use of "queer" in the mass media reflected a gay marketing strategy not on a register of identity so much as the register of lifestyle. This approach made it possible to target new market niches while retaining a universalist image, thereby satisfying the capitalist requirement of permanent expansion.[105]

The mass media's use of the term "queer" shows that this signifier was employed precisely because its meaning was unclear in French. Whereas in English the word is known to mean "fag" or "pansy" in addition to "strange" or "weird," no French TV series or show explicitly explained the English meaning. The French did not choose the English term to refer to a radical activist culture or ironically subvert a stigma. It was chosen because the word in French was disconnected from homosexual categorizations that TV executives considered insufficiently broad in appeal. Moreover, we should not overlook the wariness of the term expressed by some queer women writers themselves. By the early 1990s they realized that it was becoming a slogan. In 1994 De Lauretis referred to it as a "conceptually vacant creature of the publishing industry."[106] Thanks to the particularly plastic nature of the word "queer," it became possible to acknowledge that sexuality has indeed been taken into account without having to pay the cost of a more explicit reference to homosexuality, transsexuality, or feminism. "Queer" can therefore be either utopian or dystopian; there are spheres in which the term has been used to explore a vision of a different world and others in which it has been instrumentalized to commercial ends or to sustain the epistemologically dominant relationship between heterosexuality and homosexuality. Given this situation, the concept of queer theory itself has met heavy resistance, as exemplified by several French feminist groups and their critical view of the American model, thereby prompting reflection on the European dimension of queerness.

Queertopias

The activist, academic, and media repercussions of queer theory are part of a long Franco-American intellectual history, marked by poststructuralism and writings associated with "French theory" in the United States. Monique Wittig's situation is emblematic of the tension between idealization and rejection of queer echoes in the Franco-American world. Wittig was a cofounder of the French women's liberation movement (Mouvement de Libération des Femmes), participated in laying a wreath for the wife of the unknown soldier in 1970, and then participated in the group called Gouines Rouges (Red Dykes), which broke from the overly androcentric Front Homosexuel d'Action Révolutionnaire (Homosexual Front for Revolutionary Action, FHAR). In 1976 she left France for the United States and became a professor at the University of Arizona. Her political writings, however, were not published in France until 2001, the year an international symposium—organized by Suzette Robichon and Bourcier on the Paris campus of Columbia University—paid her a tribute. The way in which Wittig's work challenged straight epistemology was perceived as a betrayal of French universality (as purportedly demonstrated by her exile to the United States). Wittig herself played on this fear of a "Trojan horse." In her essay "The Mark of Gender," she sought to demonstrate that the pronoun "I," in both French and English, already indicated gender because the speaker is involved in a gender system that transcends strict grammatical variations from one language to another.[107] This dimension also left a strong mark on Butler's work.[108]

The idea of an American Trojan horse was widely present among French feminist theorists. Their articles and public statements against queer theory were so resonant that it was possible to envisage the presence of queerness in France as being more dystopian than utopian. This phenomenon was particularly marked among the leading figures of materialist feminism. Anthropologist Nicole-Claude Mathieu argued that queer theory reduced sex and gender to a symbolic status.[109] The emphasis on performativity purportedly relativized the bodily inscription of norms, an inscription on which masculine domination was based. In other words, by referring to performance, queer theory might deprive women of certain tools of resistance as the individual and agency were emphasized. Sociologist Christine Delphy, another cofounder of the Mouvement de Libération des Femmes and a member of the Gouines Rouges, summed up this particular rejection of queer theory:

> It seems to me that the arrival of queerness favors an individualist approach that encourages people to change categories, but without questioning those categories. I'm interested in subjectivities, so that approach should be supported in the context of every person's right to dignity, but it does not represent a political struggle insofar as it doesn't propose any change to the structures of society.[110]

Delphy's position contrasts with her attitude toward the work of Foucault himself, going so far as to assert in the second volume of *L'Ennemi principal* that she perceived "unconscious Marxist principles" in Foucault's work.[111] Furthermore, it is interesting to note that Delphy's stance against the French law restricting the wearing of Islamic headscarves aligned her with queer movements that argued for unrestricted tolerance of religious symbols in the public sphere on the grounds of self-determination.

In Quebec, feminist theorist Louise Turcotte also expressed anxiety over queer theory in the name of communitarian lesbian cultures.[112] Her comments were largely echoed in French feminist and lesbian circles, notably La Maison des Femmes in Paris. However, wariness toward queer theory was not universal among feminist theorists. For example, Liliane Kandel recalls having enthusiastically welcomed the rise of queer movements in the United States. She even hoped to translate one chapter of *Gender Trouble*, in conjunction with Michèle Kail, and publish it in the Sartrean review *Les Temps Modernes* in 1999; but, unable to get a chapter to stand alone, the plan was ultimately dropped. Even if Kandel admits to having adopted a distance from certain queer-theory-related texts, in regard to the issue of wearing the Islamic headscarf—she has notably critiqued the positions of sociologists Nacira Guénif, Éric Macé, and Éric Fassin—she nevertheless adds that Paul B. Preciado's experimentation on the body represents an interesting intersection between queer theory and materialist philosophy.[113]

The conflict between materialist feminist theory and queer theory is no longer operative for a new generation of female activists who emerged in the 2000s. They are able to relate to both materialist feminism and queer theory. Marie, an active member of Les Tumultueuses and the Marche des Tordu(e)s, explained that her militantism arose from a simultaneous reading of Delphy and Butler.[114] Several feminist theorists have fully incorporated queer analyses into their thinking. Philosopher Elsa Dorlin introduced many black feminist writings into French and has pointed out that queer movements are heirs to those feminist trends, particularly in the way they reappropriate offensive language.[115] Similarly, in the wake of Kevin Floyd's book *The Reification of Desire: Toward a Queer Marxism*,[116] political scientist Sophie Noyé presented an analysis of the logic of capitalist accumulation and its effects on sexuality, especially the transformation of the subject into "subject-value."[117] One of the most recent examples of the convergence of feminist and queer theories is the online magazine *Politiqueer*, dubbed "a site for queer and feminist analyses in French." The first issue, introduced by Charlotte Prieur and Bruno Laprade, concerned the queer francophone sphere in an attempt to "address the impact on identities of a language as heavily gendered as French."[118] This return to language and the grammatical gender of language might provide an opportunity for queer work that is more francophone than French.

Just as Belgium and Quebec were key go-betweens in introducing American political philosophy into France—even reconfiguring certain political issues there[119]—major initiatives in queer theory were undertaken in those countries. For example, a workshop on "Gender(s) and Sexuality(ies)" was launched in 2005 at Institut de Sociologie in the Université Libre de Bruxelles, Belgium, by Cathy Herbrand, David Paternotte, Annalisa Casini, and David Berliner. It often discussed queer theory when hosting the likes of Butler, Bourcier, and Eribon. The workshop further extended its network of guests to the entire globe, including speakers from India, Israel, Australia, Hungary, and Chile. This openness contrasts with the way seminars on queer issues in France mostly focused on the United States, thereby creating intellectual links that are very strong but come at the expense of more varied, more mobile networks. We must therefore relativize the view of several commentators who feel that queer theory has been globalized:[120] there exist many spheres in which queer theory is not only formulated and discussed but also fantasized in highly different ways.

In Germany, *Gender Trouble* was published in translation as early as 1991, followed in 1995 by *Bodies That Matter*. Butler's theses on performativity initially sparked a lively polemic within feminist studies, but by the mid-1990s they were progressively incorporated into studies on homosexuality and transgender identities and subsequently extended to issues of citizenship and racism, testifying to a shift of paradigm within academic feminism. In Germany, however, the arrival of queer theory was not limited to Butler's writings. Other American texts "entered the university traveling on the ticket of deconstructivism."[121]

The German example shows that queer theory assumed highly diverse forms in Europe and did not spread in a synchronous manner. Hence a pronounced tension exists between Eastern and Western Europe: in most studies on sexuality, Central and Eastern Europe are defined as being European even as they are "discursively framed as the cultural Other."[122]

Defining the European cultural sphere is itself a strategic goal for LGBT activists who seek to stimulate exchanges around shared representations of borders. It is useful to remember that the presence of queer theory was largely maintained by groups of people linked to academic institutions (doctoral and postdoctoral students as well as tenured scholars) without necessarily being fully institutionalized (for example, by awarding credits to students who attended seminars). These groups simultaneously sprang from activist associations, where many of their members got their start. Such was the case with Zoo, whose most active members had an academic profile (such as Bourcier, Dell'Omodarme, and Deschamps) even as they included other people who came from the activist LGBT sphere (Espineira, for example). Furthermore, Zoo first met in the Centre Gai et Lesbien de Paris and later on the premises of the Sorbonne without ever having the status of an official course. A similar phenomenon occurred in other European countries such as Spain.[123]

Whereas queer academic life in France remains basically oriented toward the United States, queer activists developed far more sustained transnational practices. This could be seen in festivals such as Queeruption, first organized in London in 1998 but followed by annual gatherings in other major European cities (Barcelona, Amsterdam, Berlin) as well as in San Francisco, New York, Sydney, and Tel Aviv. Queeruption was made possible through the implementation of an online platform enabling participants to communicate. Konstantinos Eleftheriadis, who has studied Queeruption and other European events such as the queer festivals in Copenhagen and Oslo and the Queeristan festival in Amsterdam, argues that the deliberate lack of hierarchy between participants and organizers, along with a desire to give everyone the possibility of suggesting workshops and other activities, favored authentic transnational exchanges.[124] Communication itself occurred in several languages, even if English remained the main tool of interaction. This use of English inevitably raises the question of power relationships among queer participants, since English appears to be the language of the theory of that name. While certain participants were uncomfortable with the idea of queer theory, others moved "toward the academic sphere itself in an attempt to change it."[125]

Given the materialist feminist critique in France and the circulation of activist ideas and practices in Europe, the simultaneously dystopian and utopian view of the American perspective was progressively relativized, a process further encouraged by the emergence of a new generation of scholars and activists. These "queer children," born at the very moment that queer theory arose, now make heterotopic use of it.[126] They seek not so much to uncover some primal meaning to which American society allegedly holds the secret, for better or for worse, but rather to transform the meaning of the realm in which they exist. This "queer twist" creates, to a certain extent, a world within a world, one with its own codes, language, and rules, simultaneously visible to all yet largely inaccessible to the uninitiated. Unlike LGBT's concern for visibility, this generation suggests appropriating the fear of betrayal and transmission of homosexuality to invent new forms of solidarity. Its work is being done through more direct interaction with American queer theory, without the mediation of French translations. As geographer Charlotte Prieur has commented, while many queer studies bearing on performativity and sexual categories have now been translated, more recent writings that address relationships to time, space, and memory are not yet available in French.[127] Prieur has completed a comparative study of queer venues in Paris (such as the bar called La Mutinerie) and Montreal; she demonstrated the fleeting nature of most queer venues and activities, halfway between the real and virtual worlds, usually sustained by open forums such as Facebook pages. Those venues no longer play the role of showcase but of initiation and critical relationship to mainstream venues.[128]

This same initiatory role is found in the sphere of arts, in particular the work of director, photographer, and performance-artist Emilie Jouvet.[129] After participating in a series of short films collectively titled *Les Contes de Queer Factory* (Tales from Queer Factory) in 2004, she made a documentary titled *Too Much Pussy!*,[130] which recorded the 2009 tour of the *Queer X Show*, an event that brought together performance artists Wendy Delorme, Judy Minx, DJ Metzgerei, Mad Kate, Sadie, Lune, Madison Young, and Jouvet herself. The film documented how the performers bonded with an audience that learned even as it watched the show. There is thus another dimension to queer practices, which means not merely carving out a new sphere of understanding in the present but also leaving traces that anticipate future queer genealogies.[131] How can these meanings be seeded in a way that renders them fertile later, thereby spawning new interpretive communities?[132]

In conjunction with media theorist Nathalie Magnan (one of the French translators of Donna Haraway's *Cyborg Manifesto*),[133] Elisabeth Lebovici, a critic of contemporary art as well as a former member of ACT UP Paris and a regular participant in the seminar on the "Sociology of Homosexualities," began studying queer texts extensively, in the light of which she examined unexplored aspects of the lives and works of various artists. She soon became interested in Eunice Lipton's work on Victorine Meurent (the artist who was also Édouard Manet's primary model).[134] In 2011 she participated in the "Let's Queer Art History" conference organized by Patricia Falguières at the Pompidou Center in Paris.[135] She asked to what extent authors and readers are linked by an unending epistemological game on queerness: Does the other know what I know? This game of heterotopic readings has even been extended to the polemic over gender theory—since 2014, parties known as "Peanut Butler" have been held in Paris to do honor to queer theory even while mocking the excessive importance placed on it in the context of the debate over gay marriage. The same effect was created by the Loud and Proud Festival held at the Gaîté Lyrique theater in Paris on July 2–5, 2015; according to festival organizers, "Queer is henceforth an activist school of thought as well as a useful analytical tool for exploring gender, social and sexual norms, and relationships of domination at work in today's society. . . . So in a way it means rendering unto RuPaul what is RuPaul's."[136] As an extension of this idea, I now discuss two heterotopic initiatives that illustrate the contribution made by France's new queer generation: La Marche des Tordu(e)s and Queer Week at Sciences Po.

The Children of Queer Theory: Les Tordu(e)s

In 2005, a small group of activists calling themselves Les Tordu(e)s organized a counter-demonstration during the Gay Pride event in Paris. Then they organized another "counter-march" the following year. The name Les Tordu(e)s is a gender-bending attempt to convey the idea of "queer" in French (*tordu* means "warped" or "weird"; *tordus* is the masculine plural form, and *tordues*, the feminine). At one point the group considered calling themselves "Dépravé(e)s" but ultimately chose the queerer term. They wanted to give weight to a politics of "disorder" through a series of actions against dominant sexual norms, beginning with the LGBT movement. Their logo itself evokes multiple layers of resistance, all interrelated in a queer approach characterized by the use of pink and black (typical of ACT UP's colors). The logo combines various symbols, literally overturning the direction and sense of letters: although the word read from left to right, the arrow underlining the term "Tordu(e)s" points left. The letter "E"—indicating the feminine form of the French word—is ironically placed in parentheses even as it points backward, as though it had flipped. This feminine indicator, running against the grain of the other letters, is the only one in pink, not only to mock social norms but also to underscore its own power. It incarnates the minority principle, since the entire linearity of language (which governs the other letters) is thwarted by its presence (as indicated by the arrow). Norms are thereby inverted and warped even in the logo of Les Tordu(e)s. This tactic of micro-resistance through language conveys the movement's twin origins in homosexual and feminist struggles and anarchist struggles: the letter "o" hosts the symbols of both male and female homosexuality, while the letter "u" hoists the Jolly Roger, indicating an unruliness typical of the anarchist movement even as it symbolizes piracy and disobedience.

Most of the participants in the first counter-march—Les Tordu(e)s preferred the term "charge"—numbering roughly one hundred people, came from the ranks of ACT UP Paris and various anarchist groups (the Confédération Nationale du Travail, Radio Libertaire). The five founding Tordu(e)s members were themselves activists in two groups, Les Panthères Roses and Les Furieuses Fallopes (Furious Fallopians). Les Panthères Roses was founded by several members of a student LGBT association, Debout Étudiants Gays et Lesbiennes (DEGEL), to protest the law-and-order drift of the 2002 presidential campaign in France. But groups of Panthères Roses also sprang up in Montreal, Lisbon, Madrid, and Brussels. They described themselves as a movement of "dykes, trans, and fags irritated by the moral order, patriarchy, sexism, racism,

FIGURE 25. Logo of Les Tordu(e)s. Source: http://tordues.quickup.org/tordues/www.tordues.org/index.html.

obsessive law-and-order, social regression, and all that."[137] The movement is known for mocking the arguments made by authority figures—zaps against a given individual or homophobic, transphobic, or racist event called for a good deal of sequins and chanting, while petitions were circulated against reactionary policies and their advocates, along with campaigns in favor of apostasy. Les Furieuses Fallopes is a "women-only radical feminist group" founded by roughly ten anticapitalist feminists. One of the group's first acts was to organize a demonstration opposing the march for life coordinated by the Catholic group Renaissance in 2003. Les Furieuses Fallopes issued numerous press releases to provide their opposing views on gender, sexuality, and social issues. The five founding women of Les Tordu(e)s were soon joined by activists from ACT UP Paris and several militant anarchists from Toulouse. The group numbered between fifteen and twenty members.

Les Tordu(e)s rallied around dissatisfaction with the commercial nature of the Paris Gay Pride event, as well as around a desire to lend greater visibility to the issues such as trans identities, the increasing pauperization of young gays and lesbians, and discrimination against migrants. The call for a counter-charge that circulated on social networks explained,

> This is a collective march of Tordu(e)s, that is, Twisted, Organized, Radical, Deconstructed, United, Exasperated, Subversive Sodomites. . . . Why this charge? To express what we can no longer express on a daily basis and what we cannot or no longer express at the Pride march. The charge is a march of nonnormative visibilities. Who wants a parade sponsored by commercial brands, by the union of gay cops (FLAG), by politicians and organizations for whom this day is an opportunity for "gay-friendly" good consciences? Visibility for all means a multiplication of places and resources: Can one exist outside the Marais neighborhood, Delarue's [the host of a sensationalist show on public television], or— once a year—the Pride March? Let us create alternative spaces governed not by consumer laws as a way of life, spaces that are nonnormative, where everyone can be what s/he wants to be.[138]

In this respect, Les Tordu(e)s echoes the American movement Gay Shame, which organized demonstrations against "the 'self-serving' values of gay consumerism and the increasingly hypocritical left."[139] Les Tordu(e)s issued similar criticisms of "gay marketing" at a time when, just a few years after legalization of civil unions, businesses were beginning to target male couples. A trade show called Rainbow Attitude, first held in 2003, spurred the founding of

Les Tordu(e)s as a group. Gay-friendly firms jointly displayed their wares and services at the Porte de Versailles trade center on the edge of Paris, seeking to connect with new partners as well as new customers. These firms claimed they were involved in a "new form of activism" based on consumerism.[140]

Les Tordu(e)s objected to this rhetoric, claiming that economic exploitation is inherent in business and that no commercial initiative can ever be synonymous with activism. Although the context in which Les Tordu(e)s emerged may be similar to that of their American counterpart, the modus operandi of their protests was slightly different. Les Tordu(e)s first decided that its march would begin where the Gay Pride march ended and head back toward Gay Pride's point of departure. The two marches would inevitably come face-to-face. The goal of Les Tordu(e)s was to block the main parade, thereby demonstrating the power a minority might assume—the demonstrators, who numbered at most one hundred, knew they would be overwhelmed numerically by a march that usually draws half a million people, yet Les Tordu(e)s activists were convinced that their strategy would be effective because a small number of people would be sufficient to block the road. They could thus impose a new balance of power, based not so much on numbers as on position. Their goal was not to appropriate new territories but to displace normal territorial relationships, especially when they are governed by the principle of the greatest number acquiring territorial privilege (that is, appropriation of the premises). However, the police refused to authorize this counter-demonstration. Les Tordu(e)s therefore finally decided to organize a different march, immediately following the main one. From Belleville, a working-class neighborhood (the Pride event mostly moved through the most bourgeois part of Left-Bank Paris) the march would end next to the Pompidou Center, right on the edge of the Marais neighborhood, the main gay commercial zone of Paris.

The strategy for occupying space adopted by Les Tordu(e)s did not entail taking possession of an existing space (the streets of Paris) but contesting the very notion of property promoted by "mainstream LGBT politics." The first Gay Pride event in France was organized in Paris in 1977 and was originally a spontaneous movement with no official affiliation. During the 1980s an organizing committee was formed, working closely with police authorities. In 1998 the name "Gay Pride" was even registered as a trademark—the use of the name henceforth belonged to the organizers, who decided who could or could not use it during the march and other officially related events. In 2001 Gay Pride was redubbed the Marche des Fiertés Lesbiennes, Gaies, Bi et Trans (Lesbian,

Gay, Bi, and Trans Pride Parade). Given the institutionalization of LGBT movements, Les Tordu(e)s had to reflect on indirect strategies for lending voice to its cause. It borrowed a certain number of approaches already developed by lesbian activist groups, such as La Coordination Lesbienne en France (Lesbian Coordination in France) and a women-only lesbian group called La Barbare (The Female Barbarian), which had already organized street demonstrations, including "Take Back the Night" marches,[141] which continue to be held on a regular basis.[142] Both groups had begun to "occupy" Gay Pride as early as 1999. Every year during the Pride March, slogans in English were painted on the sidewalks of Paris, such as "Lesbian I love you" and "Optimistic lesbian." The strategy of marking the ground evoked an idealized space, one with no physical location but one that left its traces on the sidewalk. Several participants in the Tordu(e)s movement were involved in these actions either directly or indirectly, notably the women who were members of Furieuses Fallopes. Once joined by activists from DEGEL, ACT UP, and several anarchist groups from Toulouse, they founded Les Tordu(e)s in a context where queer theory was discussed within the groups, prompting a critical gaze on the performative effects of traditional street demonstrations. Given the various activist backgrounds of members of Les Tordu(e)s, it was the queer critical stance that served as their common denominator.

Members of Les Tordu(e)s thus sought to liberate themselves from traditional forms of activism in which the organizational structure is entirely geared toward recruitment and public relations. These traditional forms imply an internal delegation of responsibilities (via specialization of roles) and an external delegation of communication (via official spokespeople). Les Tordu(e)s therefore decided against having a spokesperson, against any contact with the media—only the group itself would produce written or audiovisual statements. It thereby opted for an anarchistic, nonhierarchical form of activism. Stéphanie Kunert nevertheless emerged as a key figure in the group. She was then a PhD student in media studies at CELSA, the prestigious school of journalism (and is currently on the faculty at the University de Lyon II), as well as an author known as Wendy Delorme. Kunert performed in various queer shows such as *Kisses Cause Trouble*, *Drag King Fem Show*, and the *Queer X Show Tour*. She also lived in the United States for a while with a person who self-identified as "queer." Kunert has thus stated that she uses the term "queer" only in the American context, preferring to use *transpédégouine* (transfagdyke) in France because it seems more "abrasive."[143] She was a regular participant in Eribon and Gaspard's seminar at EHESS from 1998 to 2004. In May 2012 she wrote a manifesto-like book, *Insurrections! En territoire sexuel*, published by Au Diable Vauvert. While Kunert makes it a point of honor to function within the group just like any other member, it is her name that resurfaces in all interviews with the activists in Les Tordu(e)s. Furthermore, although Les Tordu(e)s advocated a nonhierarchical approach, its actions were feasible thanks only to support from associations like ACT UP Paris, which accept a more hierarchical division of labor. This explains how the first counter-march could be organized in just a matter of weeks.

There is little documentation on Les Tordu(e)s since the group deliberately expressed itself only in fleeting traces, in the interstices of official movements. The members used stencils to leave messages on the walls and sidewalks of Paris, taking photos of their graffiti for their own use. They were thereby creating a sphere accessible only to insiders capable of reading their messages and grasping the meaning. A key mechanism of the way minorities achieve autonomy is by establishing their own space and time (the group's actions were scheduled to offset the timing of the official march). Minorities thus expose the majority to the consequences of its own domination. They spark a curiosity, indeed a desire, for interstitial cultures, showing the majority that it can no longer understand the very people it has banished. Through stenciled messages, Les Tordu(e)s played on the spectacle of "dislocation," based on various textual strategies. Among the messages, "Your mother's a machine" (*Ta mère est 1 machine*) points to one of the characteristics of the heteropatriarchal system, the instrumentalization of women's bodies as wombs for the nation. In other words, Les Tordu(e)s argue that women's bodies are already the object of an occupation that cannot be eliminated simply through occupation of public spaces. The system itself has to be attacked (as emphasized by the use of the word "machine" and the numeral "1" for *une*).

As part of its attack, Les Tordu(e)s also resorted to a double transformation of the French language by inventing new words and using English. *Transpdgouine*, another of their stenciled messages, is a good example. "Transfagdyke" is a combination of an abbreviation (*trans*, transsexual), an acronym (*pd*, pederast, pédé, or fag), and a noun (*gouine*, dyke), all of which have been used as insults. But Les Tordu(e)s reappropriated them, seeking an alternative not only to the gender specificity of the French language but also to the overly essentialist use of the terms "gay" and "lesbian." *Transpdgouine* appeared for the first time at Zoo, Marie-Hélène/Sam Bourcier's seminar group, in 1997.[144] The neologism is characterized by its combination of divergent linguistic elements (an abbreviation, a phonetically inspired acronym, a reappropriated slur), generating an inventive strangeness.[145] Les Tordu(e)s also developed another linguistic strategy by using English to overcome the problem of translating queer terms into French. This tactic seeks to create a bond, indeed a certain intimacy, among people who grasp the reference, even as it reinforces a sense of belonging on a transnational level: for instance, use of the slogan "In Gode we trust" (*gode*, pronounced "god" in French, means "dildo").

Les Tordu(e)s claimed to oppose every norm, as made clear in its call to arms: "Who are Les Tordu(e)s? You, us, me, dykes, fags, bis, trans, queens, prostitutes, HIV positives—everyone who experiences gender and/or sexuality as something political, something that goes against any idea of norm."[146] The group's focus on language and the violation of linguistic boundaries was motivated by a desire for a global queer community. In this respect, Les Tordu(e)s was a queer group not because its members belonged to a culture that rejected restrictions but because they imparted new life to local textuality by using English as a vernacular language for minorities, the better to reinvent the public spheres from which they have traditionally been excluded. From this viewpoint, Les Tordu(e)s activists are heirs of FHAR, whose activists specifically addressed the LGBT movement and sought to critique the processes of increasing disciplinary control.[147] As Marie, a participant in the Marche des Tordu(e)s, explained:

> We also wanted to reappropriate libertarian watchwords. We obviously have certain things in common with various far-left, anarchist, and/or libertarian movements, and since these movements often employ highly virile images and representations, we thought (and still do, I think) it was important not to abandon certain turfs within the struggle; it was important to remain visible as transfagdykes—for example, on issues such as the moral order, against guys who exploit the discourse on emancipation and free love in order to have as many affairs as they like.[148]

On June 26, 2015, ACT UP Paris, OUTrans!, and Femmes en Luttes 93, along with several other LGBT, feminist, queer, and antiracist organizations, took up the torch first raised by Les Tordu(e)s and organized a "night pride" march (Pride de Nuit) on the eve of the official Pride event.[149] The organizers stated that "dancing [in a parade] is not enough—our struggles are political; they call for solidarity,"[150] and they specifically denounced the official Pride event's ties to the political party then in power, the Socialist Party. The lead banner on their night march joked about the government's repeated retreats during the polemic over gender theory: "The PS has no Pride." The use of the English word "pride" in Pride de Nuit imitated the approach of Les Tordu(e)s in its desire to subvert official language (the official Gay Pride parade had been renamed "Marche des Fiertés") by forging worldwide solidarity among minorities via the English language. Demonstrators also acknowledged their links to FHAR—signs that referred to "the fuzz" (la flicaille) and incited people to "screw the sex and gender police" were direct allusions to FHAR's denunciation of "straight-fuzz" (hétéro-flics). Other slogans claimed that "We are still the scourge of society."[151] Allusions were also made to the Stonewall riot: "Stonewall was not a foam party—fight back"; "Stonewall was a fucking riot." Furthermore, the term "queer" surfaced frequently during the demonstration: for example, "Queers against racism and Islamophobia"; "Queer as militant" (the word "folk" on the sign was crossed out, in order to distance themselves from the commercial dimension of contemporary gay cultures, as exemplified by the TV show Queer as Folk); and "Let's queer society." Here queerness was a kind of self-identification that rejected institutionally validated categories ("Proud to be the shame of the nation") and promoted internationalism ("Solidarity with Palestinian queers" read one sign, while another showed the territorial expansion of Israel since the country was founded). The Pride de Nuit combined a discourse that denounced homonationalism and pinkwashing with one that advocated solidarity with Palestinian, Moroccan, Egyptian, and other homosexuals. Queer arguments were combined with a critique of capitalism, as Les Tordu(e)s did. The same was not true of the activists who organized Queer Week at Sciences Po, whose use of the term "queer" had no explicitly anticapitalist meaning but was above all the result of student mobility. Unlike Tordu(e)s, Queer Week was media oriented; it sparked ire among members of the Printemps Français group.

The Children of Queer Theory: Queer Week at Sciences Po

Queer Week (La Semaine des Genres et Sexualités) is a series of events that has been held every year since the spring of 2010 at the Institut d'Études Politiques in Paris, best known as Sciences Po.[152] It sprang from the initiative of students who, after spending a year abroad in the United States or Great Britain, wanted to organize a week of queer events as is regularly done on American and, to a lesser extent, British campuses. The five founders, Clément Lacoin, Marine Perrin, Paul Denizeaux, Ghislain de Salins, and Marie Mesnil, had studied at the University of Pennsylvania, Bath University, Oberlin College, King's College London, and Imperial College London.[153] A key factor for all was having taken courses in gender and feminist studies, where they had encountered queer theory. Their goal was thus not just to organize a week of LGBT visibility but to build a framework for reflecting on categories, discrimination, and representations of sexual minorities pursuant to having begun this critical approach on the other side of the Atlantic or Channel. Queer Week started out as a group project or educational module that would entitle the students to course credit. They submitted the idea of a Queer Week to the school administration, which won approval from the faculty as well as the head of Sciences Po, Richard Descoings.[154] The project came on the heels of the publication, by other students, of an erotic magazine, *L'Imparfaite*, "for deviants of all persuasions," also with the school's endorsement.[155] The first issue appeared in October 2009 and featured articles and pictures that stressed the sexual continuum and explored the multiplicity of objects that can be the target of desire. Although Queer Week was marked by this prior initiative (some members of Queer Week, such as Clément Lacoin, contributed to the magazine), it focused more particularly on the problematics of sexual minorities. In this respect it was more closely linked to the LGBT association at Sciences Po, called Plug'n Play, where most of the organizers had started out.

So what was queer about Queer Week? The first year, Queer Week organized events centered on academia and queer theory itself. Eribon gave a lecture titled "Queer . . . and After?—a Future for Subversion." In it he raised the issue of recognition and the danger that the institutionalization of queer theory—by becoming course work—would neutralize the "trouble" it injected into the politics of academic knowledge. "Queer theory and politics exist as protest, or they don't exist," Eribon argued. He noted that describing Queer Week as "a week of gender and sexualities" raised a problem since, by vaguely ranging across the gamut of sexualities, it ran the risk of merely making future politicians conversant on the subject; and however useful the event might be, the week itself was "no innovation."[156] The students followed this suggestion that their critical perspective would be sharpened by thinking about the situations of people being governed rather than those of the governors; otherwise, sexuality would continue to reinforce—in the name of diversity—other forms of domination, especially social and economic.

In subsequent years, students invited other academics (including Marie-Hélène/Sam Bourcier, Paola Bacchetta, Natacha Chetcuti, Luca Greco, and Mathieu Trachman) but also made more room for artists of all kinds: for example, the patron of one year's events was singer Juliette Noureddine, composer and performer of several queer songs including "Monocle et col dur" and "Monsieur Vénus"; Louise Deville organized a drag king workshop; graphic novelist Julie Maroh presented her new book, *Le Bleu est une couleur chaude*; street artist Kashnik painted "gayfitti"; Lassein Ninja organized a voguing workshop; Céline Sciamma spoke about her film *Tomboy*; and Cherry Lyly Darling gave a burlesque performance. Activist movements were featured beginning with the first event—invited speakers included Nikita and Tiphaine from STRASS (the sex workers' union); activists from La Barbe and Les Tumultueuses; and projection of a documentary, *L'Ordre des mots*, on trans persons (including Maud-Yeuse Thomas, cofounder of the Observatoire des Transidentités, and Vincent He-Say from ACT UP). In subsequent years, Maud-Yeuse Thomas was present alongside Karine Espineira (also cofounder of the Observatoire des Transidentités), as was another STRASS activist, Thierry Schaffauser. In March 2014, Queer Week collaborated with Cineffable (an association that organizes international festivals of lesbian and feminist films in Paris) to host a show of short films outside the school at the queer venue La Mutinerie. Thus, after having established the principle the first year, the students later followed Eribon's advice by creating events in the form of workshops and performances in the school's public spaces, breaking out of the traditional context of courses and seminars.

It was precisely this break that sparked controversy. From the first year, Queer Week was supported by LGBT media such as Pink TV and Têtu and even received wide coverage in the mass media. Several dailies and weeklies reported the event, unleashing a storm of reaction. Columnist Elisabeth Lévy, who founded the magazine *Causeur*, went on the offensive: "Behind this obscure hodgepodge is one main idea, borrowed from US universities, that we must put an end to the dictatorship of the difference between the sexes, imposed on us by nature and oppression, and promote gender that everyone can choose depending on passing mood or color of handbag. If you think you're either a man or a woman, then you are either a reactionary or fettered by tradition. So just be queer—whatever you want, whenever you want."[157] It was also insinuated, in more or less veiled terms, that Richard Descoings's bisexuality was a sign of the moral corruption of public leaders and of a gay conspiracy among high-ranking civil servants (Descoings was first in a civil-union part-nership with a man, Guillaume Peppy, the head of France's national railroad company, and later married a woman, Nadia Marik, who became deputy direc-tor of Sciences Po). This argument redoubled in intensity following the sud-den death of Descoings in New York on April 3, 2012, as though two visions of homosexuality merged—a public, proselytizing one,[158] and another, more hidden one that demonstrated the disloyalty of people "in the closet" who stuck together because bound by their secret.[159] In 2014, several Sciences Po students associated with the Printemps Français group described Queer Week's work-shops and photo exhibits on social media.[160] It was taken up by several far-right websites, such as Français de Souche.[161] The Printemps Français decided to take the floor, via its spokesperson, Béatrice Bourges, during a Queer Week lecture on LGBTQ activism in France. She was driven out by several activists who were attending or participating in the debate.[162]

The polemic sparked by Queer Week coincided with the implementa-tion at Sciences Po of a gender-studies program (Programme de Recherche et d'Enseignement des SAvoirs sur le GEnre [PRESAGE]), as announced in the spring of 2010 by Hélène Périvier and Françoise Milewski, two professors in one of the school's research units (Observatoire Français de Conjonctures Économiques [OFCE]). The simultaneity of Queer Week and the launch of PRES-AGE led opponents of gender theory to view it as further proof of the influence of the gender lobby. A former conservative member of the European Parliament, Élisabeth Montfort, described Queer Week as an "initiatory event" designed to provide a "preview of gender studies."[163] Although other, similar gender-studies programs had already existed for many years in certain French universities such as Paris VIII and Toulouse Le Mirail, the fact that PRESAGE was being launched in "*the* school of government" created a lot of controversy. It was not just domi-nant academia that was being challenged but the intellectual crucible of France's national identity—how could anticommunitarianism survive if challenged in the very place where the nation's leaders were educated? In responding to the criti-cism leveled at her, Périvier had to point to the French origin of gender studies: "This field of research has been extensively developed in France since the 1970s, contrary to the stock belief that it all comes from the United States and Judith Butler. Butler drew inspiration from Foucault and Derrida!"[164]

The new student and educational initiatives at Sciences Po show that queer-ness in France challenges not only the norms and representations of gender and sexuality but, more broadly, national assumptions about the social contract and the way that contract is anchored to fantasies about American culture.

CHAPTER 2 SHOWS the actual presence of queerness in France through the many overlaps between various political, academic, media, and activist circles. I have debunked the premises of the idea of "gender theory," but I do not abandon the idea of the theory itself. The production of queer theory in the Franco-American sphere has been very intense in the past twenty-five years and has challenged theories of the State. The next two chapters explore this: What does queerness change in our perception of the transatlantic sphere and in the idea of the globalization of sexualities? What does it reveal about representation in a majority, democratic political system? How does it trigger a rethinking of the boundaries of "the community" and the idea of marriage itself? I discuss how reiteration of a highly supple signifier—in this case, repeated use of the word "queer" in the public sphere—has affected (that is, literally destabilized through *affects*) the tacit foundations of the sense of belonging. As Denise Riley has rightly put it, "Hearing something said too many times will make it rise up out of its background, suspended in relief. But what goes to determine whether irritation or boredom will be born of reiteration, rather than the saving grace of irony's attentiveness to those categories which only unhelpfully apostrophise us?"[165]

CHAPTER 3

TRANSATLANTIC HOMECOMINGS

FRENCH THEORY'S "return" to France via queer theory brings overlooked texts to light and tries to reproduce the dynamics of intellectual movements born on the other side of the Atlantic. This attempt to revive the critical potential of French theory in France itself began at the precise moment that an anticommunitarian mood took hold,[1] solidly grounded on the older idea that anti-Americanism represents a form of humanism.[2] However, the idea of a deliberate strategy of importation, which certain writers defend,[3] is too restrictive. Cultural fantasies always contain a measure of the unexpected and the offbeat.[4] A self-reflexive view of a given culture in the mirror of an "other" culture in fact means inventing yet a third culture, one that disrupts normal boundaries of belonging through the very presence of that other.[5] Therefore, I am not trying here to employ sociological data in an effort to flush out cultural similarities and differences, which are meant to reveal what makes transcultural interaction possible.[6] On the contrary, I am interested in how the response to queer theory is implicitly governed by a principle of authenticity—there are supposedly true and false interpretations, good translations and mistakes. Queer theory tends to travel in the sphere of the obvious, since it attaches itself to the concrete experience of sexuality, both sexual practices and categories of practices. Most of the activists whose careers I discuss in Chapter 2 claim to have found in queer theory a voice in which to express their struggles and explain their personal paths. Queer theory reflects their critique of dominant sexual categories and the normative world, even as it enables them to converse with people who experience the same discrepancies. In this chapter, I try to understand what is tacit in the process of appropriating queer theory, beginning with adherence to cosmopolitan values and a belief in the possibility of a radical nonnormativity.

In undertaking this task, I explore how the tension between local and global is imagined across the Atlantic. There are several dimensions to globalization, which function both independently and jointly: for example, the circulation of capital beyond State control; the revival of a cosmopolitan ideal made possible by ever-greater methods of communication; the spread of supranational policies in the context of continents that are increasingly integrated politically; the growing influence of transnational activism; and the emergence of hybrid forms of culture. Many academics have embraced this "global turn" in sexual matters—representations and practices are apparently circulating more widely through the increase in movement of people (immigration and tourism), spread of mass entertainment, and internationalization of activism.[7] Other writers have stressed the threat that globalization poses to vernacular forms of sexuality. They view globalization in terms of balance of power, showing how a new empire has arisen through the paradoxical effect of transnational gay activism combined with a more traditional form of Orientalism. This is what Joseph Massad dubs "the gay international" and Momin Rahman calls "homocolonialism."[8]

Still other commentators point to the rise of a "counterpublic" via the use of internationalized social media, stressing the intensification of forms of resistance to majority norms in each culture through the very effect of globalization.[9] Finally, an increasing number of studies reveal that legal statutes on sexuality are steadily converging. They nevertheless point to an important nuance in the process of globalization by showing that interconnections in the activist and legislative spheres occur above all at a regional, rather than truly global, level.[10] Furthermore, this legislative convergence has been the object of major protests throughout the world—new alliances to oppose the rights of sexual minorities have been formed at domestic and international levels. Thus, resort to local activism appears in many cases to be more effective than the mechanisms of basic human rights.[11] Study of the globalization of sexuality is therefore booming, a vitality further confirmed by the varieties of approaches taken to it.

I would nevertheless like to nuance this idea of the globalization of sexuality in a number of ways. First, from a longer historical perspective, transcultural flows have been the rule rather than the exception; the settling of European nation-states into their late nineteenth-century form has led us to believe that a new phenomenon has recently emerged.[12] It is also essential to emphasize that what is changing today is not so much cultural flows themselves as the meaning ascribed to them (a meaning that varies greatly depending on age, class, and cultural origin) and the form they take (virtual, rapid, fleeting, participatory). A sense of national belonging is no weaker than before but is increasingly based on the notion of culture and decreasingly on the notion of citizenship.[13] It is therefore necessary to identify the new forms on which a feeling of belonging is constructed, challenging the overly simplistic idea that that this feeling has diminished. Finally, it is important to recall, as geographer Jon Binnie has done, that "globalization has reinforced the importance of space and place precisely because places are differently impacted upon by globalization."[14] Thus, there is no contradiction between local and global but rather a shifting set—simultaneously overlapping and interdependent—of forms of attachment.

For the past decade, the central debate within queer theory across the Atlantic has been the globalization of sexuality, a debate that went notoriously public when Judith Butler refused to accept a prize awarded by the Berlin Pride event because racist attitudes had been expressed on several occasions within the organization.[15] I take a particular look at the way queerness is employed in radical critiques of nationalism, showing that these critiques paradoxically reify the identities they claim to combat. Along the way, I propose a deconstruction of the notion of "homonationalism" itself, demonstrating that it manages to critique North/South and East/West forms of domination only at the cost of misunderstanding the complex links between sexuality and sense of belonging in the Euro-American world. In conclusion, I introduce the variable of time into transatlantic queer echoes. I show that the tensions expressed over the local/global polarity in discussions of queer theory on both sides of the Atlantic tend to minimize the minority/majority polarity, which nevertheless continues to structure the exercise of power on various levels.

Sexuality and Nationalism

The legal recognition of homosexuality in Western, Iberian, and Northern Europe has led to the progressive inclusion in national governance of the "homosexual question" (among other questions such as prostitution, binational couples, and trans identities). Some commentators on current political affairs, such as Éric Fassin, call it "sexual democracy."[16] Homosexuality is no longer just an object of public policy but a tool for implementing other public policies, notably those related to national identity. In the Netherlands, for instance, candidates for citizenship are shown pictures and quizzed on their level of acceptance of homosexuality and public nudity.[17] In Germany, the state of Baden Württemberg instituted a similar profiling system aimed at Muslim immigrants in 2006, based on their attitudes to sexual issues, especially homosexuality. The questions included, "How would you feel about an openly gay politician?"[18] It should nevertheless be pointed out that there is no widespread use of the homosexual question as an instrument of local, national, or European policy on immigration. As Fassin himself concedes, it is more a question of the "rhetoric of sexual democracy" than actual "sexual democracy."[19] This discourse surfaces in LGBT movements themselves. Some LGBT associations have accused the cultures of certain immigrants—such as people of Turkish origin in Germany—as being responsible for homophobia.[20]

In France, Inter-LGBT (the greater Paris federation of gay and lesbian associations) produced two posters with patriotic overtones and a certain condescension toward racialized minorities. The first, which appeared in 2011, called on participants in the Pride March to vote in 2012, and it showed the French national mascot, a white rooster, draped in a feather boa, a symbol of gay theatricalization. The poster was withdrawn following objections by several LGBT activists and the publication of many unfavorable online reactions.[21] The second poster, dating from 2015, featured a black (or mixed-raced) Marianne, emblem of the French Republic, with the slogan, "Our struggle will emancipate you." The "we/you" rhetoric created an artificial opposition between racial and sexual questions, as well as conveying a haughty viewpoint. Presented to government minister Christiane Taubira during a public meeting, the poster sparked many demands for its withdrawal by queer groups and far-left activists.[22] The slogan was ultimately changed to: "Pride Parade: Lesbian, gay, bi and trans—many and indivisible."

The concept of indivisibility itself can be problematic, as it underpins the anticommunitarian attitude in France. The first article of the current constitution of the French Republic (1958) declares that "France is an indivisible, secular, democratic, and social republic." The idea of indivisibility leaves no room for productive tensions that arise among various minority groups and tends to promote more timid demands that may reinforce, rather than change, the legitimacy of the republican state. That is exactly what happened in 2015 with respect the rights of transgender individuals. In June 2015, Inter-LGBT decided not to back the demands of Existrans (a march for the rights of transidentity persons) for a free and easy modification of identity documents. Instead, Inter-LGBT preferred to speak of "quick, transparent" change of identity papers "based on self-determination," which might continue to require a court process rather than the implementation of a simplified administrative procedure.[23] Such republican legalism is not new within the LGBT movement, unless the history of LGBT activism is reduced to revolutionary activism alone. The association Homosexualité et Socialisme (Homosexuality and Socialism), founded in 1983 by activists within the Socialist Party, played a key role in organizing Inter-LGBT and on numerous occasions has weighed in on the positions adopted by the latter group.[24] The conservative drift of certain LGBT movements reflects the conservative drift within the entire left-wing government itself.

In a similar fashion, we should not be misled by the polemic over the far right's appropriation of the homosexual question. During a speech in Lyon on December 10, 2010, Front National (FN) leader Marine Le Pen stated, "I'm hearing more and more stories about the fact that, in certain neighborhoods, it's not good to be a woman, or a homosexual, or a Jew, or even French or white."[25] Many media headlines then trumpeted a new FN strategy with respect to gays,[26] at the very moment that the former founding president of ACT UP Paris, Didier Lestrade, published a book, *Why Gays Have Moved to the Right*.[27] The polemic flared up again in 2015 when Sébastien Chenu, the former president of Gay Lib (an LGBT caucus with the conservative UMP party) joined the FN, just when the vice president of the FN himself, Florian Philippot, was outed by the media.[28] Although some gays and some lesbians are indeed members of the FN, it would be simplistic to view it as an automatic effect of their sexual orientation. Nor is the phenomenon a new one.[29] When threatened by a homophobic environment, transferring that rejection onto other minorities is not an uncommon reaction.[30] Furthermore, the tendency of some gays and lesbians to support policies of exclusion has never prevented other homosexuals from advocating diametrically opposed positions in the very same political context.[31]

Finally, another question must be asked: Has there really been a change of attitude toward homosexuality in the FN since Marine Le Pen became head of the party?[32] The FN has always been heavily marked by France's wars of decolonization, linked to the image of its founding leader, Jean-Marie Le Pen, a powerfully built army officer who terrorized and sparked admiration among men in the ranks. On several occasions Le Pen had himself filmed while working out in the boxing ring, proudly displaying his physical strength. During the legislative campaign of 1997, he ran into opponents in Mantes-la-Jolie and assaulted the socialist candidate, boasting, "I've never been afraid of any man, or even several!" Then he shouted at one of his opponents, "I'll set you running, you redheaded faggot!" The homophobic insult does not necessarily exclude a certain virile camaraderie. Le Pen never made a secret of his affection for the former mayor of Pau, André Labarrère, a friend from youth who was an overt homosexual. In the end, FN rhetoric entertains two homosexualities: the one that reinforces the chief's virility, attractive to both men and women, and the one that is a form of weakness and moral corruption, symbolizing the feminization of society. Le Pen summed up his position in 1995: "What we don't have in the FN is queens."[33] FN leadership is keen to valorize the virile strength of others, as long as it doesn't exceed the chief's own strength. So after having been pushed aside as party leader by his own daughter, Marine, Jean-Marie Le Pen naturally went for Philippot, accusing him of having a nefarious influence on Marine. Referring to Philippot as a *gestapette* (the little Gaystapo), a label formerly applied to Abel Bonnard, minister of education during the Vichy regime, Le Pen stressed the underhandedness of snooping, talkative, overt homosexuals.[34]

Indeed, his virile strength has taken on a new body in the person of his daughter. Marine Le Pen is now the leader of the FN but, according to her father, cannot impart sufficient virility into the homosexuals around her. Marine's accession to the leadership was made possible by the inherited transmission of power. The Le Pens often refer to their political "gene." Thus, paradoxically, despite the conflict between father and daughter, Marine's leadership has maintained the old chief's virility intact, since it survives "bodily." Marine herself has played on this genealogy to establish her own autonomy, to her father's great annoyance. This self-assertion within a patriarchal constraint has led some gays to see themselves in Marine Le Pen and to run for office in her party. Many of them are also seeking class revenge, such as Steeve Briois, elected mayor of Hénin-Beaumont in 2014. Briois is the grandson of a miner; his father was a laborer, and his mother, an accountant. His homosexuality was revealed by the publication of a book just a few months before the municipal election. As it turned out, the configuration of the 2014 campaign tended to demonstrate the preeminence of class issues, thereby relativizing the argument that FN voters were influenced by the homosexuality issue.[35]

This, then, was the context—neglectful of the history of homosexualities and the sociology of voting—in which the notion of homonationalism spread through France and Europe. When Butler refused the prize awarded to her by the Berlin Pride organization as a protest against its underlying racism, she never established a substantive link with homosexuality.[36] Other scholars and organizations did. In France, several queer associations denounced the "Brand Israel" policy followed by the Israeli government since 2005 to attract homosexual tourists to the country (in particular to Tel Aviv) and to thereby create a positive image in Western media. This "pinkwashing" renders less invisible the stakes of the Israeli-Palestinian conflict and the work of queer Palestinian groups such as Queers for Boycott, Divestment and Sanctions (GBDS).[37] In March 2012, a collective called the Front du 20 Mars invited Haneen Maikey and Ramzy Kumsieh to Paris—both members of the Palestinian association Al-Qaws, which promotes sexual diversity, and both active in the GBDS campaign—in order to publicly present the issues behind their struggle.[38] Founded on March 20, 2001, the Front du 20 Mars is a collective that opposes the instrumentalization of feminism to Islamophobic ends; it was born of a joint initiative by the Panthères Roses, the Tumultueuses, the Indivisibles,[39] and another collective called Les Mots Sont Importants.[40] The front's role of providing information nevertheless took the form of generalizations—the prospectus announcing the event asserted that "all Europe is the scene of the widespread co-opting of feminist, queer, and white LGBT movements by reactionary forces against Muslims, immigrants, and all nonwhites in general." The prospectus cited as an example a kiss-in planned for May 7, 2011, in front of the grand mosque in Lyon, designed to "combat homophobia in Islamic countries and the homophobia of a small minority of Muslims in France."[41] The kiss-in was the brainchild of three college students from Lyon, who had already organized several kiss-ins in front of churches. Posted on Facebook, their call was swiftly taken up by far-right groups, notably Français de Souche (Those of French Extraction). Following a meeting with the president of Lesbian and Gay Pride in Lyon, who opposed the idea, the students canceled the event. The call for a kiss-in arose from confused thinking on several levels: the homophobia of Islamic countries was associated with the homophobia of certain Muslim individuals in France; by failing to compare homophobia in traditionally Islamic countries with homophobia in traditionally Christian countries, the call for a demonstration exonerated Christianity of all responsibility; and organizing a demonstration against a majority religion does not occupy the same discursive register as a demonstration against a minority religion that has itself been stigmatized.[42] Work on the way religions are perceived should not lead to simplification of the issues linking nationalisms to sexualities.[43]

A symposium, "Sexual Nationalisms: Gender, Sexuality, and the Politics of Belonging in New Europe," held at the University of Amsterdam on January 27–28, 2011, provided another paradigmatic example of the tensions running through the field of research into sexualities. The event was jointly organized by two research units, the Amsterdam Research Center for Gender and Sexuality (University of Amsterdam) and the Institut de Recherche Interdisciplinaire sur les Enjeux Sociaux at the EHESS. Its stated goal was to show that, subsequent to movements for the rights of women and homosexuals, the social construction of nationalism, formerly founded on an ideal of patriotic virility (the organizers cited the work of George Mosse), had evolved into a sexualization of national identity against non-Europeans. The program stated that "the refashioning of citizenship has contributed to the redefinition of secular liberalism as cultural whiteness. Homophobia and conservatism, gender segregation and sexual violence have been represented as alien to modern European culture and transposed upon the bodies, cultures, and religions of migrants, especially Muslims and their descendants."[44] But the final session of the Amsterdam symposium was boycotted by several participants who wanted to demonstrate that this type of event reproduced what it was designed to combat.[45] One panel discussion was devoted to "Homonationalism, Homoneoliberalism, Homoneocolonialism: Crises and Travels, Europe and Beyond," with papers by Jennifer Petzen, Jin Haritaworn, and Suhraiya Jivraj and chaired by Lisa Duggan. Jin Haritaworn and Fatima El-Tayeb decided not to participate in the final session and asked Jasbir Puar to speak on their behalf. They criticized the conference organizers for having invited them at a late date out of a simple concern for diversity. They explained that the symposium was dominated by white people in both number of papers and references cited, consequently reinforcing a system of citation that obliged young scholars of color to pass through a white vetting system in order to exist in this field of study.

This critique raises an important question concerning academic self-reproductive mechanisms. It reminds us that these mechanisms are not merely structural but also representational, that is, they are conveyed by individuals whose disposition (age, skin color) and sometimes even professional position (the enjoyment of a constant media presence, or a position of power on university committees, and the like) reinforce discriminations that they oppose discursively.[46] The critique spotlights the divided nature of academic comportment and reminds us that a truly minority practice remains to be invented. However, the interpretation of minority practices that it proposed was oversimplified: the protesters rallied around the concept of homonationalism advanced by Jasbir Puar and merely contrasted nonnormative sexualities with homonationalist ones. Given this situation, Eribon asks how can we reject homophobia and transphobia and advocate sexual freedom even while "struggl[ing] against the immigration policies of my government, or of other European governments, against laws directed and enforced against various immigrants"?[47] The first response is to avoid mistaking the part for the whole: while certain LGBT people support conservative policies, nothing indicates that their opinions are intrinsically guided by their sexual orientation. The second response involves examining those individuals' personal careers and taking into consideration the fact that they operate in several temporal frameworks, as suggested by Eribon's hypothesis:

> Our way of conceiving of the time of politics is too homogeneous. We could say it is a Hegelian and synthetic way of conceiving of temporality which leads us either to think in terms of the convergence of struggles, the alliance of different minorities, or to think in terms of an exclusive choice of one kind of struggle to the detriment of others, or even in opposition to others. Perhaps we should instead think of politics in terms of heterogeneity, that is in terms of temporalities that are juxtaposed to different degrees.[48]

Homonationalism's Blind Alleys

It is precisely an inability to conceptualize heterogeneous temporalities that characterizes the notion of assemblage as advanced by Puar. Assemblage smooths several systems of domination into a patchwork that is ultimately reduced to a watchword. Puar's analysis of homonationalism assembles disparate data but establishes no correlation between them. She argues that the 2003 US Supreme Court decision in *Lawrence and Garner v. Texas*, which overturned the sodomy law in Texas and, consequently, in thirteen other states, was a paragon of homonormativity "*against* the sexually nonnormative racialized subjects." Her reasoning is symptomatic: she makes a distinction, without ever demonstrating it, between the "homonormative subjects of class, racial, legal status and gender privilege" and "sexually nonnormative racialized subjects."[49] On what foundations do these two holistic, antagonist categories rest?[50] Obviously, the *Lawrence and Garner* decision was a response to the court's own 1986 decision in *Bowers v. Hardwick*, which refused to declare the state of Georgia's sodomy

law unconstitutional. In this instance, the case involved an act of fellatio between two men, which the judges assigned to the category of sodomy. Legal
expert Janet Halley rightly pointed out that this decision inevitably associated
the legal category of sodomy with male homosexuality even though the same
category was used to prosecute sexual acts between women.[51] The decision
also defined, a contrario, the boundaries of legitimate sexuality. The *Lawrence
and Garner* decision undid the categories established in *Bowers v. Hardwick*
and ruled that, in the private sphere, acts of sodomy could not be the object of
prosecution. It thereby severed the link between sodomy and homosexuality by
shifting to another topic, that of private versus public sphere. To avoid disturbing the public order, the *Lawrence and Garner* decision decriminalized homosexuality by restricting sexuality to the private sphere.

On this point, Puar's observation is perfectly valid—apart from the issue
of the inevitably public aspect of sexuality, which Michael Warner has raised
elsewhere,[52] the very possibility of enjoying a private sphere is itself most un-
equally distributed. It is difficult for minorities, especially racialized minorities,
to establish a private sphere where they are felt to be dangerous (and are thus
monitored) and where the economic conditions for creating a private sphere
are not present (due to wage disparities, educational inequality, and the like).
This profound inequality is underscored by the fact that the police were summoned to intervene in the Lawrence and Garner affair by a phone caller who
said that "a black male [was] going crazy with a gun." The *Lawrence and Garner*
decision was therefore double-edged: it established a zone of freedom not accessible to all while reaffirming a denial of freedom outside that zone. It is one
thing to make this observation, however, and another to accept the categories
of legal reasoning at face value.

John Lawrence was a fifty-five-year-old white man at the time of the incident; Tyron Garner, a thirty-one-year-old black man. Puar noted this difference in age without exploring it. She nevertheless argued that the *Lawrence
and Garner* decision was overdetermined by "the silent interraciality" and it
was "highly plausible" that the decision was influenced by the issue of interracial marriage, which had been illegal in certain states until the *Loving v. Virginia* case of 1967. Referring to the fantasy of "multicultural queerness" and
the separation of the gay and African American communities (thereby limiting
homosexuality to white homosexuality while limiting black identities to heterosexuality),[53] Puar commits a first oversimplification. On the one hand, she
admits the existence of two distinct communities without exploring them; on

the other, she fails to consider that modes of belonging to a group (whiteness in one case, heterosexuality in the other) vary considerably depending on factors of class, generation, place of origin, and complex family background.[54] In the same way, when Puar discusses the racial aspect of the accusation of sodomy through history (evoking the register of bestiality), she fails to analyze the fact that Lawrence and Garner were both exposed to it but exposed differently precisely because of the color of their skins and their ages. She simply mentions the fact that the decision referred to "values we share with a wider civilization."[55] But this reference was a response to Justice Warren Burger's decision in *Bowers v. Hardwick*, which invoked a defense of Judeo-Christian morality. That it was a "counternarrative" and that the *Lawrence and Garner* decision resulted in the acquittal of the two protagonists did not hinder Puar from arguing that

> the annexing of a black-white sodomy duo to civilization can be read in at least two ways: the ascendancy of whiteness achieved through the sexual and racial hybrid couple, a token of tolerance and diversity that now invites homosexuals despite or perhaps even because of national identity becoming more hegemonic than ever; or as surrogate citizenship to black subjects who remain economically disenfranchised to the extent of their exclusion from the model minority ethnic, proffering sexual citizenship in the face of racial inclusion.[56]

It is interesting to note that Puar not only describes the Lawrence-Garner relationship without ever giving them the floor but also uses the category of homosexuals in a generic way once again—the reader is not quite sure what it covers here. Thanks to this generalization, Puar can then conclude that the *Lawrence and Garner* decision is symptomatic of the liberal context and exacerbation of white American identity:

> The metonymic fusing of homosexuality to sodomy, a fusing that the Lawrence-Garner ruling actively sought to de-fuse, exerted its spectacular force with the Orientalist readings of Abu Ghraib. That is to say, sodomy as homosexual sex is produced outside of the ever-narrowing parameters of legitimate homosexual American subjects; those protected by Lawrence-Garner are now exempt from this fusing. This legislation compels some homosexuals into the fold of American nationalism and into collusion with contemporary U.S. expansionism.[57]

While it should be noted that, for once, Puar refers to "some" homosexuals and not the entire category, the connection she makes between the decriminalization of sodomy and expansionist American policy is too brief: the verb "compel" suggests a causal link that is not backed by any data and simultaneously overlooks another aspect, the importance of class in the adoption of nationalist values (as witnessed by enlistment in the military).[58] The distinction Puar makes between "homonormative subjects" and "nonnormative racialized subjects" borders on sophistry.[59] Not only are all sexualities traversed by norms, something that alone invalidates the binary vision she proposes, but the idea that homonormative subjects are recognized *in opposition to* nonnormative racialized subjects represents a serious oversimplification of the way norms operate. Subjectification is an inceptive process in which deconstruction of norms cannot be dissociated from their reproduction.

Thus, the fact that some gays and lesbians adhere to racist and imperialist policies in no way demonstrates that there is some ontological correlation with the category of homosexual that would justify the use of a portmanteau word. True enough, Puar explains that homonationalism does not refer to specific individuals and is therefore not designed to evaluate the behavior of a given individual but refers to a system of power. However, even as a heuristic device, the notion of homonationalism remains aporetic. On the one hand, it effects a double totalization—of homosexuality (a category thereby drained of its sociological density) and of nationalism (a phenomenon thereby drained of its historical density); on the other hand, a concept always operates on several registers simultaneously: it represents an analytical category and a political category with which people conceptualize, name, and incorporate themselves into a group (whose boundaries they define along the way). Paradoxically, there exists a real risk of reinforcing the nationalist leanings of certain gays and lesbians by essentializing them. Such accusations may ultimately render homonationalism performative: by constructing categories that are both rigid and strictly dichotomous, we perhaps run the risk of stoking nationalism by associating it with given sexual identities and practices, ultimately pushing those practitioners into its arms.[60]

If we take a look at recent debate over "marriage for all," it is possible to arrive at a conclusion quite different from one of widespread homonationalism. Opposition to the legal equality of heterosexual and homosexual couples was expressed by representatives of all the major monotheistic religions, but the opposition movement was nevertheless organized by Catholic groups close to the Vatican, and attendance at demonstrations was increased by the mobilization of provincial parishes. The argument that "we"—white, civilized Europeans concerned to protect homosexuals' rights—now oppose a "them" composed of dark-skinned foreigners, immigrants from southern lands, and second-generation immigrants from certain French urban ghettos, does not stand up to the facts.[61] The groups that fought the Taubira Act did so in the name of French and European Catholicism. In contrast, the LGBT movements stressed arguments based on fragilization, lack of legal recognition, and children born to homoparental families, as well as the discriminations that stem from outlawing same-sex marriage (including pension packages and acquisition of nationality for the foreign member of binational homosexual couples).

It was, in fact, the opponents of the Taubira Act who attempted to exploit the national identity issue by referring to the imposition on "real people" of rights that had no French tradition and by going so far as to demand withdrawal from the Council of Europe and consequently abrogation of the European Convention on Human Rights.[62] The debate that raged in 2012–13 prompts us to reflect on the protean, shifting form of discourse—the very stage on which a nationalist claim is being played out may not be national at all.[63] Furthermore, an appeal to nationalism may well be strategic, as Robert Kulpa has explained: "Lesbian and gay communities in CEE [Central and Eastern Europe] and elsewhere may well embrace national ideas . . . as one of the methods of their struggles."[64] Recourse to nationalist rhetoric does not necessarily imply adoption of those ideas but may reflect a tactical need to employ the dominant discourse to obtain legal security for one's own situation, all the while destabilizing that discourse and even introducing a new problematic. The question is therefore not one of escaping the norm, whose dominance continues to be conveyed by the very idea of escape, but to gather the resources needed to destabilize it.

Globally Gay?

The second queer echo to reach France from the United States was the notion of a "gay international" introduced by Joseph Massad in *Desiring Arabs*. The publication of a book *White Feminists and Empire* by Félix Boggio Éwanjé-Épée (a PhD student in philosophy) and Stella Magliani-Belkacem (from La Fabrique publishing house) triggered a polemic in France.[65] It argued:

> As is the case with feminism, contemporary reaction in recent years has constantly cast nonwhites as the major threat to "homosexuals." Black and Arabic men—from virile, macho "ghetto youth" to "fundamentalist" Muslims—as well as those from non-Western, particularly Islamic, cultures are depicted as a major

force in contemporary heterosexist domination. As has often been pointed out, this maneuver is employed only to exonerate white France of its structural homophobia, lesbophobia, and transphobia, as inscribed in its legislation, its educational and medical systems, and even its policy of access to health care.[66]

Éwanjé-Épée and Magliani-Belkacem denounced the stigmatization of non-whites and the exoneration of whites of responsibility for homophobia, lesbophobia, and transphobia. But their argument begins with a misleading generalization about feminism as a whole, overlooking its heterogeneity. This vagueness is what seemingly allows the two authors to advance a powerful political position: a racist stigmatization is occurring not only in the wake of LGBT movements but with their collusion. Indeed, Éwanjé-Épée and Magliani-Belkacem assert that

> what is being described here is more or less what has allowed "anti-homophobia" slogans to be adopted even by the far right of the political spectrum in order to assert a racist consensus. One of the major factors of that adoption involves a certain blindness to Western hegemony within the LGBT (lesbian, gay, bi- and transsexual) movement, plus an absence of any analysis of social and historical disparities in the production of sexual identities in different parts of the world.[67]

To bolster their demonstration, the authors compare the antiracist activism of FHAR, founded in 1971, with the racist drift of LGBT movements close to the Socialist Party. Among other examples, they cite Franck Chaumont's *Homo-Ghetto*,[68] which denounces ghetto homophobia by invoking the French republican tradition of integration. Chaumont was a former director of public relations for socialist-affiliated association Ni Putes ni Soumises, founded in 2003 by Fadela Amara, herself a member of the Socialist Party and a junior government minister for urban policies in 2007 during Nicolas Sarkozy's presidency. Although Éwanjé-Épée and Magliani-Belkacem's examples have some basis, their reasoning is skewed by the fact that they conflate groups that are politically very remote. Conversely, the actual practices of situationist homosexual groups—for example, those who produced the *Pédérama* program on the Libertaire radio station from 2003 to 2008—were as antiracist as FHAR had been in the early 1970s and employed a very similar kind of irony in their relationship to politics.[69] Éwanjé-Épée and Magliani-Belkacem write:

> Today's Orientalist view partitions the enlightened/Western world from the backward/despotic/Oriental world on the basis of what is called the "treatment

of homosexuals," taken as one humanitarian issue among others. These images reinforce the ideological arsenal of the imperialist bloc more than ever, putting a new face on its civilizing mission. Joseph Massad critiqued this rhetoric in *Desiring Arabs* by showing that, in the Arab world, the label "homosexual" is absent from traditional descriptions—of sexual relationships between members of the same sex. . . . The problem with that label is, according to Massad's argument, that homoerotic practices were common in Arab countries prior to the nineteenth century without being linked to "sexual orientations." Denouncing them and attempting to suppress them were the result of the importation of the West's Victorian morality, which equated that sexual freedom with "homosexuality."[70]

Massad's historical argument, adopted by Éwanjé-Épée and Magliani-Belkacem here, appears to hit home: Arab homoeroticism was stigmatized by colonizers via the category of homosexual, which had only recently emerged in the West. However, this argument has two blind spots. The first is that the appearance of the words "homosexual" and "heterosexual" in the late nineteenth century was not immediately followed by a change in the way people in the West were labeled by others or themselves or were perceived by the law. Until the mid-1930s, American medical dictionaries defined "heterosexuality" as an immoderate sexual appetite.[71] The terms *inverti* (sexual invert), *tribade* (tribade or lesbian), *bougre* (bugger), and *uranien* (Uranian) continued to be used after the category of homosexual was invented. The hetero/homosexual distinction not only took a long time to be adopted in practice but also coexisted with other types of self-naming. All these various categories circulated in European colonies, and all helped shape subjective perceptions. Furthermore, in France, the criminalization of homosexuality (that is, the raising of the age of consent for homosexual relations) was not introduced until 1942, by the Vichy regime. No Western categorical bloc exists; there are simply "historical interarticulations and complications of Eastern and Western bodies, desires, aesthetic traditions and analytical paradigms."[72] The second blind spot concerns the question of borrowings, hybridizations, and conflicts surrounding representations and norms of sexuality in non-Western areas. That issue has been addressed by Joseph Allen Boone in *The Homoerotics of Orientalism*. Boone explores the circulation of representations of homoerotism not only between East and West but also within those two spheres:

> In bringing eastern and western archives into conjunction, my intention is not to argue that one culture's representations directly influenced or shaped those of

the other. Rather, reading these cultural manifestations contrapuntally, listening to the echo-effects they create, adds a density of texture that illuminates the staying power, connotative energies, and accretion of meanings that emanate from them.[73]

Boone discusses the many paths and interpretations of the concept of sexuality, especially throughout the nineteenth and twentieth centuries, and also introduces the idea of postmodernist irony regarding Orientalist stereotypes in both East and West. He thus expresses regret that Massad leaves no room for human agency or the unexpected nature of sexuality whenever sexuality is confronted with multiple, changing norms and representations.[74] In contrast, Massad tends to criticize individuals in Arab countries who identify with LGBT categories for colluding with the system of Western domination, thereby acting against the interests of their own people. A contradiction arises because denouncing this complicity means recognizing the existence of a collective identity (if only defined by a shared refusal to be identified according to sexual practices). When asked by Éwanjé-Épée and Magliani-Belkacem about the accusation that he is thereby rendering invisible Arabs who identify themselves as gay, Massad replied that "the tiny number of gay-identified Arabs organized in Gay Internationalist organizations are complicit with an imperial sexual regime that rearranges the world along the hetero-homo binary, which they fully adopt without questioning and insist on reproducing and disseminating across the Arab world as the road to liberation."[75] The accusation of complicity stems from a fantasy of authenticity that requires a hermetic culture. At an individual level, this fantasy excludes any possibility of human agency, while at a collective level it invents a mythical past in which sexuality played no role in identity. In addition, when Massad refers to "Gay Internationalist organizations," he evokes organizations driven by imperialist fantasies.

But sociological research into social movements reveals more complex motivations behind such organizations.[76] In fact, Massad's work lacks a deeper analysis of the policies of non-Western states with respect to sexual relations between persons of the same sex, mainly those who invoke human-rights activism to justify a discursive rejection and penal repression of homosexuality and/or homosexual acts. Such an analysis would avoid attributing a single cause to that repression. Massad argues, "Also, most Arab and Muslim countries that do not have laws against sexual contact between men respond to the Gay International's incitement to discourse by professing antihomosexual stances on a nationalist basis. This is leading to police harassment in some cases and could lead to antihomosexual legislation."[77] In other words, Massad describes an implacable repressive machinery in which Arab and Islamic states are merely a passive cog. As historic proof, he cites the case of Lebanon, whose penal system allegedly stems from French colonial law, which apparently imposed the criminalization of homosexuality in the 1930s.[78] Yet, as I pointed out earlier, France decriminalized "unnatural acts" in 1791, and they were only criminalized again in 1942 by the collaborationist Vichy government. Furthermore, it is useful to distinguish here between criminalization and a policy of monitoring society. During the French Mandate Lebanon was influenced by conservative families who had arrived from France and whose policy was to close certain places of prostitution, especially those aimed at men. It should be pointed out that Article 534 of the Lebanese penal code, which later outlaws "unnatural acts," is not a strict copy of the 1942 Vichy measure that merely raised the age of consent for homosexual relations (to twenty-one, as opposed to thirteen for heterosexual relations; today the age is fifteen). It would therefore be wise to examine the complex resonances between moral notions of sexuality in France and Lebanon. Nizar Saghiyeh comments, for example, that nonconsent to homosexual acts was not viewed in the same way by French and Lebanese jurisprudence after 1942.[79]

I do not wish to engage in further discussion of Massad's arguments here. Valérie Traub has already accomplished that task, revealing that Massad resorts to certain generalizations concerning existing literature even as she notes his interesting angle on the way sexuality is rooted in the Western modernist project.[80] Massad offers a highly sophisticated intellectual and cultural history of Arab and Islamic countries, but the absence of legal, political, and social analyses leads him to unilateral conclusions. It is precisely those conclusions—rather than his scholarly analysis of Orientalist homoeroticism—that were echoed in the realm of queer theory in France. Although studies of the imbrication of racism and sexual stereotypes are not new, Massad's interpretation has helped trigger new research more specifically centered on the homosexual community. Thus, Maxime Cervulle, explicitly acknowledging Massad's work,[81] analyzed homosexual pornographic films since the 1980s, explaining how many of them are marked by a commodification of Arab boys:

> *Harem* [a 1984 pornographic film by Jean-Daniel Cadinot] promotes the concept of a political solidarity formed by dissident desire and activated by sexual

relations in a manner not unlike that of Jean Genet, who self-consciously recognized the erotic significance of his political commitment to the Black Panthers in the 1960s. But while this model of sexual/political solidarity could potentially lead to an awareness of race, class, and gender as multiple sites of oppression, it does not allow for an intersectional account of such politics. Caught between the politics of porn and the erotic charge of politics, the nonwhite subject is reduced to a body to be exploited by white pornographers and revolutionaries alike as both a sign and a mode of exchange, as both a battlefield and a playground.[82]

Cervulle leaves no room for agency here. His analysis was criticized in *Minorités*, an online magazine launched in 2002 by Laurent Chambon and Mehmet Koksal, to which ACT UP Paris founder Didier Lestrade is a regular contributor. *Minorités* raises issues of cultures and practices marked by gender, sex, sexuality, race, class, and so on by jointly examining individual and collective practices.

It is also interesting to note that Massad's approach has spread beyond the question of homosexuality. Sociologist Nacira Guénif-Souilamas has described her work as similar to Massad's, "at the junction between queer and subalternist approaches."[83] Guénif-Souilamas shows that daughters of migrants in ghetto suburbs are the object of a special investment—made both by institutions and the families themselves—designed to integrate their families into the French Republic. However, they "experience integration via emancipation as an imposition or constraint, not as a liberation. First of all, normative assimilation tolerates only one model of conformity—meritocratic success—and only one form of allegiance—citizenship via nationality—and expects proof of both to be expressed physically as well as verbally."[84] Similarly, she explains that the integration system legitimizes its investment in girls by reproducing representations of Arab boys as heterosexuals dominated by their predatory nature. Paradoxically, then, sons of immigrants are really recognized by the French Republic only when they reinforce the violent stereotypes imposed on them. In Guénif-Souilamas's analysis of institutional performativity, the agency of boys is thereby reduced, and the material consequences of violent stereotypes tend to be elided by explanations that hinge on collective constraints: "By confining themselves to the enclave of a sexuality that is destructive for themselves and for the women they subjugate, some immigrants' sons thereby demonstrate their normative integration: they are doing exactly what is expected of them."[85]

Another interpretation often borrowed from *Desiring Arabs* is the idea that homosexuality does not exist as a category—whether of self-identification or institutional—in most areas outside the West. Houria Bouteldja, spokesperson for the decolonial and anti-Zionist organization called Parti des Indigènes de la République (Party of the Indigenous of the Republic) has adopted this idea:[86]

> Claiming to be gay, that is, to claim a gay political identity, is by no means a universal act. It exists in Europe, it exists in the United States, but it doesn't exist in the Maghreb. . . . In the Maghreb, homoeroticism was long tolerated until colonization imposed the norms of a rigid homo/hetero binarism. Here I recommend that you read the work of Joseph Massad. . . . One can claim to be Arab and homosexual/lesbian because such identities exist in Europe. They exist. What I'm saying is that you cannot go defend men or women on the basis of their homosexuality if they themselves don't claim or assume it as an identity. That might be considered sexual imperialism.[87]

Arguing that the category of homosexuality does not exist in the Maghreb, even as she is obliged to admit that some individuals identify themselves Arab and gay in Europe, Bouteldja insinuates that two entirely separate cultural blocs exist. This belief allows her to give credence to the idea of sexual imperialism. Moroccan writer Abdellah Taïa has publicly replied to Bouteldja. Drawing on Arabic literary tradition, he retorts that the very existence of himself and other Moroccan homosexuals makes homosexuality a de facto political category.[88] Other studies show, in the French-speaking context, that the category of homosexuality is used in numerous ways in Arab and Islamic countries.[89] Even though the criminalization of certain types of sexual behavior such as sodomy or acts in public is not exclusively aimed at sexual relations between men in most Arab and Islamic countries, it nevertheless primarily targets such relations, as witnessed by the prison sentences given in June 2015 to two young Moroccan men accused of kissing in public. Article 489 of the Moroccan penal code incriminates "any person who commits obscene or unnatural acts with another person of the same sex." Algerian law refers to homosexuality even more explicitly. Article 338 of its penal code states, "Anyone guilty of an act of homosexuality is punishable by imprisonment from two months to two years and a fine of 500 to 2,000 Algerian dinars." Given this situation, it would appear difficult to continue to claim that no process of subjectification is operating on the basis of the category of homosexuality, if only to avoid a statutory offense. The penal codes of Morocco and Algeria, as just two examples, were adopted after independence.

What is therefore required is a joint study of the impact of colonial discourses that stigmatized bestiality in the colonies based on the criminalization of homosexuality in the West and how those discourses were turned by post-independent states against those people who, within the newly independent populations, had been "contaminated" by the West. With respect to Mali, anthropologist Christophe Broqua has demonstrated this dual tendency to denounce the West and then adopt its categories in the name of national identity.[90] The same logic was behind Mahmoud Ahmadinejad's statement at Columbia University on September 24, 2007. "In Iran we don't have homosexuals like in your country. We don't have that in our country. In Iran, we don't have this phenomenon. I don't know who has told you that we have it."[91] Yet in the city of Mashhad in northeastern Iran two teenagers, aged sixteen and eighteen, were publicly hanged on July 19, 2005. Officially, they were convicted of raping a minor; unofficially, it was the homosexual aspect of the act that was punished. Article 111 of the Iranian penal code stipulates the death sentence for any act of penetration or "rubbing" between two adult males, if even sound of mind and consenting.[92] Several associations, including the Iranian Queer Organization, have reported ongoing violence and arrests.[93] The Iranian example shows that while the influence of international gay associations should be queried, the responsibility of states themselves cannot be overlooked. Otherwise, we would have a particularly paradoxical situation in which critical analysis, as useful as it may be, ignores—or at least considers as a secondary importance—the repression exercised against people because of their sexual practices, whether or not those people identify themselves as homosexuals. Any simplification of perceptions of the Occident also means simplifying perceptions of the Orient, and vice versa.[94] It also leads, as was largely the case in France, to ignoring the complex power relations within the global South.[95]

All this raises the question of the analytical framework. Indeed, there is something contradictory about minimizing the repression of sexual practices between men while conversely taking the State as the main analytical framework for pinkwashing. The latter is in fact based on a flow of tourists that largely concerns big cities. Shouldn't we question the networks being created between major urban zones and consequently ask how some gays and lesbians are helping create those networks? The idea of globalization will then take on a different meaning, not so much the imposition of a single model of identity as the growing presence of *certain* images of homosexuality in various large cities. Pride parades are a good example of this phenomenon. They in no way reverse the fragility of recognition of LGBT cultures, because they sometimes coexist with policies of cleaning up sex venues in the name of principles of health and morality.[96] We need an overall analysis of the spectacular presence of homosexuality and the many ways of appropriating space and mobility. Marianne Blidon and France Guérin-Pace have pioneered this path in France by showing that the relationship of gays to the city and to the countryside cannot be grasped without taking into consideration the age of coming out, the number of migratory stages, the moving of couples to less urbanized areas, and the effects of visibility on a professional career, as well as strategies of remaining anchored to one's hometown (including strategies of partial distancing).[97] Only by grasping multifarious situations is it possible to obtain a better understanding of the commercial and political strategies that target gay men around the world. Indeed, these strategies also produce complex forms of subjectification and even subjection. In an article on male prostitution in Patpong, a red-light district of Bangkok, Sébastien Roux notes that the category of gay is now common in Thailand but does not refer to a permanent identity. The term is associated with urban life in contrast to the more traditional femininity of *kathoeys* (ladyboys). In the case of prostitution, this identity is acquired on contact with international customers and other, older prostitutes and does not exclude heterosexual practices elsewhere.[98] It might be useful to explore the hybridization effects mentioned by Roux among Western customers and expatriates themselves. How does it affect their relationship to the category of gay and its gender implications?

My intention here is not to deny that nationalist strategies exploit certain aspects of gay and lesbian culture (especially tourism) and that some gays and lesbians adopt a swaggering patriotism to the detriment of the variety of the sexual practices and identities around the world—far from it.[99] Understanding multiple, diverse strategies calls for refined analytical tools, however. A queer analysis might explore the complex weave of modes of self-identification based on institutional categories, language, material constraints, erotic practices, and so on.[100] Valérie Pouzol, for example, has noted the importance of language in political mobilization, using queer activism in Palestine as an example:

> The activists of Aswat and Al-Qaws had to carry out a veritable task of linguistic research and adaptation to express sexual difference and to exhume from Arabic culture words and writings able to convey homosexuality. Old expressions belonging to medieval Arabic (*suhakiya* for lesbian) or pejorative in connotation

("children of Lot," linking homosexuality to sodomy) were rejected by the activists, who criticized their religious or clinical references. . . . They preferred the expressions *mithliyun/mithliyat* or simply *methliya jensiya*, "those who have the same sexuality." The Western term "queer," which was long ignored, is increasingly used by activists who emphasize above all its performative and political usefulness.[101]

Another crucial aspect of a critical approach to queerness involves not using national borders as the point of departure for an analysis that seeks, precisely, to reveal unconceptualized elements. During the first Intifada, for example, sexuality, morality, and sovereignty were conceived in a mode very similar to the way they are in the West, thereby yielding the idea that sexual minorities collaborated with the enemy.[102] The stakes behind transnational queer analysis require that we note the multiplicity of systems of identification not to oppose them but to show how they may take on several meanings simultaneously, without those meanings being necessarily logical or coherent.[103]

Intersectionality Is Not Enough

The reservations I have expressed with regard to homonationalism and the gay international are rooted in the way the notion of intersectionality has been treated in France. Several queer scholars associated with Marie-Hélène/Sam Bourcier have in fact seized on the notions of homonationalism and the gay international insofar as they both raise the issue of whiteness. Maxime Cervulle has thus pointed out that his research involves the sexualization of race and the racialization of sexuality. Cervulle describes the "second wave" of queer theory in France as one that sheds light on the whiteness of the first wave, as emblematized by Judith Butler.[104] This chronology raises certain problems because, as discussed in Chapter 2, queer theory first emerged in the United States as a "queer of color" theory. Gloria Anzaldúa at the University of Santa Cruz was one of the first people to formulate a queer critique, her terminology having been taken up by Teresa de Lauretis in 1989 and 1990 and then applied to the work of Sedgwick and Butler. The work of each of these women was therefore rife with resonances for studies of sex, gender, race, class, sexuality, religion, and more. As Cervulle acknowledged, Sedgwick's study of *Billy Budd* is an analysis of race.[105] The same is true of De Lauretis's studies on cumulative oppression, themselves inspired by Audre Lorde's *Zami*. Butler was therefore the one primarily criticized for not including race in her analyses, which purportedly explained her popularity in France. Bourcier even argues that contact with France changed Butler—previously open to an analysis of performative chains in which the "I" is constantly put back into play, she apparently became dangerously Cartesian, positing an "I" as preliminary to any analysis:

> Simone de Beauvoir's intentionality, will, and "I" were strictly eliminated from *Gender Trouble*. . . . The ability to act rested on the impersonal nature of performative repetition. . . . In *Undoing Gender*, we see a radical change at the level of utterance. The "I" of the philosopher, Butler herself, enters the stage, even more powerfully when she addresses France, the eldest daughter of Europe's philosophical tradition.[106]

This is a largely distorted interpretation of Butler: neither her early articles on Simone de Beauvoir, Monique Wittig, and Michel Foucault; her thesis on Hegel; *Gender Trouble*; nor *Bodies That Matter* dissolves the subject. But her work offsets a reading of the Cartesian "I think" with an analysis of "I speak." Bourcier criticizes Butler for entertaining a dialogue with a repressive corpus (he cites Levinas and Freud as well as the California-period Foucault still in the "SM closet"),[107] which Bourcier claims led Butler to rigidify gender, as witnessed by Butler's attachment to notions of melancholy and mourning that "pathologize" gender,[108] thereby preventing genders from proliferating as they had in the past. But only because Bourcier effected a highly distorted reading of Butler does he now regret he is no longer able to project onto the author of *Gender Trouble* his own call to radicality—what he labels, at the risk of a logical impasse, a "post-identitarian identity politics."[109] This also leads Bourcier to argue that emphasis on a critique of the binary heterosexual/homosexual system made Butler blind to the issue of racialization. Yet, on the one hand, Butler discussed the question of racialization in the early 1990s, as witnessed by her article on Rodney King;[110] on the other hand, in her *Bodies That Matter* (1993, not translated into French until 2009), she analyzed how the gendered body was used as an interpretive grid of race, based on the documentary film *Paris Is Burning*.[111] While *Gender Trouble* brought Butler a wider readership, it was not her first book to be translated into French. *The Psychic Life of Power*, *Excitable Speech*, *Antigone's Claim*, and *Precarious Life*, as well as a collection of articles (in conversation with Gayle Rubin), had already been published in French. The very idea of a first and second queer wave needs to be relativized. Finally, another criticism emerges from the issue of racialization: scholars who claim to be part of a second queer wave seem uneasy with demands for same-sex marriage, a demand they describe as white and bourgeois. As Bourcier plainly states:

> They harp on gay marriage to the point of overlooking the politics of marriage, to the point of embarking on a linear process along lines that are disturbing, to say the least. Marriage will inevitably be followed by homoparenthood—marriage, family, and country—that's the familial holy trinity toward which this unprecedented reprivatization of sexuality is leading us. Oedipus loves you! . . . How did we get from the politics of the pink triangle to the politics of familial triangulation?[112]

The criticism that Butler's theory is too removed from the real stakes means supposing that some lives are queerer than others, without ever explaining in what way they are. Once again we encounter a highly idealized, almost Romantic vision of the fringes as being beyond the law, even though they are a product of it.

This discourse also artificially separates the stakes behind the struggle for equal sexual rights from the "decolonization" of social practices. Bouteldja's positions are emblematic in this respect:

> I have no opinion as to whether homo demands are legitimate or not, but I have an opinion on the universality of the demand for homosexual identity. I'll tell you pretty straight—this discussion doesn't concern me. This discussion doesn't concern me because what I have to say is very special, is specifically located somewhere. There are a certain number of positions being expressed here, and in France when you speak out on this issue, either you're on the right or on the left; either you're liberal or you're reactionary. As far as I'm concerned, I have nothing to do with all that. I'm outside all that, in fact, because what I have to say is politically situated somewhere. I'm situated in the history of postcolonial immigration and working-class neighborhoods. If I'm asked about this issue, here where I'm at—because I don't have a universal opinion—here where I'm at, I say, this issue doesn't concern me. Because if you take a mike and wander through the housing projects—Le Mirail in Toulouse, Le Mas du Taureau in Lyon, La Cité du Luth in Gennevilliers—and you ask people, "What kind of problems do you have?," the spontaneous answers will mainly be about housing, police harassment, discrimination, unemployment, a whole heap of questions related to everyday life. This issue [of gay marriage] won't even come up, I'll bet.[113]

The stereotype that associates the law with privilege, without taking into account the materiality and performativity of the law, is precisely that which seeks to accredit reactionary movements against sexual minorities.[114] The economic and social aspects of marriage, along with its impact on acquiring French nationality, make reform of marriage a locus of change in the norms governing couples and sexuality as well as professional, economic, and racial relationships.[115] It would therefore be useful to return to a less dichotomizing, less monolithic, less static approach to the notion of intersectionality. Kimberlé Crenshaw's article "Mapping the Margins" was translated into French in 2005 by Oristelle Bonis.[116] Unlike Bouteldja's understanding of intersectionality, several French scholars have provided an intersecting analysis of class, sex, and race in a materialist vein.[117] Their work interrogates the consubstantiality of social relations. Research by Sirma Bilge, a sociologist from the University of Montreal, also made its way into French academia; she warned of an "ornamental intersectionality" that appeared to be form of "diversity" but did not question conceptual categories themselves.[118] This critical approach was precisely what drove Crenshaw's pioneering article. Intersectionality is not merely a question of interweaving several factors. It does not mean racializing sexuality or sexualizing race, which would merely reify one variable in order to study another, to open a new front by closing another. As Crenshaw put it, "I should say at the outset that intersectionality is not being offered here as some new, totalizing theory of identity. Nor do I mean to suggest that violence against women of color can be explained only through the specific frameworks of race and gender considered here."[119] If Crenshaw argues that intersectionality cannot provide a total explanation, she does so because it is itself the locus of several dynamics, themselves at the intersection of other dynamics. She therefore proposes to study only the effects of such convergences.[120]

Without that caveat, the notion of intersectionality runs the risk of essentializing the categories under study by implying that they preexist their intersection. Jasbir Puar shares this perspective but fears that intersectionality, as such, may be hindered by essentialization. She thus regrets that Crenshaw took the experience of black women as the point of departure for her article. "'Mapping the Margins,'" writes Puar, "may well be driven by anxieties about maintaining the 'integrity' of a discrete black feminist genealogy, one that might actually obfuscate how intersectionality is thought of and functions differently in different strands of black feminist and women of color feminist thought." Puar also regrets the fact that intersectionality has become so mainstream that it may be nothing more than "a way to manage difference that colludes with dominant forms of liberal multiculturalism." She furthermore feels that analyzing tensions and accidents at the intersection of multiple categorical systems may ultimately invoke the law as arbiter: "There is emphasis on motion rather than gridlock, on how the halting of motion produces the demand to locate. The accident itself indicates the entry of the standardizing needs of the juridical; is there a crime taking place? How does one determine who is at fault?"[121]

This fear of the juridical is expressed especially in terms of international law, which is increasingly incorporating intersectional discriminations in its field of action. Puar pleads for deterritorialization against juridical territorialization, because she feels that grasping experience through legal categories—and through the framework of representational politics—may obliterate the nonrepresentational referent of materiality itself.[122]

> No matter how intersectional our models of subjectivity, no matter how attuned
> to locational politics of space, place, and scale, these formulations—these fine
> tunings of intersectionality, as it were, that continue to be demanded—may still
> limit us if they presume the automatic primacy and singularity of the disciplinary subject and its identitarian interpellation.[123]

Thus, she proposes the term "assemblage" as a complement to the intersectional approach. Assemblage is an "awkward translation of the French term *agencement*," a term borrowed from Gilles Deleuze and Félix Guattari.[124] Puar shares Deleuze and Guattari's deep suspicion of identitarian sedimentation, yet she overlooks a key aspect of their work: "minority evolution" (*le devenir minoritaire*).[125] Deterritorialization is possible only through the frictions and bumps generated by minority developments. And that is exactly the source of Crenshaw's article, built on cases of violence to black women. As this points out, Puar viewing assemblage as a complementary approach to intersectionality comes at the cost of a fragmentary vision of Deleuze and Guattari's *agencements*: "Intersectionality attempts to comprehend political institutions and their attendant forms of social normativity and disciplinary administration, while assemblages, in an effort to reintroduce politics into the political, asks what is prior to and beyond what gets established."[126] I would argue, on the contrary, that there is no "prior to" or "post" politics. We are always, and forever, caught up in power relationships.

Queer Theory: Radical *and* Normative

The radical fantasy of transcending norms is suggested by the term "queer" itself. In French, "queer" is not synonymous with LGBT, as it sometimes is in English. It refers instead to ideas, practices, or individuals that expressly adopt a distance from the categories of homosexual, gay, lesbian, bisexual, and, to a lesser extent, transsexual and transgender.[127] Bourcier, as a leading figure of the Zoo collective, said several years after the workshop was launched that queer theory was fundamentally nonacademic, whereas lesbian and gay studies had been overtaken by academicism. "Queer theory is a political and cultural act in reaction to institutional practices that favor heterocentric fields and to gay and lesbian studies that risk being dominated by the field of history."[128] In contrast, Eribon constantly claims that his work is located within both gay/lesbian studies *and* queer studies insofar as the latter label is above all strategic. The distinction is nevertheless sharpened in the media by the presence of protagonists who stress the spectacular nature of queer theory as opposed to canonical fields. In a book that sought to "undress" French literature by looking at it through the "glory hole," François Cusset explained:

> Contrary to the assigning of identity assumed by the word "gay," "queer" enjoys the uncertainty of play, in the sense of provocation and the enlarging of a field. "Queer studies," when applied to literature, sees itself as a way of questioning in a more transgressive manner, especially when compared to the circumscribed approach characteristic of "gay studies." Whereas the latter seeks to establish a homo counter-corpus, as canonic in the end as the official corpus (and traveling parallel in literary history from Shakespeare to Oscar Wilde, from Virginia Woolf to Proust), the former does not limit its field of investigation to any pre-established criteria, explicit thematic, or author biography, preferring not the celebration of difference, but rather the insinuation of constant doubt, and the political, playful, and insatiable erosion of the usual borders between homo and hetero. Just as we would all be a little bit that way, all literary texts are too.[129]

Cusset's comparison is highly revealing: on the one hand, some analyses purportedly escape all predestination; on the other, some research is conditioned by a concern to manufacture difference and is therefore locked into the specificity it has produced. In other words, Cusset manages to discredit gay studies insofar as they are minoritarian, whereas queer studies are unlimited precisely because they have universalized the minority principle ("we [are] *all* a little bit that way"). He thereby incorporates queer theory into the universalist, anti-identitarian attitude that governs academic life in France, whereas critiques of identity in other national contexts—where anticommunitarianism does not have the same hold—encourage above all greater reflection on a sense of belonging.[130] This depoliticization of "minority evolution" constructs a system that devises a categorical rigidity for gayness in order to demonstrate how radical queerness is. This rhetoric has now become commonplace and paradoxically may reinforce inequalities and discrimination, as it begins with the principle that queer is, by definition, nonnormative and is therefore not very vigilant with regard to people's material situations.

It would be highly useful to reject the radical distinction between queer studies and gay/lesbian studies, just as Biddy Martin has done with respect to queer studies and feminist studies: "I *am* suggesting that we stop defining queerness as mobile and fluid in relation to what then gets construed as stagnant and ensnaring, and as associated with a maternal, anachronistic, and putatively puritanical feminism." Martin continues, "Queer or perverse desires do not seem very transformative if the claims made in their name rely on conceptions of gender and psychic life as either so fluid as to be irrelevant or so fixed and punitive that they have to be escaped." She stresses that diametrically opposing fluidity and rigidity leads to dropping the question of rights and law, which the "radical" stance holds to be overly burdened by social norms and reproduction. Furthermore, it causes us to limit psychic life to a simple "interiorization of a punitive outside and to suppose, somewhat paradoxically, that the psyche is therefore easily manipulable or a mere ruse that discursive change, awareness and/or desire will help us overcome."[131] In France, this fantasy of transformation through performance runs throughout the work of Bourcier, who has elevated "queering" to an anti-identitarian agenda carried out in a performative or punning mode.

I disagree with Bourcier's call to "queer heterocentric places, fields, and methods of knowledge-power without forgetting the sexual-political roots of the term: such might be the agenda of a 'queer subject'—inevitably a 'poor student,' simultaneously 'out' and anti-assimilationist—who seeks to exploit the resources of the fringe."[132] According to Bourcier, "sexual-political roots" would henceforth function only as memory, kept outside any social interaction itself. The specter of identity (in the form of incorporated memories, transfer, paranoiac reflexes) is the very locus of power relationships. The way we are haunted by the lives we have not lived constitutes the social relationship itself.[133] Furthermore, setting oneself up as a counter-model of academic orthodoxy (with its rites of passage, its pretentious modes of communication, and so on) means stamping out institutional razzmatazz without truly stamping out the strategies of power that riddle the institution. It means flaunting representations and stimulating our senses but failing to make the pleasure last. It is too limiting to place all faith in the magic of anti-assimilationist performance and hope that reality itself (which, in this scheme of things, preexists the performance) will be automatically affected. On the contrary, it is the very status of what is real and what is fiction that the queer problematic interrogates. This is particularly true in regard to laws of kinship, whose fictional nature is the very basis of its power. Bourcier's radical stance raises a political problem, for as Biddy Martin ironically puts it when noting many queer writers' wariness of family issues, "radical anti-normativity throws out a lot of babies with a lot of bathwater."[134] Bourcier indeed denounced the normativity of gay parenting—"soppy homoparents"— at a symposium on "Homosexualities in the Plural" hosted by the Université de Lausanne in 2006.[135] In my view, queer analysis is interested in what makes human lives simultaneously ordinary and extraordinary. That is the angle from which queerness can critique State power based both on the myth of heroic founders and on a presumption of the docility of the masses.

Minority Evolution

In her seminal article on queer theory, Teresa de Lauretis writes:

> The project of the conference was based on the speculative premise that homosexuality is no longer to be seen simply as marginal with regard to a dominant, stable form of sexuality (heterosexuality) against which it would be defined either by opposition or homology. In other words, it is no longer to be seen either as merely transgressive or deviant vis-à-vis a proper, natural sexuality (i.e., institutionalized reproductive sexuality), according to the older, pathological model, or as just another, optional "life-style," according to the model of contemporary North American pluralism.[136]

Although de Lauretis conceives of queer theory as distinct from a specific power system from which stem—and to which contribute—the categories of gay and lesbian, she does not seek to undermine lesbian and gay studies themselves but to render them more critical. De Lauretis does not set lesbian/gay

studies against queer studies but proposes a queer *theory*. She seeks to open
new horizons conducive to social change. The notion of theory should be
understood as a "speculative project" rather than a corpus.[137] Nearly twenty-
five years after that founding act, queer theory has spread into many spheres
of social life. It is no longer merely a speculative project but is also a uniting
category that is not free of norms itself. Can queer theory be anything other
than a moment, without reproducing what it hopes to change? How can this
project continue to welcome multiple demands, analyses, and practices? That
was Butler's initial concern:

> If the term "queer" is to be a site of collective contestation, the point of depar-
> ture for a set of historical reflections and futural imaginings, it will have to re-
> main that which is, in the present, never fully owned. . . . As expansive as the
> term "queer" is meant to be, it is used in ways that enforce a set of overlapping
> divisions: in some contexts, the term appeals to a younger generation who want
> to resist the more institutionalized and reformist politics sometimes signified
> by "lesbian and gay"; in some contexts, sometimes the same, it has marked a
> predominantly white movement that has not fully addressed the way in which
> "queer" plays—or fails to play—within non-white communities; and whereas in
> some instances it has mobilized a lesbian activism, in others the term represents
> a false unity of women and men.[138]

This queer changeability is reflected in its history. Discussing the case of
Queer Nation in San Francisco (founded in June 1990 but folded in December
1991), Elizabeth Armstrong shows that the notion of queerness was quickly
assimilated by homosexual organizations, to the extent that queer soon became synonymous with the categories of lesbian and gay and subsequently
extended to other struggles, first transsexual and later bisexual.[139] Rather than
perceive a diminution of activism, Armstrong notes a fragmentation of the
organizational sphere, first because these groups were marked and defined by
relations they developed with local authorities and commercial organizations
(in a kind of chameleon effect) and then because they were less dependent on
earmarked funds (especially by health institutions). The rise of multiple categories led to unique rearrangements that themselves produced new forms of
belonging to peer groups.[140] A queer critique thus calls for reflection on what
succeeded and what failed in this new attachment to multiple categories. A
politically rigorous queer theory does not reject all use of categories as identities, once those categories can also be turned against themselves. Such is the

condition of a truly democratic queer politics—understanding the inevitable link between reproduction and deconstruction.[141]

IN THIS CHAPTER I have shown that the tension between local and global is a structuring axis of the presence of queer theory in France. The United States has served as an echo chamber for French fantasies of the global, but that fascination has also embodied a paradoxical wish to eliminate American culture. Insistence on the idea of cultural translation and the radical nature of queer theory and nonnormative practices in opposition to the nationalist drift of LGBT movements in France masks the fact that reifying an external origin also means—the very moment a given reference is borrowed—trying to eliminate one's debt toward that culture.[142] This is a trick of history—the cosmopolitan arguments underpinning the critique of homonationalism are obliged to reify the state and national borders as the foundation of their analyses. How can we resist these forms of cultural hegemony without essentializing the object of opposition?[143] I argue that there is no specifically French origin of queer theory any more than queer theory is today American. The idea that French theory has returned to France via queer theory is a transatlantic cultural fantasy that postulates the existences of two distinct, stable territories defined through their exchanges and oppositions. The "traffic in queer representations" should instead be understood in terms of minority evolution.[144]

A minority, it should be recalled, is a group of people defined by a relationship of domination. What constitutes a political minority is the transformation of that power relationship through the deployment of dominated cultures. I am therefore using the term "minority" in a problematic rather than theorematic way. If the notion of minority is raised in a static way, defined by its content, it immediately becomes self-contradictory. This is what Deleuze ironically terms "the submission of the line to the period, the submission of movement to memory," because "there is no history but of the majority, or of minorities as defined in relation to the majority."[145] As Michael Warner puts it in his introduction to *Fear of a Queer Planet*, "The tension between globalizing and localizing arguments is different from the universalizing/minoritizing tension analyzed by Eve Sedgwick; there are globalizing arguments about minority interests, just as there are localizing arguments about quasi-universal interests."[146] Queer theory analyzes the resonances in each individual of multiple forms of affiliation and disaffiliation, of subjectification and subjection. Ultimately, it holds that each individual is a territory whose borders oscillate with those of the world. It resists the way majoritarian norms and institutions reify some of these borders. Queer theory therefore constitutes a challenge to contemporary definitions of citizenship based on preestablished criteria, whether inherited or acquired. How does it operate in the context of French politics? In the following chapter I show that the minority/majority polarity destabilizes the idea of belonging and representation, even as it potentially welcomes new political alliances.

CHAPTER 4

THE SPECTER OF QUEER POLITICS

QUEER THEORY challenges the notion of sexual identity as a fixed political category that would reflect some biological essence. It undertakes an analysis of identity as a performative event in a discursive chain: each identity copies other identities and therefore carries multiple instances of place and time within itself. Queer theory does not reject the concept of identity, whose political utility it recognizes. It simply notes the immanent, proliferating nature of identities. From that perspective, it then questions how identity becomes inscribed in a community. What is the basis on which a "feeling of belonging" is built? What are the epistemological conditions that enable an immanent category to be reproduced, learned, and imitated?[1] Queer theory argues that identification and deidentification work in tandem. The theory therefore runs afoul of how belonging exclusively to the nation is posed as a condition of citizenship in France, both in public discourse and in law. In the French Republic, "communitarianism," acknowledging a basic loyalty to a given community (whether ethnic, religious, cultural, or sexual), is viewed as a democracy-corrupting illness. Across almost the entire political spectrum, from far left to far right—with the exception of minority trends within the ecology party and the Radicaux de Gauche (Radical Party of the Left)—France is described as living under the constant threat of disintegration as a result of the effect of communitarianism. This fear of communitarianism has a long genealogy related to a pathologizing of sexuality as a health risk and to a fear of a homosexual cabal against the interests of France. In line with the work of Eve Kosofsky Sedgwick, I argue that the crises currently triggered by the homosexual/heterosexual distinction continue to structure, even today, the construction of citizenship in France.[2]

Although anticommunitarianism constitutes a central axis of France's system of civic regulation, what Foucault called the "disciplinary regime,"[3] it can take highly varied forms. Sexuality, in fact, is an important vector of anticommunitarianism beyond sex-related policies themselves (contraception, HIV, sex education, abortion).[4] It makes it possible to express verbally and meaningfully other issues such as immigration, health, kinship, political representation, and secular society. The contrived perception of the wearing of an Islamic headscarf as a threat to French republican values was possible due to the mobilization of intellectuals who defended a model of French-style flirtatiousness and sex appeal that they felt structured the public sphere itself.[5] During the term of conservative president Nicolas Sarkozy, the hardening of immigration policies was based on generating anxiety over the idea that an apparently loving couple was a confidence trick (the government invented the notion of "marriage of contrivance" [*mariage gris*] to refer to marriages in which one spouse took advantage of the other to become a French citizen, whereas "marriage of convenience" [*mariage blanc*] implies mutual consent).[6] Sexuality thus becomes entangled in multiple histories. Not only does it contribute to the delineation of other political issues, but it shifts position along with the reconfiguration of debates in which it participates. Disciplinary regimes are thus multiple for the simple reason that, "after all, to identify *as* must always include multiple processes of identification *with*."[7] Furthermore, it should be added that the power of a disciplinary regime resides in its contradictions and blind spots as well as in its ability to impose its beliefs.[8]

Although France's condemnation of communitarianism is part of a long history of fear of betrayal by enemies within, that fear has frequently changed course. For example, around 2005, several articles that received great media coverage sought to establish the idea that France and the West were threatened by foreign cultures that hated women, Jews, and homosexuals.[9] Former "enemies within" thus became standard-bearers of the French nation. This discourse is particularly pernicious because rejection of foreigners is justified in the name of cosmopolitanism: since the barbarians reject open-mindedness, civilized people purportedly have a duty to cloister themselves to preserve their model of openness.[10] This discourse was inflected anew in the context of the economic downturn: as I have already shown in the debate over marriage for all, both right and left issued pressing calls for a return to "the real issues." In other words, sexual minorities were once again perceived as dangerous because they managed to polarize public debate on social issues at a time when the nation should have been uniting to address the real stakes, the growing pressures of increasingly global capitalism.

France's rejection of communitarianism thus raises the question of the epistemological conditions of sovereignty and how it is exercised. For example, it is striking that, despite legislative reforms and a wider acceptance of homosexuality, the national self-image remains tightly linked in the collective imagination to traditional heterosexual roles—a seductive, boundlessly ambitious male, or a mother of many children who attends to social issues, or a good father who is also a local elected official, and so on. Unlike in other European nations such as the United Kingdom, few French politicians are openly gay.[11] Only five national representatives have publicly acknowledged their homosexuality.[12] It is on this precise point that queer theory interrogates the unspoken assumptions of France's social contract. By reflecting simultaneously on types of affiliation and disaffiliation, and by investigating not just the constituencies but also the counter-constituencies of public policies, it derealizes belief in a universalist perspective.

THIS CHAPTER is devoted to the various discursive registers that, in regard to sexuality, shape a sense of belonging: the fear of betrayal by minorities, the fantasy of the death of French culture, alarm at the theatricality of nonheterosexual pleasure, resistance to contamination through "sameness," failure to recognize multiple identities, and the myth of the impossible community. Studying these disciplinary regimes sheds a different light on the debate over homosexual marriage. Fear of a queer invasion from the United States was so extensively echoed precisely because the sense of national belonging was already structured along immunological and sacrificial lines. I begin by showing how fear of betrayal by "perverts" in the government, like fear of Jews and colonial subjects, led to a condemnation of communitarianism throughout the twentieth century.[13] This disciplinary regime was long defended by conservative parties and movements in the name of the State's moral and political authority, yet it has also taken the form of a plea for alterity within the left wing of the current government on a register that is both moral and psychological: recognizing the "other" and his or her differences is viewed as essential for transcending one's own attachments with a view to the common good.

Several experts and groups of experts associated with the Socialist Party even believe that learning about sexual difference is the primal experience of all difference, an experience that alone creates an ability to perform the democratic process of transcending the individual self. Other experts think that the very potential for eroticism depends on this fantasy of alterity. In this manner, experience of the individual, personal body is linked to the constitution of the body politic. This link basically hinges on sacrifice. Any practice that seems to depart from it is branded as dangerous: adoption of protest cultures, corruption of youth, the madness of a sexually confused world, homosexual contamination, negation of the future, "impossible" communities. I analyze these various disciplinary registers, concluding the chapter with a demonstration of why queer practices force disciplinary registers to confront their own limits. By combining several ways of labeling oneself, by merging several time frames and spaces, queer practices nurture an ability to reconceptualize the social contract in a nonsacrificial form. From a queer perspective, a community is not the result of impossible expectations of universal "communion" within the republic but of a critical reexamination of one's own experience, which reformulates the relationship of memory and affects and consequently reconnects minority lives. Some of the main political consequences of this critical reexamination are that it renders obsolete the partisan system of majority representation and raises the possibility of critical alliances between class theory and liberal political thought.

The Specter of Betrayal

Using sexuality as the point of departure for a genealogy of anticommunitarianism in France means sidestepping the canons of institutional history. The evolution of constitutional texts often seems to suffice for an understanding of the stages in the democratic life. However, the foundations of a given political authority are largely invented retrospectively, through processes of mythification of constituent factors (the rhetoric of "founding fathers," the valorization of philosophical ideals and patriotic symbols), even when the main players were not necessarily aware of the changes they were effecting.[14] Furthermore, a change of regime does not necessarily lead to a change of the entire legal system. The rules governing the economy, administration, family, civil society, and penal regime remain largely unchanged. Most of the political and administrative personnel also remain in place. Changes to political regime are often described as moments of historic renewal because their promoters need to assert as much to establish their own authority. A political history cannot be reduced to its institutional arrangements; it is an ongoing operation of categorization.

Sexuality is at the heart of this operation, precisely because it authorizes a transfiguration of individual bodily experience into a collectively imagined body politic. During debate over gay marriage in France, fear of an American invasion and the spread of homosexuality, along with condemnation of any expression of communitarianism, showed that homosexuality remains an idea on which French identity has been formulated and its political history fantasized. I demonstrate here that political regimes have been legitimized in part, since the late eighteenth century, by the fantasy of a secret society. That society is allegedly governed by its own norms, cultural references, and language—just the opposite of a universalizing ideal. Furthermore, this secret society purportedly colludes with other spheres abroad in a transnational solidarity that undermines the foundations of sovereignty itself. These spheres, although in open view, are purportedly inaccessible to the uninitiated (what Foucault called a "heterotopia").[15] In the passages that follow I thus show that while the fear of homosexuality as a personal aversion has largely diminished in the past twenty or more years, it retains a structuring role as a political totem. My analysis converges with those of historians who have discussed how homosexual groups have been dreaded and persecuted at key moments in Western history insofar as they were suspected of failing to fulfill the usual mechanism of governmental power. David Johnson, for example, studied the McCarthy purges in the United States in the 1950s and concluded that homosexuals were persecuted because "homosexuality is a psychical disturbance that leads to communism."[16] More recently, Michael S. Sherry has reexamined the fear that certain gay artistic circles were conspiring to overturn the mass-consumer culture, to the detriment of the United States and the advantage of the Soviet empire.[17]

In France, the crime of sodomy was removed from the law books in 1791. The Napoleonic penal code of 1810 made no mention of it. Thus, no act between people of the same sex was considered illegal until the Vichy regime. Yet homosexual practices were constantly "monitored" by the government because the State could not tolerate situations that contravened the traditional family order on which the political order rested.[18] Prosecution of "infractions" committed in cruising spots were frequent, even though homosexual behaviors were not acknowledged in the family sphere.[19] Until 1981 the French police conducted investigations in numerous port areas—including Toulouse, Brest, and Nice—as places of prostitution and cruising and kept detailed ledgers on the people who frequented those places, all under the aegis of the prefecture.[20] Similarly, judges—even though they possessed no legal arsenal for prosecuting homosexuality—meticulously recorded homosexual practices whenever a case involving homosexual acts came up before them. By the first half of the nineteenth century they also began resorting to psychiatry and forensic medicine to prosecute perversions. As historian Laure Murat has shown in her study of police ledgers,[21] labeling homosexuals as a category of individuals predated 1870, the point at which Foucault claimed that homosexuals became a "species."[22] The period between the two world wars was marked by a greater focus on homosexuality as a lifestyle;[23] in this context pederasty was the subject of major publications beginning with André Gide's *Corydon* (published anonymously in 1910, then again under Gide's name in 1924), and several associations and confraternities looked to Greek pederasty as their model.[24] Homosexuality was also monitored through the censorship of publications judged licentious, such as the magazine *Inversions* in 1924 and Victor Margueritte's novel *La Garçonne* in 1925.[25] The fate reserved for *Futur* magazine exemplifies continued censorship after the Second World War: published from October 1952 to April 1956, and marked by its allusions to antiquity, the magazine was successfully prosecuted for subversion of public morals and incitement to homosexuality.[26]

Given these already repressive measures, one might wonder why the Vichy government introduced new penalties for homosexuality. Historian Marc Boninchi examined unexplored archives to reveal that penalization of homosexual acts was already being considered in the days of the Third Republic.[27] On April 14, 1942, the staff of Vichy's minister of the navy, François Darlan, submitted a memorandum on the prosecution of homosexual prostitution in port zones. Some commentators—such as Jean Le Bitoux, in his notes on the wartime deportation of homosexuals[28]—view this memo as proof of the fascist origins of the law promulgated on August 6, 1942, which established the age of consent for homosexual relations at twenty-one (the age of consent for heterosexual relations was thirteen at the time).[29] This argument was used in 1982 to justify depenalization of homosexuality not only by gay associations but also by members of the government (starting with minister of justice Robert Badinter).[30] In fact, numerous police reports on homosexual cruising in the 1930s led the ministry of the navy to adopt repressive measures as early as 1934 (only sailors were subject to disciplinary proceedings). After several cases had been brought before the appeals court in Paris, a judge named Médan drafted a note recommending that the age of consent be raised for homosexual relations, given young people's weaker powers of "discernment." This report was transmitted to the chancery, which passed it to the French premier,

Édouard Daladier of the Radical-Socialist Party. Daladier approved of raising the age of consent, but it was too late to include the measure in the packet of executive decrees then being prepared (which required preliminary authorization by the French parliament). Médan's report thus remained moot yet served as the basis of the Béraud report, commissioned by the Vichy chancery and made public on January 7, 1942. It was this report on which the law of August 6, 1942, was based.

The measure was maintained in the postwar period following a decree by General Charles de Gaulle on February 8, 1945. Those years were characterized by an intense campaign to increase the birth rate and protect youth from corruption. The provisional government sought to restore the authority of the State where Vichy had failed.[31] Judges also faced difficulties when assessing acts that might come under the remit of the 1942 law, especially concerning relations between women.[32] The reestablishment of the State's authority in 1945 therefore included defending morality more efficiently than had the previous regime. Penalizing homosexuality was one aspect of the disciplinary regime of redemption via the monitoring of sexuality; another was shaving the heads of women accused of "horizontal collaboration" with the enemy.[33] Reparation involved first of all a reparation of the corrupted body, sapped by the traitors, the enemy within.[34] Furthermore, after 1945 penalization of homosexuality was reinforced by increased prosecution for obscenity. In 1949 the Prefecture of Police in Paris banned dancing between two people of the same sex. Parisian homosexuals then had to meet in places outside the city, as exemplified by a bar in the suburban area of Les Yvelines, run by a former member of the Resistance nicknamed "La colonelle" (Colo-Nelly). The train heading from Montparnasse station in Paris to Les Yvelines was dubbed the "queen train."

Several newspapers were also censored, beginning with the bulletin of the homophile association Arcadie, founded in 1954 by a former seminarian, André Baudry. The newsletter was convicted of corrupting morals even though Arcadie's stated goal was to promote a better understanding of homophilia—the group rejected the overly sexual connotations of the term "homosexuality"— and to win recognition from public authorities.[35] On July 18, 1960, the Assemblée Nationale passed an amendment proposed by Gaullist member Paul Mirguet that described homosexuality as one of the "scourges of society" alongside alcoholism and tuberculosis. At this time Arcadie was still trying to obtain repeal of the Vichy law of 1942, but the parliamentary amendment was promoted in the name of public health, so the administration did not oppose it. The Mirguet amendment thus represented a blunt rejection of the efforts of some homosexuals to constitute a pressure group.[36]

The mechanisms for monitoring and punishing homosexual practices extended across all political systems, even if each regime sought to draw a specific legitimacy from them. It is perhaps even possible to argue that also at stake was a battle against the constitution of homosexual associations. Sexual stereotypes were the foundation of the political discourse on national identity. Early twentieth-century caricatures often depicted the political sphere as a form of homosexual relation. The magazine *L'Assiette au beurre* showed Tsar Nicolas II as a prostitute while his ally Edward VII robs his client, the French president, Armand Fallières. Aristide Briand, who held many ministerial posts including premier, was known for his pacifist policies and thus was often shown in a pose of sexual submission, for example, licking the boot of the German president, Paul von Hindenburg.[37]

Allusions to homosexual relations in political caricature were not limited to sophisticated commentary but also circulated widely in public imagery. In the early 1900s satirical songs often played on the themes of the inversion of gender roles or of sexual submission, indeed on the idea of the homosexual couple busily carrying on domestic life, as exemplified by the "Chanson de l'armée allemande" (Maurel and Vilbert), "Les Petits Soldats de Guillaume" (Soubeyran), and "Scandale teuton" (Péheu).[38] Such representations played on fantasies of treason and were thus often combined with anti-Semitic caricatures. The stereotype of the effeminate Jew appeared extensively in the far-right press from the 1920s to the 1940s, especially targeting Jean Zay, Pierre Mendès-France, Georges Mandel, Emmanuel Berl, Alfred Naquet (a legislator behind the 1884 law on divorce), Maurice Sachs (who was himself homosexual), and above all the socialist premier, Léon Blum. Jewish dandyism mirrored homosexual dandyism, triggering a fear of passing: to survive, Jews and homosexuals had "to perfor[m] their disappearance" and could easily be seen as contaminating agents.[39] According to numerous articles in *Gringoire et Gilles* (written by Pierre Drieu la Rochelle), Jews procreated solely in the goal of reproducing other Jews, thereby undermining the French nation. They were the enemy within, serving only their own cause. Historian Jérémy Guedj explains, "The heterosexual act performed by a Jew, preferably with French Christian women, was aimed at procreation, demeaning the nation that had welcomed him; if he sought to seduce women, it was only to take the place of French men and to demonstrate his superiority here as in all fields. Yet the true nature of the Jew is homosexuality."[40]

The idea of treason was reinforced by the fact that several fantasies concerning homosexuality were interlinked: the "pederast" was drawn by the masculine display of enemy forces even while being naturally feminine ("inverted") and therefore unable to resist. The German soldier was active and virile in an environment of male bonding that rejected homosexuality, whereas passive, effeminate French homosexuals wallowed in their own vice. These two images, however, were not set in a homosexual context that might involve friendship, multiple partners, or pedagogy but rather in a straight conjugal context: France was depicted as an impotent husband, betrayed by his spouse (the passive homosexual) and unable to compete with his handsome rival (the enemy soldier). The frustration associated with defeat in love in fact shifted the responsibility to the unfaithful wife, avoiding any questioning of the idea of the virility incarnated by deceived husband, which historian Carolyn Dean has called the "redemption of virility."[41]

Just after the Second World War, Jean-Paul Sartre conceptualized this imaginative construct of defeat in love and politics in a text titled "Qu'est-ce qu'un collaborateur?" (What Is a Collaborator?)[42] He asserted that pederasts were "among the best recruits" for collaboration[43]—he was perhaps thinking of Abel Bonnard. Whatever the case, it is certain that the trial of writer Robert Brasillach for treasonous collaboration weighed heavily on Sartre's comments, for he explicitly referred to it.[44] Although there is no formal proof of Brasillach's homosexuality, his work is riddled with homoerotic allusions: in 1931 he published *Présence de Virgile*, a biographical study of the poet Virgil, whose writings are at least implicitly homosexual; most of Brasillach's novels involve a ménage à trois in which the conjugal relationship is subsumed by the intense masculine friendship. Brasillach and his brother-in-law Maurice Bardèche were nicknamed "Brasillèche and Bardach" by their former classmate René Etiemble, whose merger of their two last names suggests they were a "cute couple." During his trial, Brasillach managed to refute most of the charges of collaboration brought by the prosecuting attorney, Marcel Reboul. Although he published many anti-Semitic articles in the newspaper *Je suis partout*, actual acts of collaboration were harder to prove. Brasillach was nevertheless very destabilized when Reboul described his attraction to the occupying forces as "a love that dare not speak its name."[45] By employing several metaphors of penetration, Reboul landed decisive blows against Brasillach,[46] who was convicted and had to face the firing squad on February 6, 1945. The provisional French government viewed the execution as a sign of the country's moral recovery.

Given that context, what do Sartre's comments mean? Clearly, by failing to discuss the mechanisms that prompted hundreds of homosexuals to join the Resistance, and those mechanisms that prompted others to collaborate, Sartre's analysis is largely biased.[47] His comments are not without interest, however. Sartre did not claim that pederasts have an ontological propensity for treason but that the dilemma of authenticity in which they were trapped[48]—to speak, or not to speak, of their sexuality—might have led some pederasts into collaborationist behavior. In a society that was particularly repressive of all forms of weakness, an extreme investment in values socially perceived as masculine might be considered a refuge for certain homosexuals, which might explain why some fascist and anti-Semitic circles attracted Left-Bank lesbians (such as Gertrude Stein and Natalie Barney),[49] as well as male closeted homosexuals (Marcel Jouhandeau and Pierre Gaxotte, the latter having introduced Georges Dumézil into the Action Française sphere, which has recently led Eribon to query the nature of male bonding in the entourage of Action Française leader Charles Maurras).[50] Sandrine Sanos has developed a thesis with deep historical foundations: beyond mere social networks, far-right movements (notably that of Maurras) developed an entire notion of "Frenchness as aesthetics" by basing the idea of a body politic on fantasies of classic French literary forms, themselves marked by homoeroticism.[51]

Has the image of a homosexual as someone trapped in a dilemma of loyalty completely disappeared today? When Jean-Marie Le Pen refers to Florian Philippot, current vice president of the FN, he mockingly uses the nickname "the little Gaystapo." When the mayor of Toulon was assassinated in 1995, Le Pen asserted, "There is no surveillance of 'zippers' in the Front National. . . . If every homosexual was assassinated in France, it would be a desert, particularly in the world of the media, politics, and the arts."[52] The idea that homosexuals— and, more broadly, certain minorities—are to be found everywhere in government and other spheres of influence largely extends beyond the limits of the far right. It entails pitting "real people" against a separate category of people, powerful minorities who defend their own interests even beyond the borders. Since around 2010 a discourse of "cultural insecurity" has arisen on the French left, a notion coined by political scientist Laurent Bouvet, a former editor in chief of the *Revue Socialiste* and a member of the Jean Jaurès Foundation, an advisory group close to the Socialist Party. The concept of cultural danger refers to a fear of being threatened in one's own system of beliefs by foreign cultures. This cultural insecurity externalizes culture, merely adopting xenophobic discourse without deconstructing it. The culture that sparks fear is the culture of the other, the foreigner, the minority lobby, the media, and so on. In other words, the concept of cultural danger dissociates subjectification from the invention of tradition.[53] Bouvet thus asserted in 2012:

> We are under no illusion: if François Hollande proves to be as powerless as his predecessor in halting the spiral of deindustrialization and unemployment, we can count on the social-issue lefties, massively represented in the media, to incite people to open the floodgates—measures to allow foreigners to vote, charters for regional and minority languages, and "marriage." Over the years all these measures have become the identifying signs of a left that has no shared vision because it has no roots in society, and they will be brought to the fore to serve as a smokescreen. Once again people will try to camouflage their resignation over the way things are going by putting on a bold face. The problem is that no one, apart from a few editorial boards and a few grant-aided associations, believes in this phony facade.[54]

Minorities versus the "real people": that is, the alleged impasse facing the French left today. The real people are not simply the ones who exist but those who embody a primal nature, in this case the heterosexual order. In reply to a comment on his blog, Bouvet explained: "When it comes to the equality of heterosexual and homosexual couples in marriage, I'm for it. The problem arises with the adoption of children and, later, medically assisted procreation, because that destroys the legal fiction based on heterosexual reproduction. That's also why I'm against adoption by single parents, which is already legal."[55]

Fear of betrayal by homosexuals—rife among reactionary movements, present in working-class imagery, and central to phases of constitutional transition in France throughout the twentieth century—can still be detected in today's anticommunitarian rhetoric. What interests me particularly is how the left-wing government, which up until the mid-1980s retained an ambivalent relationship to the idea of the republic (criticizing it in the name of transnational class interests even as it accepted its institutions), wound up essentializing that idea.[56] While a suspicion of treason weighed on Jews and homosexuals throughout the twentieth century, that suspicion was also cast on left-wing political parties. Inspired by the idea of an International, these parties were long attacked by conservatives as liable to betray the French Republic at any moment (or, at the very least, to bend the republic to their own ends). The complex relations between the French left and the institutions of the French Republic have already been documented, on topics ranging from the party's social climb during the Fourth Republic[57] to the left's strategic endorsement of the Fifth Republic[58] via a path of "political conversion" from the left to the far right[59] and the fascistic tendencies of Christian leftists, particularly intellectuals.[60] One must remember that the republic's institutions have known an infinite range of configurations,[61] but also the fear of disintegration of the nation under the weight of group solidarities has not been restricted to republican regimes. Stanislas de Clermont Tonnerre argued that Jews should be granted citizenship during debate on December 23, 1789: "We must deny the Jews everything as a nation but grant the Jews everything as individuals; . . . they must not constitute either an order or a body politic within the State; they must be citizens, individually."[62] While France was still a constitutional monarchy, a law adopted on June 14, 1791 (Loi Le Chapelier) abolished guilds and stipulated that there would henceforth exist only "the particular interest of each individual and the general interest."[63] There then arose a "nobility of State," an administrative corps legitimized by the king yet no longer dynastic, which became self-legitimizing through exclusion of other, intermediate corps.[64]

But if anticommunitarianism has not been restricted to the republic, the disciplinary regime traditionally associated with the republican right, which entails defining the government through its moral authority, its concern for public health, and its pro-birth policies,[65] metamorphosed into new disciplinary mechanisms concocted by left-wing intellectuals and politicians when they came to power for the first time in 1981. These included, on the institutional level, monitoring social movements and using socio-anthropological expertise to legitimize institutional decisions and, on the substantive level, mooring citizenship to the notion of the difference between the sexes and the biologicalization of the law. In *The Politics of Adoption* I discussed this cultural construct (citizenship and law) as a "second nature."[66] Historian Camille Robcis, in *The Law of Kinship*, has traced the links between networks of experts in family issues and the way that they became key references for the Socialist Party in what she called "Republican structuralism."[67] In particular, she shows how "Social Catholicism" paved the way for an ideological merger between left and right throughout the Third Republic, from the early censuses on birth rates to the family-planning structures implemented by the Fourth and Fifth Republics, toward which socialist leaders such as Jacques Delors worked so hard.[68] Here, I focus on the upshot of this convergence between right and left, showing how the disciplinary regime spurred by and around the

Socialist Party directly echoes the idea of human ecology promoted by reactionary movements during the debate over extending the rights of marriage and adoption to homosexual couples.

The Specter of "Sameness"

The Socialist Party was initially hostile to the institutions of France's Fifth Republic, founded in 1958, but in the 1970s it developed a strategy for winning elections based on acceptance of "republican" mechanisms to the point of underscoring certain constitutional principles and symbols. The party thus has made a point of honor, since it first won the presidency in 1981, of emphasizing the nation as the sole, totally inclusive community. It is even possible to argue that the reforms instituted by the socialist president, François Mitterrand, with a view to decentralizing government, played a significant role in the condemnation of communitarianism. Indeed, legislative debate over the measure sparked sustained opposition in the name of the risk of territorial fragmentation and a loss of national identity; furthermore, the decentralization process, which included new local elections, at first resulted in a series of victories for right-wing parties, which were more prepared and better organized locally.[69] The Socialist Party reacted by stressing its concern to maintain territorial and civic cohesion; thus, it not only contributed to the French "civic republican tradition" of stripping power from intermediate bodies and local government,[70] but it also reinvented this tradition "as a tool of governmentality designed to uphold the racial and sexual boundaries of the nation."[71]

The phenomenon became even more pronounced with the electoral rise of the far right during the 1980s. In municipal elections held in Dreux in 1983, the mainstream conservative and Gaullist party (Rassemblement pour la République, RPR) allied itself with the FN for the first time; there ensued a very clear ideological shift within the Socialist Party, which employed an anticommunitarian discourse to distinguish itself from the patronage tactics of the right. In so doing, the Socialist Party not only abandoned the anti-authoritarian tradition it had embraced in the 1960s when it still opposed the centralized institutions of the Fifth Republic, but it also moved away from the minority groups that had elected it to government. Socialist governments now criticize such groups for being inward looking and agree to recognize them only if they divest themselves of their own specific identity and history, or at the very least express that identity through the prism of the party line.

The principle of uniting one and all, as explicitly stated in a declaration of principle issued by the PS in 1990, has had the paradoxical effect of "deobjectifying" minority groups that might have sought to use the party as a grandstand.[72] What is true for workers is also true for immigrants and sexual minorities. Unconventional voices within the PS, often rooted in local experience, have been marginalized. Such was the case regarding key figures in the recognition of LGBT rights, such as Françoise Gaspard (a former socialist mayor of Dreux, national legislator, and European parliamentarian who had promoted a women's section within the PS in 1979 yet was denied a ministerial post by François Mitterrand during his first term because of her sexual orientation) and Patrick Bloche (a national legislator from Paris, former member of the Homosexualité et Socialisme group, and codrafter with Jean-Pierre Michel of the bill legalizing civil unions). The fear of communitarianism led the socialist legislature to proceed with stealth: on October 9, 1998, socialist members of the Assemblée Nationale did not attend the session in sufficient numbers to pass the civil union bill, thereby sabotaging the first draft of the law. In 2004, the PS criticized the wedding of a gay couple performed by the mayor of Bègles and would commit itself only to legalization of gay marriage if the issue of adoption were excluded. In 2012, socialist president François Hollande supported extension of the right of MAP to single women and lesbian couples, then backtracked in 2013 by referring the question to a national ethics commission (Comité Consultatif National d'Éthique [CCNE]) that had always strongly opposed the idea.[73] Its flip-flops on such issues has exposed the PS to suspicions of succumbing to patronage pressures—opponents of marriage for all thus criticized the party for precisely what it was trying to avoid.

Social change has thus come largely from outside the ranks of the PS—the bill on civil unions was drawn up thanks to the joint efforts of the AIDES association and homosexual activists such as Jan-Paul Pouliquen. Although other proposals for civil union had already been mooted by socialist politicians such as Senator Jean-Luc Mélenchon in 1990, they were not backed by the PS (Mélenchon later left the party and now opposes its political line). The PS has accepted and implemented social reforms such as civil unions and gay marriage; however, it has systematically excluded others, consequently reinstating inequalities targeted by the reforms it eventually adopted. After consulting a number of "official experts," including sociologist Irène Théry[74] and law professor Françoise Dekeuwer-Défossez,[75] the PS made sure that civil unions would not lead to joint adoption of a child by two people of the same sex because such an adoption would contradict—according to the minister of justice of the day,

Élisabeth Guigou (who cited Irène Théry's reports)—the fundamental anthropological distinction between man and woman, the only one on which kinship should be based.[76] Regularly consulted by the PS on issues of family rights since the mid-1990s, Théry developed her arguments in the review *Esprit*, explaining her opposition to "unisex" marriage and kinship ties in order to "preserve culture" and avoid reducing the other sex to a simple "purveyor of life."[77] Her opposition to what would become civil unions was also a way of forestalling other reforms: adoption and MAP. Today Théry expresses support for both, but only if these processes are accompanied by a systematic recognition of the role of the biological parents, since unisex kinship is still unthinkable for her.[78]

Other opponents of equal rights were also consulted during debate first on civil unions and then on gay marriage. With alacrity they referred to structural anthropology in support of their opposition to the bills being drawn up. Anthropologist Françoise Héritier claimed that there exist "invariants"[79]—the difference between the sexes being foremost among them—without which any society would be doomed to vanish and therefore same-sex unions were "unthinkable."[80] In regard to psychoanalytic theories, those that essentialize the Oedipal triangle argued along the same lines, as defended by psychoanalyst Jean-Pierre Winter and legal theorist Pierre Legendre. Oedipal principles, as incorporated into legal statutes, purportedly demonstrated that "sameness" (homosexuality) is incapable of constructing— inculcating—"otherness."[81] Finally, reactionary philosophers also entered the argument. Several writers, such as Marcel Gauchet (editor-in-chief of *Le Débat* magazine), condemned the empire of individualism—the individual, through an infinite extension of individual rights, would spell the end of social mix. This doctrine targeted minorities but in fact attempted to stem the tide of the invention of new lifestyles that necessarily questioned established privileges. In 2014, *Le Débat* devoted an entire issue to the moral and political excesses generated by the extension of marriage to homosexual couples.[82]

This discourse, which links the corruption of culture to an individualism that rejects the natural order, is similar on almost every point to the argument employed by experts on the Manif pour Tous side. François-Xavier Bellamy, a teacher of philosophy close to Manif pour Tous, claims—when pleading on behalf of the transmission of culture—that

> the civilizations from which we descend have all, in fact, developed discourses,
> rites, clothing, customs, and works around sexual alterity: by inciting us to see
> them as an artifice, inherited from a necessarily archaic past that hampers our

choices, people manage to spark "gender trouble" and, in the end, to make the difference between man and woman disappear completely. . . . Once "gender stereotypes" have been deconstructed, once they become vague, we will reconstruct our identity by ourselves, with no trace of cultural heritage influencing our choices. The concept of gender therefore opens a new field of battle in the war against culture.[83]

The notion of culture is indeed understood here as a second nature. It is a heritage that expresses the givens of nature in a way specific to each civilization.[84] The deconstruction of stereotypes would thus mean the end of civilization itself. Gender trouble is undermining civilization itself in what Bellamy calls the "battle against culture."[85] Note the striking resonance here with Théry's argument that we must "preserve culture" and resist individualism.

Thus, when successive socialist prime ministers Jean-Marc Ayrault and Manuel Valls argued that they wanted to avoid conflict around the notion of gender and hence withdrew several proposed bills on education about sexual diversity, they were simply adopting the same recourse to "experts" enshrined by their predecessors (particularly Lionel Jospin) to favor a natural order over the rights of individuals in the name of the survival of "culture." The first victims of this attitude were trans people. The promise to free change of sex status from complicated medical *and* court procedures never took place, nor did the introduction of a criterion of "gender identity" in the fight against transphobic discrimination and violence, despite an opinion to the contrary by the Commission Nationale Consultative des Droits de l'Homme (National Consultative Commission on Human Rights), which further stated that such an introduction would allow France to bring its legal system "in line with European and international law,"[86] especially recommendation 1728 of the Council of Europe's parliamentary assembly, the Thomas Hammarberg report,[87] and resolution 2048, adopted April 22, 2015.[88] Nor has there been any public policy providing adequate medical coverage for hormonal and surgical procedures that lie outside a psychiatric context, directly or indirectly.[89] In 2016, a government bill to modernize the justice system included a clause permitting a Tribunal de Grande Instance (county court) to order a change of gender marker for transgender people on the basis of "sufficient proof" of the "alleged gender."[90] This clause excludes minors unless they have been emancipated. Only a change of first name can be effected, even by minors, through declaration to an administrative officer in the local town hall. Self-determination for transgender persons is therefore not yet on the cards. As had already happened during debate over civil unions, several national and local elected officials reminded the administration of its promises, but they remained the exceptions within the party.[91]

The Socialist Party's reliance on expertise on family matters entails more than occasional consultation. It was institutionalized during debate over bioethics in the 1980s. The socialist administration charged minister Jean-Pierre Chevènement with setting up several permanent commissions of experts to address philosophical issues raised by new reproductive technologies (including CCNE, founded in 1983). Given their largely conservative composition—senior medical and religious representatives were systematically included but not patients and service users—these commissions recommended on several occasions that MAP be restricted to cases of medical infertility. The upshot was a 1994 law that followed CCNE recommendations by outlawing surrogate pregnancies and restricted outside-donor inseminations to heterosexual couples married (or living together) for at least two years. When prime minister Ayrault's administration decided not to press for extension of MAP to single women and lesbian couples, it did so after submitting the question to CCNE. In 2005, CCNE had argued that "the deliberately asexual term 'homoparenthood' denies any significant difference between the sexes. What is at stake here are the paternal and maternal roles and their complementarity in nurturing kinship relations that are humanly edifying."[92]

Finally, the Socialist Party closely monitored homosexual associations, even though it considered them to be external to the party. "The PS lost touch with the associations especially because it tried too hard to control their initiatives," commented Rémi Lefebvre and Frédéric Sawicki.[93] The gay socialist group Homosexualité et Socialisme (HES), founded in 1983, is not part of the party itself. And those of its founding members who might still hope for an executive post within the party are not very open about their earlier commitment. It is therefore not surprising that gay groups associated with conservative parties (such as Gaylib, founded in 2002 within the UMP) became an integral part of the party structure. During the presidential campaign of 2007, candidate Nicolas Sarkozy's UMP team launched La Diagonale, a support group seeking to unite left-leaning Sarkozy supporters. The first Diagonale meeting, held in the Bains-Douches in Paris, was attended by Sarkozy; the group directly and explicitly appealed to the gay community even though Sarkozy's conservative platform, which included neither gay marriage nor gay adoption, was more discriminatory toward homosexuality than that of the rival candidate, Ségolène Royal.

Meanwhile, LGBT associations and experts close to the Socialist Party continued to condemn the idea of a homosexual community, periodically expressed through highly mediatized publications. Such was the case regarding Frédéric Martel's book *Le Rose et le Noir*. Martel railed against the idea of a gay community, against homosexual ghettoization on the allegedly American model. He adopted a rhetoric of "the right to be indifferent," which allowed him to place responsibility for stigmatization on the stigmatized people themselves.[94] During a television program that featured Martel's book, which aired on May 6, 1996, discussion centered on the American model.[95] Jean-Pierre Michel, the national legislator who had drafted one of the bills on civil unions, defended Martel and accused Didier Eribon of wanting to Americanize French society at the expense of the "French model."[96] An internal Socialist Party report on "civil unions and new rights for couples outside marriage," completed on May 30, 1996, and co-drafted by ten contributors (including Martel and Stéphane Martinet, president of HES) under the editorship of Adeline Hazan (who held the post of national party secretary for social issues), argued that a civil union open solely to homosexuals "would represent a brutal break with the history and mechanisms of the French Republic. After two centuries of republican universalism, of state neutrality through secularism, we would be opting for American-style communitarianism."[97]

In 1999, the policy committee of Inter-LGBT, the federation of many Parisian homosexual associations that organized the Pride event (Inter-LGBT was called Greater Paris Lesbian & Pride at the time), published *Livre blanc 2000* (A white paper for 2000), a set of proposals submitted to Lionel Jospin's socialist administration. The drafting of the *Livre blanc* was the scene of political jockeying: members of HES managed to suppress all direct criticism of the government and aligned the report with an anticommunitarian discourse. It stressed that "promoting, indeed imposing, a given community identity, whether based on religion, ethnic origin . . . sexual orientation, or membership in any other given 'community,' is necessarily discriminatory."[98] This position provoked the resignation of Franck Delaire, then president of Greater Paris Lesbian & Gay Pride (and himself a contributor to Pédérama), since he disagreed with this text. Similarly, when Inter-LGBT adopted a stance against the plan for civil unions being proposed by Sarkozy in 2007 (a plan restricted to homosexual couples, conferring rights inferior to marriage and lacking the right to joint parenthood of children), it did so in the name of anticommunitarianism.[99]

Not all gay associations were hostile to the idea of community, nor have some of them always been so. During the early years of the Euro-Mediterranean summer seminars, several activists, including Christiane Jouve and Jacques Fortin, invoked community solidarity in the context of the decline of the revolutionary activist groups of the 1970s—they adopted a deliberate position in an effort to revive the activist sphere.[100] Similarly, ACT UP Paris has always defended the idea of community as a form of political solidarity, even while working toward the deconstruction of anticommunitarianism.[101] When Philippe Mangeot, a former president of ACT UP Paris and, in his own words, "an avid reader of Foucault,"[102] pushed his association in the direction of open minority resistance, he was taking a path rejected up to that point by the association's founders, particularly Didier Lestrade. "I decided right from the start," wrote Lestrade, "that it was crucial I avoid reading Foucault if I wanted to be president of ACT UP Paris. Foucault's philosophy had so influenced the early associations in the fight against AIDS that I had to steer clear of it. . . . Foucault could have announced that he was HIV positive, in any way he wanted—he was rich and famous."[103]

It would seem that the two former presidents of ACT UP were referring to two different Foucaults. Mangeot was talking about Foucault's writings on sexuality, on friendship as a lifestyle, and on the invention of new lifestyles (many of which were written in the United States or at least marked by his American experience). Lestrade was referring to Foucault as a public figure and to his influence, after he died,[104] on associations combating AIDS (one of the main French associations, AIDES, was founded after Foucault's death by his partner, Daniel Defert).[105] Lestrade was promoting the political importance of the notion of homosexual community, while Mangeot was stressing the deconstruction of anticommunitarianism.[106] Many queer groups have also been founded on a community basis, combining local solidarity and expertise, a basis described by Marianne Constable in a different context as a "new politics of association."[107] Such was the case concerning Queer Food for Love and, more recently, a Paris bar called La Mutinerie. Here the notion of community entails the idea of a self-governing group that seeks to establish a type of solidarity based on the experience of subjectification. Where a critique of identity can motivate a rejection of the notion of community on a macropolitical level, that critique can be the very motivator of a community on the local level. The idea of community emerges from the echoes produced by a critical perspective on people's own subjectification, against the totalizing idea of community as a mini-society that is greater than the individual.[108]

The Specter of Queer Theatricality

The disciplinary regime of anticommunitarianism is indissociable from the rhetoric of the difference between the sexes. This double register is reflected in Manif pour Tous's obsession with trans identities: the fear of—and the fascination with[109]—"indifference to the difference" between the sexes and simultaneously the fear of secession through "excess of difference." The dual registers reflect two intertwined forms of stigmatization: a condemnation of the madness of a lack of sexual markers and distrust of the different ways that sexual minorities pass on their culture. I intend to show how the question of eroticism lies as the intersection of these two registers. In what way is queer theory perceived as a threat to the eroticism of the difference between the sexes? And how does that eroticism get politicized?

The fixation on the notion of difference as crucial to sex is a historically contingent development. The difference between the sexes is not an invariable that dictates destiny, something that Sylviane Agacinski attributes to nature,[110] jurist Pierre Legendre attributes to the dogmatic aspect of law,[111] and Lacan attributed to the symbolic instance of the unconscious.[112] Human reproduction is based on sex, but sexuality does not have to be organized according to a principle of difference in order to function. Debates over marriage provide a good example. "The marriage form," writes Jacqueline Stevens, "exists to maintain ongoing political communities, not humanity itself."[113] The imaginative construct of biological membership informs national affiliation, even when citizenship is not based on blood.[114] Here, the social function of the difference between the sexes is to neutralize the mingling of blood, to reabsorb any idea of differentiation even before it surfaces (in this instance, the differentiation that distinguishes the children's biological existence from that of the parents). The difference between the sexes thus symbolically sustains the idea of *re*production (the production of something identical), whereas birth is always a production. This organicist imaginative construct of the difference between the sexes is directly linked to the imaginative construct of the biological permanence of the body of the nation.[115] When the issue of the difference between the sexes is raised in the French public sphere, it is national identity that is called into question. France has been described as a repository of the difference between the sexes, a guardian of all of humanity's destiny thanks to the universality of its values. Its mission has been defended in the name of a model of seductiveness based on sexual dissymmetry. One paradigmatic example is Mona Ozouf's *Women's*

Words, which links "French-style" sex appeal to an acquired mode of public—especially political—life.[116] She defines the French model in counterpoint to an American model of equality within the couple, wherein democratic aspirations supposedly undermine romantic and marital life.

The fantasy that links national identity to the difference between the sexes has also been directed against feminist movements and queer theory, both accused of having deconstructed the categories of male and female to the point of posing a threat to heterosexual seductiveness. This thesis has been taken up in the mass media and often defended by television commentator and essayist Éric Zemmour.[117] It also surfaces in more subtle forms, which shift the fear of ruining sexual pleasure to ruining the pleasure of texts. Anne Emmanuelle Berger, in a book devoted to Franco-American exchanges on issues of sexuality, raises the problematic of the "social body" from the standpoint of language. Berger is amazed that a "certain social neutralization of the difference between the sexes as an erotic difference seems to have opened the way to a desexualization of the heterosexual relation."[118] Playing on linguistic coincidences (queer/*cuir*, drag/*drague*) and pithy shortcuts ("comedy, and thus in a sense, 'sexuality'"),[119] she concludes that "heterosexuality . . . is no longer a sexuality."[120] Queerness, she claims, has extended its empire, its theatrical vision of identity, over heterosexuality itself, to the point that the latter is left only with the expressive tools of pastiche, comedy and play. The result, Berger argues, is that sexuality is no longer sexual but a comedy. Waxing ironic over queer performer Wendy Delorme—one of the members of Les Tordu(e)s—Berger explains that her play on self-presentation fetishizes sexual attire and reveals an "indifference to (the) sex(es), and even to sexual pleasure."[121]

Berger then slides from queer artist Wendy Delorme to transsexual persons, quoting Jean Baudrillard in one of those generalizations so typical of him: "The transsexual is both a play on non-differentiation (of the two poles of sexuality) and a form of indifference to *jouissance*, to sex as *jouissance*."[122] Since Baudrillard reduces pleasure to a specific form of genitality, Berger concludes that queer artists' play on sex objects testifies to a culture of the "look" and seeks to serve as the medium of "images and discourses that circulate on the World Wide Web of instantaneous information. The Web 'speaks' English, as Wendy does. Let us say, rather, that Wendy speaks the English of the Web, from which she 'descends,' to a certain extent."[123] Berger's tone—"the English of the Web," to "descend" almost in the sense of "humans descending from the apes"—allows her to conclude that a queer artist like Delorme mimes and quotes but never translates. Delorme, argues Berger, thereby forsakes the rich-ness of the process of translation, a noble task par excellence that does not remain glued to its object but creates a zone of difference between the original and the translation.

I argue, on the contrary, that performing always means translating—there is no distinction between the droning English found on the Web, devoid of any critical distance, and a canonical English worthy of translation. The careers of minority subjects show, in fact, that the use of English and the resulting make-shift language also enable them to challenge the norms imposed by the lan-guage of their own country. This work may be intuitive or more strategic, but in any case, it is a mental operation. That is exactly what troubles Berger in regard to using English on both sides of the Atlantic: from French to English then English to French, grammatical gender is profoundly affected by queer echoes: "The English language, which no longer refers back to a unified place or cul-ture, is today both the paradoxical location and the vehicle of this generalized dislocation."[124] According to Berger, the damage done to sexual pleasure by its queer theatricalization also means damaging textual pleasure because biologi-cal sex and grammatical sex both shape destiny. In other words, fascination with the "container" (writing and translation) triggers fantasies of a "content" (the difference between the sexes) without taking into consideration that we constantly translate the meanings we assign to our own words and those of others. We would in no way be condemned to wander in the limbo of language were we to be deprived of the symbolic impact of the difference between the sexes.[125] On the contrary, it is within the very plasticity of the text that we con-struct our sense of belonging.

The Specter of Multiple Identities

How does sanctification of the difference between the sexes, as the very condi-tion of eroticism, relate to the sanctification of marriage? I have already de-scribed how the Socialist Party relied on "expertise" and "responsibility" on this question. Here I discuss a factor inherent in the institution of marriage itself. The problem raised by the absence of a difference between the sexes and by the theatricalization of pleasure is that it challenges the principle of ex-clusiveness. Being a man allegedly excludes the possibility of simultaneously being a woman, and vice versa.[126] This possibility is further excluded, within a couple, by the requirement of faithfulness. Prohibiting multiple sexual and amorous relationships ensures that the identities of the spouses are constructed solely as mirror images. Although debate over extending marriage to homosexual couples did not question the external dimension of conjugal exclusiveness,[127] the construction of male/female roles as mutually exclusive within a married couple is challenged de facto by the extension of marriage to same-sex couples.

This disturbance explains many of the arguments marshaled against the Taubira Act by Catholic activists. Marriage has in fact been the tool through which the Catholic Church concentrated its fortunes by strictly regulating the transmission of heritage. Faithfulness was born from a need to divide neither wealth nor paternal power among several children born of several mothers.[128] Business having originally been practiced in a family context, the principle of exclusiveness was steadily extended to property and even was eventually perceived as a natural right: every human, through his or her work and exchange, has an exclusive right to acquire goods whose value is based on their scarcity. This paradigm progressively made "lucrative activities honorable" by viewing the lure of money as a "peaceful passion" within the family context.[129] Philosopher Charles Fourier argued that the inequalities stemming from the principle of economic scarcity can be overcome only by addressing the various forms of amorous exclusiveness in marriage.[130]

Adoption itself was long feared by the Catholic Church because the procedure authorized recognition of adulterous, abandoned, and orphaned children, thereby competing with the only legitimate adoption: adoption by God through the act of baptism. The threat of adoption has been contained, in a way, by the biological representations of the family that have flourished in France in the past thirty years. Bioethical laws passed in 1994, which legalized MAP only for heterosexual couples, reinforced a model of kinship limited to a biparental, heterosexual model (furthermore, the procedure for certifying parental candidates for adoption now lasts nine months). Extending adoption to homosexual couples thereby rekindles the threat of adoption itself by abandoning the need to mimic procreation. It restores, so to speak, the very logic behind adoption, which establishes kinship in the absence of a biological link between parents and children and, in so doing, creates the possibility of having from one to four parents.[131] Debate over marriage and homoparenthood is thus also shaped by the challenge to the principle of exclusiveness. Opponents of the Taubira Act were fully aware that this one was of the problematics conveyed by queer theory. That theory therefore became a perfect target.

Queer theory tackles the question of feeling "at home," a "sense of belong-ing,"[132] of being in the right place thanks to a weave of family and friends in relationships of greater or lesser closeness. When queer theorists argue for a greater profusion of spaces and greater mobility of places, they do not imply that a feeling of exclusivity is less strong or less useful politically. As Jack Halber-stam has pointed out,

> Alternative kinship has long been a cause célèbre among gay and lesbian groups and queer scholars. . . . Some call for new models of family (Butler's Antigone as a substitute for Oedipus, Weston's chosen families as a substitute for blood bonds); others call for the recognition of friendship ties as kinship; and still others ask that we recognize the difference that gay and lesbian parents make to the very meaning of family. But few scholars call for a de-emphasis on family or a rejection of the family as the form of social organization par excellence.[133]

In my view, "a queer sense of belonging" involves neither an internal transfor-mation nor a rejection of kinship any more than it entails the invention of a utopia or heterotopia; it incorporates all of that simultaneously. The existence of multiple disciplinary regimes goes hand in hand with the invention of mul-tiple forms of resistance that, in a collective, shifting way, constitute the queer sense of belonging.

Multiple homosexual identities emerged in urban niches in the nineteenth and first half of the twentieth centuries,[134] when jobs called for greater move-ment, distance from the family, and new ways of organizing time.[135] From 1970 to 1990, homosexual populations largely contributed to the gentrification of city centers in both North America and Europe, marginalizing other populations with lower income who were therefore subject to greater invisibility or greater stigmatization. Urban culture thus became the source of numerous myths within LGBT cultures.[136] Nowadays, the weariness of the activist generation most directly affected by AIDS, the legal recognition of homosexual couples and families, and new technology favoring online encounters—as well as the social view of homosexuality[137]—have transformed this relationship to public spaces to the point that Denis Altman wonders if we are witnessing "the end of the homosexual."[138] Yet it is possible to question these changes as the sign of a queerer relationship to one's self and one's environment in the sense that they show how subjectification rests on disengagement as much as engagement.[139] Queerness would not then be experienced as a radical stance but as the ac-ceptance of an ambiguity linked to multiple positions, a strategy made necessary by the mobility of disciplinary regimes.[140] As Sylvie Tissot has shown with respect to Boston's South End, gay friendliness is conditioned by an absence of communitarian assertiveness: the gays who live in the neighborhood do not compete with straight gentrifiers (by, for example, setting up a neighborhood gay association), given a shared social view based on identical economic interests. However, "this integration was accompanied by subtle forms of exclusion, or at least an injunction to discretion, the requirement to abstain from behavior considered too identity-bound or having excessive sexual connotation."[141]

For sexual minorities, there is nothing new about this multipositionality. Throughout the twentieth century, homosexual circles were troubled by the question of "home." In the shady cabarets of Pigalle and Montparnasse in the 1920s,[142] and in the clubs and bars in Lyon in the 1970s,[143] for example, the establishment of a community was always crucial. These communities sometimes took the form of sexual networks or fleeting social links that had to remain secret. Yet sometimes they lasted: groups of friends functioned as second families for many lesbians and gays.[144] One of the features common to these various homosexual homes is that they replay kinship relationships in a mode steeped in distance and sacredness, as illustrated by both literary fiction and historical documents. For example, two men might define themselves as spouses, as sisters, as brothers, as mother and daughter, or as father and son, without attributing significance to age or generation. Jean Genet's *Our Lady of the Flowers* is constructed around the relationship that Divine cultivates with Mignon, which he describes as that of a "married woman."[145]

Two women can entertain relations of kinship and romance without any serious suggestion of incest. In Marina Tsvetaeva's novel, *Mon Frère féminin* (My Feminine Brother), conjugal ties are designated by borrowing from the full range of family relationships *except* that of sisters, which would have been too desexualizing since the two characters unite and test each other in their desire to give birth together: "My child, my friend, my darling, and (your inspired quip, Madame) my feminine brother, but never—sister."[146] In these fictional homosexual "houses," to paraphrase Genet, couples and their desire to pass on a heritage always play an important role. Artist Rosa Bonheur's real-life testament provides another fine example: down to the tiniest details, it bequeaths her property to her last partner, Anna Klumpke; and should Klumpke herself be deceased, it is her sisters who will inherit Bonheur's wealth, thereby creating "the potential for a new genealogy of independent women."[147] Bonheur, who often wore a suit and who materially supported her parents and friends, so thoroughly exemplified a new lifestyle based on independence and solidarity among women that dolls of her were made in the United States and became fashionable among female couples, simultaneously symbolizing their union and their desire for parenthood.[148]

This critical, simultaneous adoption of several identities represents a major challenge for the legal system.[149] Whereas adversaries and opponents of marriage stressed the transformative effects of extending it to homosexual couples,[150] queer theory raises the fundamental question of the coexistence of multiple legal statuses. Multipositionality effectively challenges one of the roles that Western societies have assigned to the law, the symbolic marking of territory via genealogy. The law fences in proliferating forms of life by defining them, consequently assigning them a temporal, geographic, and physical mooring.[151] But it also prompts new forms of life to emerge. The legal denial of multiple identities creates not only a gaping hole in queer lives but also an insatiable appetite for history.[152] To avoid being overwhelmed by a permanent consuming pain induced by past battles,[153] reparation takes the form of micro-resistances where new collective memory is invented.[154] Transmitting a shared heritage then takes the form of a daily deciphering of majority references, coded exchanges with peers, forms of identification with elders, and erotic practices that are not immediately inscribed in a family context.[155]

The multiple forms of identification within LGBT cultures represent a challenge to the French State insofar as the State's model of national belonging is based on transforming intermediate bodies, local allegiances, and peer groups through the law of the will of the majority. The way that queer theory valorizes multiple attachments issuing from LGBT cultures may thus be described as a critical response to majority interpellations. This questioning of the majority's power explains why the response to queer theory in France is based on a fear of contamination by the minority.

The Specter of Contagion

The anxiety of interpellation by majority categories is indissociable from the phobic fear gripping the majority group. Indeed, the emergence of minority cultures may trigger an unbearable feeling of having lost one's sovereignty, having lost control over a culture perceived as inaccessible, and thus being excluded through the effect of having excluded others. Eve Sedgwick provided a perfect illustration of this fear of minority cultures and practices in her analysis of *Billy*

Budd.[156] She showed that the male bonding that reigned on the ship was designed to circumscribe homosexuality, but by constantly holding up the specter of that sexuality, it also generated a state of generalized paranoia: Who will succumb to the temptation, and when? Homosexual irony, or camp, makes fun of this paranoia, displaying it like a trophy and drawing new strength from it. Irony challenges the assignation of the character of "homosexual" since it combines a quest for recognition (in social interaction) with a questioning of that notion (by revealing the contingent nature of the interaction). The constitution of the relationship to the community is therefore always the product of a tension.[157]

In France, this tension was long held at bay by viewing minority sexualities in a pathological light, as witnessed by the monitoring procedures described at the beginning of this chapter. The pathologizing tactic survives in the more latent form of a fear of contamination. The reason that queer theory has been labeled "puerile," "individualistic," and "sterile" is to disqualify the forms of transmission explored by that theory, which are not strictly genealogical. Thus, it is argued that there exist both majority sexual cultures, which are responsible, healthy, and concerned to transcend the self for the benefit of future generations, and minority sexual cultures, which are ill, wrapped up in their immediate interests, and oblivious to the future of the nation. Extending marriage would therefore mean weakening this key distinction. The paradox, however, is that if majority cultures can be contaminated by minority cultures, it is precisely because the latter are considered irresistible. Queer theory is simultaneously feared and desired.

The idea of a queer invasion is an extension of the fear of contamination already expressed by the spread of the AIDS virus, a fear itself based on a populist Freudianism that associates male homosexuality with short-lived pleasure while simultaneously denying the possibility of lesbian pleasure.[158] The imaginative faculty for linking male homosexuality to narcissism and the negation of difference was largely revived by the AIDS epidemic from the standpoint of both pathology and sublimation,[159] what Jeff Nunokawa called the "morbid delineation of gay identity in current construction of people with AIDS."[160] A certain misuse of psychoanalysis in public debate tended to equate life and the future with sexual reproduction, similarly equating sexual bliss with fleetingness.[161] Homosexuality, by nature infertile, thus appeared to present a risk to society as a whole by promoting a form of life geared solely toward the present. A rejection of the erotic, social, and political function of the difference between the sexes was thus perceived as a rejection of "the other" both in the present (due to the social homogeneity of a communitarian type) and in the future (via a rejection of child bearing and family life, that fantasized factor of homogeneity).[162] AIDS confirmed this equation of homosexuality with social barrenness. The rise of demands for homosexual parenthood should have demolished, logically enough, that fantasy. Such was not the case, however, since lesbians and gays were suspected of promoting homogeneity and a focus on the present,[163] since homoparenthood allegedly sought not sexual reproduction but self-reproduction, that is, the manufacture of more homosexuals.[164]

The lasting association of homosexuality with social barrenness is interesting for three important reasons. First, it raises the question of how one transmits a heritage as an imaginative construct, how projection into future generations is associated with the imaginative construct of blood ties.[165] Next, it redraws the borders of the national community by introducing a criterion of immunity into the sense of belonging distinguishing between healthy and contaminated blood.[166] Finally, as a counter-example, it legitimizes heterosexual eroticism as having a restorative effect on a body politic weakened by communitarianism. Heterosexuality comes to be perceived as a second chance, a way to deal a new hand to future generations. It was precisely on this register that certain gay cultures sought to fight back, by either demystifying the experience of HIV (the work of Hervé Guibert being one of the most striking examples in the French context) or transforming the very sense of contaminating practices:[167] there have arisen advocates of bareback sex—such as Guillaume Dustan and Erik Rémès—who defend unprotected sex regardless of the partners' HIV status.[168] In a recent book, David Caron argues that a community is created through contact and that positive HIV status consequently transforms this mechanism, since it no longer fulfills the imperative of getting outside yourself that informs the French republican ideal.[169] Caron shows that French objections to communitarianism are made possible by a certain aesthetics of the collective body that transfigures individual bodies who conform and excludes all others.[170] Rejecting the communitarian logic of barebacking, ACT UP Paris sought to propose a different model of community.[171] Plastering the streets of Paris in 2004 with a poster titled "The Community We Seek," it publicly opposed abandoning preventive measures.

But is it really possible to combat the fantasy of social infertility by reinvoking the alternative community model? The strategy is of doubtful use unless it is combined with an etiological analysis of homosexual practices themselves. Though many of these practices challenge sexuality as the locus of the production of the self,[172] French republican ideals, obsessed by the question of roots, perceive only meaningless and destructive behavior. Yet they involve not so much an experience of destruction as an experience of abandonment of self-sovereignty. Queer ethicist Lee Edelman has tried to show as much in his book *No Future*. Rather than challenge the notion of future, as his title might imply, what he tackles is the fact that the future is always associated with forward projection: "This is the ethical burden to which queerness must accede in a social order intent on misrecognizing its own investment in morbidity, fetishization, and repetition . . . to figure an unregenerate, and unregenerating, sexuality."[173] Edelman reverses the very terms of the fantasy of destruction by showing that such a fantasy actually survives in the idea of the future and hence is threatened in the very queer practices where it is usually located. Less problematized, however, is Edelman's appeal to a "we," a group that seems rigidified by the power relationship that constituted it,[174] rather than being in the making.[175]

It is precisely this counter-hymn to the community that was targeted by opponents to marriage for all, who perceived queer theory as a conspiracy by a homosexual collective driven by its destructive impulses. Marguerite Peeters stated that the undoing of civilization by queer theory takes place in three phases: first, the death of the father ("paternal love and order," as she puts it),[176] then the death of the mother (through a "contraceptive mentality" and a dissociation between pregnancy and maternity), and then the death of the child because "children have also ended up being treated as pure citizens with full rights, a 'child of the Republic' in the same way as all other 'citizens.' But they thereby lose their right to be a child—a son or a daughter with a father and mother."[177] Borrowing the title of Lee Edelman's book, she concludes that "the path of gender, queer theory, and post-gender represents a dead end for humanity. It can lead only to the death and end of humanity."[178] The notion of human ecology developed by the Vatican is designed to counter queer theory's supposedly lethal deconstruction by reestablishing a natural, God-given balance. Peeters believed that gender considerations were particularly threatening insofar as they were becoming "a global culture."[179]

The Specter of Death

A morbid vision of homosexual desire is being expressed beneath the fear of homosexual desire. This vision is rooted in a perception of the couple promoted by much of the literary and philosophical output in France. From this perspective, opponents of queer theory have invented nothing new; they have simply relied on a truism already highly regarded in intellectual debate over the notion of community. In the context of the collapse of the communist bloc, several French intellectuals, including Maurice Blanchot and Jean-Luc Nancy, struggled to rethink the notion of community. To avoid the impasse of "commonness" as a project of collective property inspired by Marxism (the "co" in community),[180] they defined community as a structuring principle of social ties yet did not assign it a specific content: they referred to "negative," "impossible," "unavowable," "idle," or "evasive community."[181] In *The Unavowable Community*, an essay first published in French in 1983, Maurice Blanchot deconstructs what he calls the myth of "the common world." He argues that the community is indissociably linked to the (contingent, unstable, tessellated) relationship that we maintain with it: "The community is not the place of Sovereignty. It is what exposes by exposing itself. It includes the exteriority of being that excludes it."[182] According to Blanchot, community is the fluctuation through which individuals explore their own limits. Blanchot employs an example that seems surprising at first glance—*The Malady of Death*, a novel published by Marguerite Duras in French in 1982. The book is a theatricalization—which in 1986 would in fact be turned into a play titled *Les Yeux bleus, Cheveux noirs* (Blue Eyes, Black Hair)—of a hopeless love story between a heterosexual woman (the narrator) and a man who loved "those like [him]self."[183] (At the time, Duras was living with Yann Andréa, a young homosexual she had met in 1980.)

Blanchot decides to make this relationship the archetype of a "community of lovers" (even though he himself plays on the romanticism of that label). The lovers are simultaneously cut off from the world and inaccessible to one another, as though the unconventional nature of their relationship excludes any illusion of eternity in the love affair—as though death itself is standing there between them. This situation creates an ethical relationship in which "the other" is not assimilated to oneself (to a shared life) but instead sparks self-interrogation through a feeling of responsibility toward another.[184] That is probably why two types of pronoun coexist in Duras's text: "She" (referring to the narrator) and "You" (when the narrator addresses her lover). The upshot is an irreducible sense of distance ("We" is never used), accompanied by a certain empathy (generated by the parallel use of these forms). This tension is sustained to the end of the novel. When the lovers part, what they lose had never really been won. "Even so you have managed to live that love in the only way possible for you. Losing it before it happened."[185] For this reason, according to Blanchot, every community is fleeting.[186]

Yet this interpretation seems to overlook the shifts that punctuate Duras's text: the malady of death is homosexuality itself, implicitly described as a form of denial of *the* difference between the sexes. "You don't love anything or anyone, you don't even love the *difference* you think you embody. All you know is the grace of the bodies of the dead, the grace of those like yourself."[187] The glorification of the heterosexual couple as a "union of opposites" is a fairly ordinary attitude.[188] As Duras would explain in *La Vie matérielle* (Material Life), "Heterosexuality is dangerous—that's where you're tempted to seek desire's perfect duality. . . . Homosexuality's passion is homosexuality. What a homosexual loves like a lover—like his country, his creature, his land—is not his lover; it's homosexuality."[189] In this context, Blanchot is mistaken when he relegates the confrontation between male homosexuality and female heterosexuality to a vagary of Duras's narrative.[190] Duras claims that *The Malady of Death* is primarily a mad love affair. In July 1982 she sent a letter to Yann Andréa saying that she placed death on her side, because wild passion represented a risk for her, a risk precisely because she was unaware of its mechanisms and effects.[191] While Andréa's homosexuality clearly informs Duras's writing, she seeks to apply the idea of death to a framework of passionate love as a whole and to any nonsexual relationship. The fact that she introduces a new character—a heterosexual man—in *Les Yeux bleus, Cheveux noirs* could have confirmed this. However, the young gay man seems to have fully embodied the malady of death since the possibility of desire is still fully "determined in both cases by anatomical difference."[192] Consequently, Blanchot exploits the idea of the couple (two rather than many)[193] and otherness (the difference between the sexes—whether expressed in heterosexuality or homosexuality—as a source of social heterogeneity) to conceptualize community. He cites the Nazi Sturmabteilung (SA) as an example of "makers of groups" who transfigure their "homosexual leaning, . . . [whether] sublimated or not" to produce social bonds.[194] According to Blanchot, the death drive can be productive only if homosexuality itself is contained.[195]

Lesbians and gays have thus been assigned an impossible choice, because they can exist socially only by disavowing what constitutes them, by being "neutralized" in advance. Demanding a guarantee of their harmlessness means resignifying their dangerousness.[196] In fact, no death drive is intrinsic to either homosexual or heterosexual desires. The idea of a death drive simply allows those who have disavowed the possibility of homosexuality to be reassured of their practices. It also explains why, inversely, homosexuality must be "avowed."[197] This situation calls for personal soul searching in the sense of the French phrase *retour sur soi*, a literal and figurative turning back on oneself. This turn is not only a backward look but an emotional shake-up, churning up feelings that have shaped a life's path, structuring it inside and out. This is not a question of transcending oneself but, to borrow Eve Sedgwick's words, of experiencing a "convoluted overlap."[198]

The Specter of Class

I have shown that the fear of homosexual communitarianism—whether couched as betrayal, invasion, lack of difference, corruption, or contamination—remains a cardinal aspect of the construction of citizenship in France. However, this fear has been somewhat displaced following the legal recognition of homosexual couples through civil unions (PACS), marriage, and adoption. The integration of gays and lesbians into the French republican universe makes it harder to point to them as a threat to the republic. Given this situation, it is interesting that fear of the community is expressed increasingly often in relation to class: minorities theoretically constitute a new class based not on economic and social criteria but on their own subjectivity. Sociologist Irène Théry continues to condemn minority subjectification as embodying the danger of unbridled individualism: "Some proposals for solutions via transgender identities occasionally give the impression of refining [the identitarian approach] in an increasingly desperate way, in the hope of ultimately dissolving in its own logic: each individual becomes a class in himself or herself alone."[199] Reactions of opposition to the extension of marriage and joint adoption to homosexual couples share this vision: the law must resist the empire of individual willfulness, in this case the all-powerful desire of adults to marry whomever they want and to have children even if they cannot conceive them together.

Opponents of the Taubira Act thus aligned themselves against a libertarian vision of the law. In fact, civil union and gay marriage in France were both conceived by several academics who were fervent advocates of individual liberty. Jurist Daniel Borrillo, for example, came up with a contract for civil unions within the AIDES association, contributed to the critique of conservative expertise, and launched the mobilization to back the gay marriage rite performed in Bègles. But here a subtle distinction must be made: while opponents of gay marriage argue that the traditional family is "disintegrating" under the onslaught of selfish desires,[200] some advocates of the Taubira Act close to the Socialist Party share the rhetoric of the all-powerful individual will, while acknowledging certain exceptions. Hence there are purportedly good LGBT citizens who gratefully accept the new legal system offered to them and militant hard-liners who, despite everything, continue to criticize the norms. Théry argues that the latter have been trapped for the past fifteen years in an "artificial" mind-set and a form of "egotistical individualism."[201] Claiming that an attachment to individual liberties combined with a critique of legal norms can define a class of citizens has one direct consequence: it effaces the real stakes behind class and the way those stakes are related to sexuality in developing a multi-tiered system of citizenship.

The polemic triggered by the publication of a recent novel by Édouard Louis, *En finir avec Eddy Bellegueule* (The End of Eddy),[202] reveals the extent to which seeing things through the joint prism of class and sexuality has become taboo in France.[203] The novel offers a paradigmatic analysis of identity and belonging that underscores the multiplicity of affects as well as minorities' difficult relationship to collective memory. First published in 2014, this autobiographical novel (Bellegueule being Louis's original family name) tells a tale of homophobia at home and school as experienced by a working-class lad in northern France in the first decade of the 2000s. (In this way, the novel follows the trail blazed by Didier Eribon when he narrated his own childhood in *Returning to Reims*,[204] first published in 2009.) Eddy, the main character, tries to conform to family and social expectations but ultimately flees a milieu that fails to recognize him:

> Fleeing was the only path open to me, the single one to which I had been reduced. I wanted to show how my escape was not the outcome of a plan constantly on my mind, as though I had been some animal deprived of liberty and had always wanted to escape, but on the contrary how running away was the last resort, considered only after a series of self-defeats.[205]

For Louis, running away is not an act of rebellion but the only option afforded by a family and environment whose expectations he cannot meet. In a way, he is expelled by a milieu whose contradictions he embodies, even before he seeks to escape the fate imposed on him. We thus realize that, paradoxically, social reproduction is also perpetuated through the careers of anyone who escapes its hold, because even renegades define—through their very departure—the borders of the community they leave behind. The French republican model is masterful in its scrutiny of these renegades, elevating them to the level of exemplar to prove that all worthy individuals can transform their lives. But the result is to reduce their impact. Democratic meritocracy functions as a decoy: by ascribing a change in status to individual qualities, it deflects recognition of the need for collective change. The role of meritocratic rhetoric is to contain any seeds of social change that a renegade might sow. By showing affect to be a collective construction, a construction that minorities must forgo (which implies first forgoing the embodied norms), Louis's novel raises a radical question: What are the social, political, economic, and epistemological conditions that would make a society truly elective?

Within weeks of its publication, Louis's novel was receiving lively media attention. Struck by the impact of certain scenes, several journalists, academics, and writers—beginning with Eribon himself and including Annie Ernaux and Chantal Jaquet—praised the young author's literary power. Others intensely rejected the novel, viewing it as merely a hoax and claiming that the scenes described by the author could not have taken place.[206] All that allegedly remained were his raw descriptions of the working class and provincial town, which attested to the classism of Louis, who had by that time become a student at the prestigious ENS in Paris.[207] A class renegade must inevitably be a traitor to the community assigned to him by birth. The reason that young Eddy's path through homophobia and social stigmatization seemed inconceivable to so many commentators is that it challenged the very idea of an exemplar, an idea that lies at the heart of the republican ideal. Chantal Jaquet asks, "How can there be an imitation of what is nonreproducible? The antinomy is patent. One must be able to picture or imitate extraordinary destinies, but how can you picture or imitate what escapes the general rule?"[208] Noting the relevance of assimilated economic constraints,[209] personal encounters,[210] and the family setting,[211] Jaquet contributes an even more original hypothesis: "A certain form of ignorance and self-blindness might paradoxically be the origin of extraordinary destinies, whereas wisdom would have instead counseled giving up higher education in order to avoid the risk of failure."[212]

Jaquet offers a counterpoint to Pierre Bourdieu's notion of homosexual "reflexivity." Bourdieu underscores the fact that lesbians and gays brought up as heterosexuals develop "a kind of cognitive and evaluative dissonance tending to contribute to their special perspicacity,"[213] because they have interiorized the society's dominant viewpoint. If a sense of belonging is, as queer theory demonstrates, a simultaneous product of rejection and acceptance, it is also the fruit of a tension between illusion and lucidity with respect to belonging. Regarding the boys at school who regularly beat him, Louis writes, "The big redheaded guy and the other, stooped shouldered, delivered a last blow. Then suddenly left. Making bland, everyday comments. This observation hurt—I counted less in their lives than they counted in mine. I focused all my thoughts and fears on them the minute I woke up. Their ability to forget me so quickly affected me."[214]

What the reaction to Louis's book reveals, and the perspective it offers, is that the specter of a policy of the queer self, one that incorporates ambiguities with regard to a sense of belonging, is still highly operative in France even after legalization of marriage for all. By accepting his own ambivalences, Louis— via his character Eddy Bellegueule—undermines the supposed coherence of the republican system. He proposes a reading of identity that does not erect personal issues in reaction to State governance. State governance calls for the erection of a symbolic dividing line between public and private, exercising its own power while giving individuals the illusion they are sovereign entities.[215] What *The End of Eddy* demonstrates, in contrast, is that any form of transmission remains attached to the balance of power that created it—it is not a dialogue between several sovereign subjects but the demonstration of several unattainable sovereignties.[216] What then emerges is the possibility of establishing critical alliances between a queer conception of belonging and the system of representation itself.

Queer Belonging and Representation

How can we conceptualize forms of citizenship that authorize a relationship to the group that is more critical, more complex, and more mobile? Does a State system even permit such a process? In France, the State historically preceded the nation—a sense of national identification grew only from reforms such as the Villers-Cotterêts decree of 1539, which made French the official language for print, or the education bills promoted by Jules Ferry in 1881–82, which established free, mandatory, secular schooling for all children aged six to thirteen. Adoption of transcendental symbols such as language and schooling have long been at the heart of the process of belonging. The social contract was validated through a *symbolon*: like the shards of pottery from a broken vase that once stood for the unification of people or families in ancient Greece, it showed that the parts were interdependent. But is this sort of artifact still necessary today? Don't all symbols always become sacrosanct once stripped of their initial materiality? From a queer perspective, it is the challenge to, rather than adoption of, this use of symbols that generates a feeling of belonging. The feeling of belonging is not the result of comparing shared references that might confirm a contract, fictional or not, but the questioning of the very idea of contract itself.

The obsession with homosexuals as a "secret society" is located within this tradition of the State's wariness of the advent of any new form of democracy. Indeed, homosexuality involves an experience of displacement (since lesbians and gays are raised in a largely heterosexual society) and shows that attachment to the inherited community (via family structures) is not unconditional. For lesbians and gays, subjectification means learning that they are simultaneously within and without. This relationship to borderlines is problematic for the State both metaphorically (because it introduces uncertainty into the staging of national genealogy) and materially (because it shows that the simultaneous adoption of several belief systems is possible). Homosexual subjectification therefore challenges the two main dimensions of a state: territory (defined as sovereignty, recognized by other states, over a given population) and a judicial-administrative system (as legitimized, in its modern liberal form, by the principle of political representation). It is not a question of accepting or rejecting the idea of representation on the argument that it merely reproduces various forms of domination but of creating spheres where the notion of representation is redefined through the encounter of several clashing senses of belonging.[217]

QUEER THEORY has brought us to the threshold of that project. How can multifarious feelings of belonging become a factor of transformation? In other words, how can they invent new theories and practices without turning inward on themselves? How can they convey unique and sometimes contradictory visions of the world? "Governance for the future" is an attempt to model efforts at subjectification and thereby limits potential approaches to life that are not strongly tied to the model of the heterosexual couple. When new critical theorizations such as queer theory emerge, they shake the very foundations on which lives unfold. Judith Butler has demonstrated as much by raising the question of the epistemological conditions of mourning. The impossible community, a "malady of death" that prevents even those people it unites from establishing mutual links, is also a malady of death in the literal sense. The dead are mourned according to the way their lives are perceived. It is necessary to invert the analysis advanced by Maurice Blanchot. Those whose very existences were rendered pathological truly entered death under a regime of community. That was the case of all the people who died from AIDS anonymously because they did not meet the criteria of either family or national mourning. If they truly constitute a community, the reason is not that they shared something (every life, hence every death, is characterized by its incommensurate singularity) but that they produced and continue to produce a feeling of belonging among those who *might have been* in their place. One of the mechanisms by which "us" is expressed rests on what Butler called "unlived possibilities."[218] The union of multiple feelings of belonging stems from both the person we are and all those we might have been. The twin foundations of the modern liberal State are thereby reconceptualized. In this perspective, sovereignty over a given population constitutes just one aspect of State power. This power also concerns all the possibilities of life that motivate citizens in a spectral manner.[219]

Raising the question of the State makes it possible to deconstruct the cultural bases that underpin belief in its authority. By rejecting the idea of an "undivided subject into the discourse of power,"[220] the principle of representation can no longer be mystified as a simple delegation, transparent unto itself, in which the representative "speaks for" the represented. Insofar as the person represented is already steeped in numerous lives that are not his or her own, the mandate by which one person substitutes for another is always an appropriation. Representation is not just a process of substitution; it is also a site of portrayal.[221] In other words, a queer theory of power interrogates not the mimetic aspect of representation but representation as the stage on which each subject compares and contrasts an entire set of unlived lives to his or her own.[222] It is the stage, not the individual as such, that is globalized. When the social and economic environment offers access to a greater flow of information, we may find ourselves exposed to new potential lives. But among all those lives within which we articulate our own, we continue to prioritize some rather than others. We remain governed by entire sets of preferences and obligations, largely forged by our immediate environment (be it family, work, or place of residence), which constrains the frequency, extent, and intensity of our attachments. The *scopic* mechanism of representation continues to be pressured by very direct power relationships.[223] Majority versus minority life: we each arbitrate, internally and in view of all, according to the means at our disposal, ranging from those who "can" to those who "cannot" speak to and for us.

The "speaking" majority can indeed bear the cost of its own disappearance once its speech act ceases—the majority voice has no need to prolong itself in time, to outlive its echo. It does not even need to say anything in order to speak, because speech itself is embodied in the majority.[224] The minority voice, meanwhile, must "dare speak its name." The "speaking" minority could say that it's speaking without knowing whether it has spoken, since it does not know if it has been heard. A minority subject does not seek to "resolv[e] the dilemma of group membership" in a multicultural perspective,[225] but it lends that dilemma body, literally brings it to life. Such is the issue facing queer politics in France: it must play on the spectral form to which republican ideology has assigned it in order to reinvent the very idea of belonging and representation.

CONCLUSION

THROUGHOUT THIS BOOK I have analyzed political uses of the notion of community based on the French response to queer theory. My work has shown that there is no reference specific to each culture but rather a set of representations and values that are constantly being redefined through the simple *presence* of other cultures. I therefore seek to interrogate the very notion of culture, all the while rejecting the alleged globalization of categories.[1] Debate over queer theory in France is not a carbon copy of that in America. Nor can it be encapsulated as a strategy of empowerment in relation to the nationalist trend of sexual politics in France and, more broadly, Europe. On the contrary, I argue that queer theory destabilizes the very concepts of global and local insofar as it sheds light on the concomitance of affiliation and disaffiliation with the group. That is why it muddies the picture of a national sense of belonging. There where the nation-state—and the multinational state—seeks to objectivize the framework of citizenship by linking genealogy ("vertical" affiliation to a lineage) to community ("horizontal" affiliation to a group), queer theory views kinship as a way of simultaneously belonging and *not* belonging. Queer theory approaches citizenship from the perspective of the norm's failures, gaps, and inability to fully grasp reality. It analyzes the way in which a feeling of belonging stems from a challenge to, rather than a sanctification of, the social order.

It is therefore a critical presence in a given social context rather than any categorization that constitutes the basis of community from a queer perspective. Contrary to a preconception that reduces it to an abstract exercise in the deconstruction of discursive categories, queer theory is a deconstruction anchored in the body's relationship to its environment. Its conception of politics is based on an experience of dispossession, a term that "marks the limits of self-sufficiency and that establishes us as relational and interdependent beings."[2] At the same time, it reminds us of our primal vulnerability, our body's exposure to the violence of this world. Queer theory therefore seeks not to escape the norm but, in a more demanding way, to develop "the art of not being governed quite so much."[3]

My own approach thus sidesteps canonical analyses of reception theories. My work is not conceptualized in terms of transmitter and receiver, of flows and trajectories, but in terms of presence. Analysis of the social conditions of the circulation of ideas has difficulty grasping transcultural influences in the absence of real interactions. Yet many activists, academics, and politicians who explicitly refer to queer theory or its main protagonists know very little—or, more often, nothing at all—of the texts and discussions to which they refer. Above all, they invoke the specter of American culture. While there have indeed been efforts to translate queer texts (which found conscientious readers), those efforts are not sufficient to explain the importance American culture has assumed in discussions of queerness, gender theory, and marriage for all. Such debates are the expression of much older cultural fantasies, particularly the idea of a self-sufficient homosexual community and, more broadly, the danger to the state posed by groups and genealogies that do not fit into a strictly national framework. This book has demonstrated the persistence of a straight mind in the nation despite major changes in the law and in everyday behavior with respect to sexual minorities. In France, the heterosexual nuclear family remains the symbolic cement of the national community.

In 1998, opposition to the establishment of civil unions had been built around the notion of a symbolic order: because they recognized a kind of marital bond that claimed no connection to the biological function of fertilization, civil unions were attacked for purportedly relativizing the difference between the sexes and consequently of all forms of difference.[4] Civilization itself was allegedly threatened, since without the notion of otherness no stable form of identity could exist.[5] Then, in 2012, with the arrival of the debate over gay marriage and adoption, this public discourse over the symbolic aspect faded into the background, although did not completely disappear. What came to the fore was anti-Americanism, expressed as a denunciation of gender theory. So what happened between 1998 and 2012? Why were the anti-gender arguments developed by the Vatican in the mid-1990s not taken up again until fifteen years later? The two first chapters of this book have provided several pieces of the puzzle. One concerns the collapse of the theories designed to thwart civil unions—the law authorizing them became an accepted part of the landscape so quickly that several political opponents of the bill admitted that they had been mistaken.[6] The people who continued to oppose minority rights therefore had to seek other arguments. The second concerns the Europe-wide nature of the debate over gay marriage. Since legalization of marriage for homosexual couples was spreading steadily from one country to another, arguing that such changes were masterminded from the United States made it possible to challenge their inevitability, even as the idea of national identity was reinforced (from this perspective, criticism of gender theory also drew on other debates about French identity, debates that already swirled around American counter-models, for example, questions of sexual harassment, wearing the Islamic headscarf, artificial insemination techniques, surrogate motherhood).[7] The third piece of the puzzle involves the publicity over the queer phenomenon in France in the early years of the twenty-first century. Whereas opposition to gender theory had remained very limited, once a broader public was exposed to the term "queer" and became aware of the existence of new demands regarding sexuality, those opposed could more easily convince themselves and others that a paradigmatic change was truly occurring in France. All the pieces thus fell into place for protesting gay marriage in the name of a theory, an *American* theory, a *queer* American theory. For lack of a specifically American corpus, one had to be invented.

This invention would not have been possible, however, had it not rested on two major contradictions: first, the paradoxical trend within queer theory to essentialize sexual categories the better to denounce the domination implied by their circulation in various countries of the world; second, the way French citizenship has been constructed against minority communities in the long history of the French Republic, in the recent history of left-wing governments, and in the past three decades of theoretical work that has conceptualized the idea of community solely in negative terms. Those two political and conceptual contradictions are the object of the analyses in Chapters 3 and 4, which show how the critique of LGBT imperialism conducted on both sides of the Atlantic echoes the older fear of homosexual contagiousness whose transnational ramifications might undermine the state. This fear of a minority conspiracy, today expressed in the rhetoric of anticommunitarianism, is more broadly inscribed in an immunological vision of the nation, a vision that promotes the institution of marriage itself. Marriage, in fact, is entirely elaborated around principles of exclusiveness (noninterchangeable roles, faithfulness, lineage). Queer theory proposes a reading of belonging that challenges the notion of exclusiveness because it describes how minority lives are caught up in multiple spaces, memories, emotions and, ultimately, identities. Opponents of the Taubira Act believed that extending marriage to gay couples meant pulling down one of the main barriers protecting them from nonexclusive cultures.

How, then, should we conceptualize the notion of community? In the wake of Maurice Blanchot, several intellectuals have attempted to propose a notion of community freed from its familial, nationalist trappings. This notion of community would be compatible with a universalist framework without necessarily being essentialist in the manner of the myth of "communism" and the abolition of class. Those intellectuals include Jean-Luc Nancy, who describes a community as unavowable, negative, idle. A community is an ever-elusive shadow—the underside of life. What we have in common is having nothing in common except death (commonality dies with the individual, at the very moment it appears attainable). Such a philosophy nevertheless remains warped by a major conceptual oversight: minorities do not have the luxury of experiencing idleness the way that majorities do because minorities do not benefit from the same degree of institutionalization, and given the relationship of domination that has produced them, they must manufacture vernacular references to which they simultaneously refuse to be limited.[8] For minorities, the community is less an unattainable horizon than a critical reflection on their practices. The latter oblige us to jointly reconceptualize belonging and representation. I argue for a minority philosophy in which presence in the social world requires no delegation of power but starts from the principle that we already carry within ourselves the voices of minoritized subjects.

On September 23, 2014, the former conservative French prime minister Alain Juppé commented on gay marriage: "Let's focus on the real issues. . . . Let's put aside debates that ultimately concern only minorities."[9] I have taken precisely the opposite tack. A minority democracy does not imply reversing the numerical relationship between the most and least numerous, replacing one norm by another, a move some philosophers would dub the "tyranny of minorities."[10] On the contrary, minority democracy involves recognition of the minority aspect of all practices of majority government. The philosopher Nicolas de Condorcet demonstrated that once a choice is no longer reduced to a binary (for/against, yes/no), no decision is mathematically possible; in other words, it is possible to prefer A to B, B to C, and simultaneously C to A. The complexity is paradoxical because it yields combinations that are coherent in isolation yet contradictory on a macropolitical level. Condorcet did not therefore reject decision making by majority vote; instead, he drew attention to the fact that a majority is nothing other than the imperfect and temporary accumulation of minority experiences.[11] Acknowledging this aspect of every political system rather than seeking to overcome it through transcendental symbols is a crucial task for LGBT people because, however full their legal recognition may be, they will nevertheless remain a numerical minority. It is not only a question of compensating for discrimination (the liberal approach par excellence), of recognizing cultural identities (the multicultural approach), or of allocating specific spheres (a community-based approach) but also of constantly challenging the rule itself. This means conceptualizing norms based on the critical experience of minorities who, given their relationship to the majority context, must continue to critique themselves.

Unlike certain writers, I claim no ideal generic content based on minority experiences. Like all social groups, the homosexual community is full of contradictions. There is no reason to assume it will provide society with "good" values or "bad" ones.[12] "The evidence of experience" is an obstacle to self-reflexiveness and might thereby represent a thoroughly haphazard principle of government.[13] My plea for a minority democracy therefore refuses to view the emergence of new social movements as an emancipatory factor in and of itself. Placing oneself on the side of the governed, of course, allows us to hear voices previously drowned out by national anthems, official discourse, and majority views. But thinking that minority expression alone suffices to transform norms can be counterproductive: hoping that the spontaneous uprising of minorities against all forms of subordination (such as ethnocentrism, nationalism, and capitalism) will overwhelm the powers that be means refusing to see that minorities themselves contribute to the political field that constrains them.[14]

Today in both France and America many queer theorists denounce gay and lesbian complicity in majority norms by invoking notions of global gayness, homonationalism, homonormativity, or pinkwashing. This exercise in public debate is highly profitable because it allows people to keep an eye on critique itself, to denounce abuses by a minority that has constituted itself through a critique of majority norms yet can eventually adopt what it has battled. That denunciation, though, may paradoxically idealize minority experiences, which are always and immediately informed by majority norms. Taking that radical stance entails essentializing minority experiences and then assigning minorities a subversive function that they do not assign to themselves in order to later denounce their abuses. But which homosexuality are we talking about? Which nationalism are we discussing? When this type of critique rests on a belief in the spontaneity and communion of minority struggles, it tends to efface their specificities and "to place all kinds of oppression and domination in the same bag, and [to employ] a single tool for dealing with them, such as 'anarchy' or 'intersectionality.'"[15] Although conservative abuses obviously require deconstruction, ascribing their cause to some essence—the "homo" in homonationalism, the "pink" in pinkwashing—constitutes a major stumbling block for any queer analysis.

A queer reading of norms entails an insistence on the multipositional nature of minorities. This is an approach already advocated by the Front Homosexuel d'Action Révolutionnaire in a special issue of the magazine *Vive la révolution*, subtitled *Tout* (Everything). "What do we want?" was asked in the April 21, 1971 issue. "Everything!" was the reply. Today, a gay man who defines himself in a relation of sisterhood with other male homosexuals may simultaneously and accurately define himself as the father of a child, for whom that specific relationship will be primordial. Children now live daily with several mothers and several fathers, whose roles are sometimes interchangeable and sometimes unique. Transsexual women become mothers by employing sperm they store before transitioning. These situations, to cite only a few, invent new forms of life that combine several types and levels of identity. They do not pit subversion against assimilation, a dichotomy that represents a trap for minorities, thwarting their inventiveness and restricting them to a dialectic of inside versus outside. We must rethink democracy in terms of multiple positions, points of passage, comings and goings. We must invent new rights that are at once personal (accruing to individuals) and relational (accruing to members of various communities). Multipositionality is part of a system of switching places, which calls for limits on the gaps between the lesser and better endowed in economic, social, and environmental capital. It is thus a question of class.

When we apply these reflections to this book's point of departure, the debate over the extension of marriage to homosexual couples in France, what emerges is an entirely different approach to the institution of matrimony: the deconstruction of that institution's hegemonic nature. Why does marriage bestow rights that do not come with other types of status? Why can't couples in civil unions adopt children jointly? Why does a childless married couple enjoy tax breaks denied to childless single individuals? Why should it be unthinkable to be married to one person and have a civil union with another? Why not be married to several people?[16] Because they redefine certain kinds of relationship to oneself and others, not because of some imaginary virtue or transcendental symbol, sexual minorities can lay the groundwork for a minority political system that recognizes multipositionality and is organized around the minority aspect of every majority.

Such a system would not be a new version of a Rawls-like "veil of ignorance" that would become more attentive to individual relationships. The multipositionality I am advocating is not the capacity to project oneself in an unknown situation under the hypothesis that one might one day experience it for oneself. That fiction is already the remit of Western legal systems. Rather, I am beginning here from the idea that we are constituted by the lives of the others in us. I am therefore arguing for a much more demanding political system, one that makes it possible to hold several personal statuses simultaneously, recognize collective rights, organize representation as a provisional form of delegation based on the resonance of "unlived lives," avoid major divergences in resources among individuals and groups of individuals, and recognize that a critique of belonging lies at the very core of citizenship. This minority democracy implies the deconstruction of the very norms that it produces, including the knowledge that stems from such deconstruction.[17] This does not mean that we must incessantly rewrite the rules of the game.[18] But minority democracy requires us to identify and eliminate the many appropriations of speech, rights, resources, and ultimately power; to hold out against the empire of majority norms by working to make them undecipherable;[19] to allot ourselves the space and time to allow our queerness to live.

trine of the Faith, to the Bishops of the Catholic Church on the Collaboration of Men and Women in the Church and in the World," May 31, 2004, http://www.vatican.va/roman_curia/congregations/cfaith/documents/rc_con_cfaith_doc_20040731_collaboration_en.html.

24. See the Pontifical Council's detailed report on the "ideology of gender": *Lexicon: Ambiguous and Debatable Terms regarding Family Life and Ethical Questions* (Vatican: Human Life International, 2006).

25. Ulrich Beck, *Risk Society: Towards a New Modernity* (London: Sage, 1992).

26. Although John Chrysostom, Saint Augustine, and, later, Saint Peter Damian issued moral condemnations of sodomy, it was above all Thomas Aquinas who transformed it into a veritable question of faith. By comparing sodomy to bestiality, he permanently furnished Christian theology with a rhetoric of nature and of unnatural acts. See John Boswell, *Christianity, Social Tolerance, and Homosexuality* (Chicago: University of Chicago Press, 1980), 311 ff. See also Daniel Borrillo and Dominique Colas, *L'Homosexualité de Platon à Foucault* (Paris: Plon, 2005), 114–23.

27. "Pope: Who Am I to Judge Gay People?," BBC News, July 29, 2013, http://www.bbc.co.uk/news/world-europe-23489702.

28. Ben Tufft, "Pope Francis Warns that Same-Sex Marriage 'Threatens the Family' and 'Disfigures God's Plan for Creation,'" *The Independent*, January 18, 2015.

29. Joshua J. McElwee, "Francis Strongly Criticizes Gender Theory, Comparing It to Nuclear Arms," February 13, 2005, http://ncronline.org/news/vatican/francis-strongly-criticizes-gender-theory-comparing-nuclear-arms.

30. Mary Anne Case, "The Role of the Popes in the Invention of Complementarity and the Vatican's Anathematization of Gender," *Public Law and Legal Theory Working Papers*, no. 565 (2016): 1–17.

31. Doris Buss, "Robes, Relics and Rights: The Vatican and the Beijing Conference on Women," *Social & Legal Studies* 7, no. 3 (1998): 339–63.

32. Doris E. Buss, "Finding the Homosexual in Women's Rights," *International Feminist Journal of Politics* 6, no. 2 (2004): 257–84; Doris Buss and Didi Herman, *Globalizing Family Values: The Christian Right in International Politics* (Minneapolis: University of Minnesota Press, 2003), 115.

33. Dale O'Leary, *The Gender Agenda: Redefining Equality* (Lafayette, LA: Vital Issues Press, 1997).

34. The scientific inaccuracy of Burggraf's reasoning has been demonstrated by sociologist Odile Fillod: "L'invention de la 'théorie du genre': le mariage blanc du Vatican et de la science," *Contemporary French Civilization* 39, no. 3 (2014): 327–30.

35. Monsignor Anatrella, "La théorie du genre et l'origine de l'homosexualité," *ZENIT–Le Monde vu de Rome*, June 5, 2012, http://www.zenit.org/fr/articles/la-theorie-du-genre-et-l-origine-de-l-homosexualite-par-mgr-anatrella.

36. Michel Schooyans, *The Gospel Confronting World Disorder*, trans. John H. Miller (St. Louis, MO: Central Bureau CCVA, 1999); Michel Schooyans, *The Hidden Face of the United Nations* (St. Louis, MO: Central Bureau CCVA, 2001).

37. Anthony Favier, "La réception catholique des études de genre: le genre, ap-

proches dépassionnées d'un débat," Archives-ouvertes, September 2012, https://halshs. archives-ouvertes.fr/halshs-00765786/document.

38. Marguerite A. Peeters, *Le Gender, une norme mondiale? Pour un discernement* (Paris: Mame, 2013), 7, 17, 18.

39. Ibid., 31.

40. Ibid., 35.

41. "Gender theory is now carrying out a decisive escalation by transforming itself into queer theory" (ibid., 2).

42. "2008 Joint Statement," ARC International, December 18, 2008, http://arc-international.net/global-advocacy/sogi-statements/2008-joint-statement.

43. "Syrian Statement: Response to SOGI Human Rights Statement," December 18, 2008, http://arc-international.net/global-advocacy/sogi-statements/syrian-statement.

44. As shown by David Paternotte, there are multiple motives behind mobilizations against gender theory. Not only is the Catholic Church a multilevel institution, but Catholic activist groups also used the Taubira Act to revive their networks (against abortion, for instance). However, their discourses and practices were indubitably imbued with the rhetoric of the Vatican hierarchs. See David Paternotte, "Habemus Gender! Autopsie d'une obsession vaticane," *Sextant*, no. 31 (January 2016): 17–18.

45. "(Le Baiser de la lune:) lutte contre l'homophobie ou contre l'hétérosexualité?," *Causeur*, February 8, 2010.

46. For a complete history of the polemic over gender in textbooks, see Odile Fillod, "Genre et SVT: copie à revoir," *Allodoxia* (blog), August, 15, 2012, http://allodoxia. blog.lemonde.fr/2012/08/15/genre-svt/.

47. "Programme d'enseignement spécifique de sciences de la vie et de la terre en classe de première de la série scientifique," *Journal Officiel*, September 30, 2010, http:// www.education.gouv.fr/cid53328/mene1019701a.htmlf ; and "Programme d'enseignement spécifique de sciences en classe de première des séries économique et sociale et littéraire," *Journal Officiel*, September 30, 2010, http://www.education.gouv.fr/cid53323/me ne1019645a.html.

48. Xavier Lacroix, "Le gender dans les programmes scolaires," in *L'Éducation à l'âge du "gender": construire ou déconstruire l'homme?*, ed. Michel Boyancé et al. (Paris: Salvator, 2013), 41–42.

49. Fillod, "L'Invention de la 'théorie du genre,'" 325, 326.

50. Tartakowsky, *Les Droites et la Rue*, 166.

51. "Mgr Barbarin contre le mariage gay: 'Le Parlement n'est pas Dieu le père,'" *Le Progrès*, August 13, 2012.

52. Vincent Trémolet de Villers and Raphaël Stainville, *Et la France se réveilla: enquête sur la révolution des valeurs* (Paris: L'Artilleur, 2013), 39ff. The two authors of this book—both journalists at the conservative *Figaro* newspaper—have written a celebration more than an analysis of the organizations opposing the Taubira Act. However, as conservatives close to Catholic circuits, they also gathered important factual data that they have made publicly available, which is the reason I cite their work here.

53. Mathieu Deslandes, "Anti-mariage gay: qui est la caution 'de gauche' de Frigide

Barjot?," *Rue89*, January 9, 2013, http://www.rue89.com/2013/01/09/anti-mariage-gay
-qui-est-la-caution-de-gauche-de-frigide-barjot-238409.

54. Bongibault later compared supporters of the Taubira Act to collaborators under
the Vichy regime, and François Hollande to Adolf Hitler. Giuseppe Di Bella, "Xavier
Bongibault dérape à propos de la rafle du Vel d'Hiv: scandaleux et ignoble!," *L'Obs Le
Plus* (blog), July 17, 2013, http://leplus.nouvelobs.com/contribution/908550-xavier-bon-
gibault-derape-a-propos-de-la-rafle-du-vel-d-hiv-scandaleux-et-ignoble.html.

55. Sophie Rétif, "Ringards, hypocrites et frustrés? Les militants des associations
familiales catholiques face à la réprobation," *Politix*, no. 106 (2014): 85–108.

56. Journalists Sylvain Mouillard and Kim Hullot-Guiot have provided a useful
overview of these networks in "Manif pour Tous, la vraie photo de famille," *Libération*,
September 13, 2013.

57. "Manifeste: au mariage pour tous, nous disons oui," *L'Obs*, January 24, 2013.

58. A document originating from the local Languedoc Roussillon chapter of Manif
pour Tous demonstrates the key role of religious networks in recruiting demonstrators
against the Taubira bill. The better to oppose "the ideology of minority groups," the
document detailed methods for getting to Paris (bus, train, car) and asked that its call to
action be largely distributed among "friends, clubs, associations, parish organizations,
and other communities, religious or not." *Manif pour Tous–Acte 10: la mobilisation, c'est
parti!*, December 6, 2012, http://www.afc-montpellier.org/documents/manifpourtous/
Email%20ACTE10%20-%2003dec12.pdf.

59. "Béatrice Bourges, l'autre égérie des anti-mariage gay," *Le Monde*, April 19, 2013.

60. "Le manifeste du Printemps Français," accessed May 18, 2016, https://www.face
book.com/media/set/?set=a.739657909500835.1073741884.275129749286989.

61. "'On ne lâche rien!' Manifeste du Printemps Français" (site discontinued).

62. "Frigide Barjot: 'Hollande veut du sang, il en aura!,'" *L'Obs*, April 12, 2013.

63. "Le Printemps français joue à l'arme secrète," *Le Monde*, May 22, 2013.

64. The bill was passed in the Sénat in an initial form on April 12, 2013, and filed that
same day with the Commission on Constitutional Laws. The final form was debated in
public session on April 17.

65. "Frigide Barjot fond en larmes en direct sur D8," Dailymotion, April 16,
2013, http://www.dailymotion.com/video/xz1zg9_frigide-barjot-fond-en-larmes-en
-direct-sur-d8_tv.

66. Karl Zéro, "Lettre à ma belle-soeur Frigide Barjot," *Le Huffington Post*, April 15,
2013, http://www.huffingtonpost.fr/karl-zero/lettre-ouverte-frigide-barjot_b_3081428.
html.

67. "Ludovine de La Rochère: 'La Manif pour Tous poursuivra sa dynamique.
Nous ne lâcherons rien,'" *Atlantico.fr*, May 26, 2013, http://www.atlantico.fr/decryptage/
ludovine-rochere-manif-pour-tous-poursuivra-dynamique-ne-lacherons-rien-737166
.html.

68. "Lancement du Grenelle de la famille," La Manif pour Tous, September 15,
2013, http://www.lamanifpourtous.fr/actualites/lancement-du-grenelle-de-la-famille;
"2e Université d'été de la Manif pour Tous: Bronzez intelligent," La Manif pour Tous,

July 29, 2014, http://www.lamanifpourtous.fr/actualites/2e-universite-d-ete-de-la-manif
-pour-tous-bronzez-intelligent.

69. "Manif pour Tous: querelle de chiffres sur la mobilisation à Paris," *L'Obs*, October 5, 2014.

70. See John D. McCarthy and Mayer N. Zald, "Resource Mobilization and Social Movements: A Partial Theory," *American Journal of Sociology* 82, no. 6 (May 1, 1977): 1212–41.

71. "La Manif pour Tous (Français de l'étranger)," Facebook, accessed February 7, 2015, https://www.facebook.com/LaManifPourTousFDE.

72. Henrik Lindell, *Les Veilleurs: enquête sur une résistance* (Paris: Salvator, 2014), 71–107. Lindell, who is a journalist at Radio Notre Dame (a conservative Catholic radio station), has written a very indulgent book on Les Veilleurs—I cite it here only for the accounts and comments he has transcribed.

73. Sarah D., "Taubira à la Sorbonne: prise en otage du débat," YouTube, March 18, 2013, https://www.youtube.com/watch?v=by-_sQ6Ooek&feature=youtube_gdata_player.

74. Lindell, *Les Veilleurs*, 69.

75. "Anti-mariage pour tous: *Les Veilleurs pour la famille*" de Nice, YouTube, April 26, 2013, https://www.youtube.com/watch?v=654y-YsJc-I&feature=youtube_gdata_player.

76. "Mariage pour tous," gender . . . coup de gueule du Père Daniel-Ange," YouTube, June 3, 2013, https://www.youtube.com/watch?v=VGygGgq_4r0&feature=youtube_gdata_player.

77. Le Manifeste des Antigones, accessed February 16, 2015, http://lesantigones.fr/manifeste-antigones/.

78. Ibid.

79. In French republican symbolism, a man's "unveiling" of a woman is associated with a quest for truth. The Hommen's reaction was therefore aimed less at the Femen's nudity than at the fact that the baring was the women's own doing. On the relationship between nudity and truth in the public sphere, see Geneviève Fraisse, *Les Excès du genre. Concept, image, nudité* (Paris: Lignes, 2014), 75–76.

80. Hommen–Officiel, accessed February 16, 2015, http://hommen-officiel.tumblr.com/?og=1.

81. Pierre Bourdieu, *Masculine Domination*, trans. Richard Nice (Stanford, CA: Stanford University Press, 2001), 56.

82. See Eve Sedgwick's study of this homosocial paranoia, *Between Men: English Literature and Male Homosocial Desire* (New York: Columbia University Press, 1985).

83. The ambivalent relationship to gender was not limited to the youngest activists. Leaders of the main movements opposing the Taubira Act were mainly women who unhesitatingly altered standards of femininity in the public sphere, notably when taking the floor. Ludovine de la Rochère was also called "Ludo" by her friends, a typically male nickname for Ludovic.

84. Bloc Identitaire, Facebook, accessed February 17, 2015, https://www.facebook.com/blocidentitaire.

85. The Action Française movement was founded in 1899 in the context of the Drey-

fus affair. Denouncing Jewish elites and left-wing intellectuals, Action Française took a monarchist and counterrevolutionary turn under the influence of Charles Maurras. Advocating for Roman Catholicism as a factor of social cohesion, Action Française gained influence among young people thanks to its youth movement, Les Camelots du Roi. In 1926, Pope Pius XI condemned Action Française, which competed with the Church's institutional and spiritual power.

86. Gaël Brustier, *Le Mai 68 conservateur* (Paris: Cerf, 2014), 98.

87. See, for example, Christopher Lannes, "Sommes-nous en février 1934?," *Le Bréviaire des Patriotes*, February 7, 2014, http://www.lebreviairedespatriotes.fr/07/02/2014/histoire/sommes-nous-en-fevrier-1934/.

88. See Camille Pollet, "6 Février 1934 et 'Printemps Français' 2013: le parallèle a ses limites," *Rue89*, April 22, 2013, http://blogs.rue89.nouvelobs.com/echos-histoire/2013/04/22/6-fevrier-1934-et-printemps-francais-2013-le-parallele-ses-limites-230177.

89. Danielle Tartakowsky, "Un parfum d'années 30?," *Le Huffington Post*, February 6, 2014, http://www.huffingtonpost.fr/danielle-tartakowsky/6-fevrier-manif-pour-tous_b_4728489.html.

90. In the 1930s the Vatican had kept its distance from Charles Maurras, who was not a believer and invoked the Church only for its moral authority over the French right.

91. Brustier, *Le Mai 68 conservateur*, 10.

92. "Allocation familiale: pourquoi la réforme va couper la France en deux," La Manif pour Tous, October 22, 2014, http://www.lamanifpourtous.fr/la-presse-en-parle/allocation-familiale-pourquoi-la-reforme-va-couper-la-france-en-deux.

93. Brustier, *Le Mai 68 conservateur*, 10.

94. "Une demande de discrétion religieuse dans la vie collective," *Sociovision*, November 2014, http://www.west-info.eu/french-dont-want-religious-symblos-in-schools-and-offices/socio-2/.

95. Alain Renon, "Une prière du 15 août très politique en France," *RFI*, August 15, 2012, http://www.rfi.fr/france/20120814-une-priere-15-aout-tres-politique-france/.

96. Villers and Stainville, *Et la France se réveilla*, 115.

97. "L'entretien du Cardinal," February 1, 2013, http://www.paris.catholique.fr/L-entretien-du-cardinal-du-samedi,26418.html (the interview is erroneously dated February 1, 2015).

98. Céline Béraud, "Un front commun des religions contre le mariage pour tous?," *Contemporary French Civilization* 39, no. 3 (2014): 339.

99. Assemblée des Évêques Orthodoxes de France, "Communiqué," October 2, 2012, http://www.aeof.fr/uploads/files/AEOF-CommuniqueReunionPeriodiqueOctobre2012.pdf; Conseil de la Fédération Protestante de France à propos du "mariage pour tous," October 13, 2012, http://www.protestants.org/?id=33257.

100. "Mariage gay: le grand rabbin de France dénonce un cheval de Troie," *Le Monde*, October 26, 2012.

101. Conseil Français du Culte Musulman, "À propos du projet de loi 'Mariage pour tous,'" November 2012, http://www.lecfcm.fr/?p=3127.

102. "Mariage homo: l'UOIF y voit un 'risque de zoophilie,'" *L'Obs*, November 15, 2012.

103. "Mariage pour tous: résumé de l'audition des représentants de culte," *La Chaine Parlementaire*, November 29, 2012, http://www.lcp.fr/videos/reportages/142825-mariage-pour-tous-resume-de-l-audition-des-representants-de-culte (site discontinued).

104. "Audition de Mme Marie-Stella Boussemart," Sénat, February 12, 2013, http://www.senat.fr/compte-rendu-commissions/20130211/lois.html#toc5.

105. Ramsès Kefi, "À la Manif pour Tous: 'C'est bien que vous soyez là, les Musulmans: nous, on est trop gentils,'" *Rue89*, February 2, 2014, http://rue89.nouvelobs.com/2014/02/02/cest-bien-les-musulmans-soyez-est-trop-gentils-249576.

106. "Audition de M. Gilles Bernheim," Sénat, February 12, 2013, http://www.senat.fr/compte-rendu-commissions/20130211/lois.html#toc4.

107. For a full account of this development, see Brustier, *Le Mai 68 conservateur*, 103–24.

108. "'Manif pour Tous,' la grande illusion," *Le Monde*, March 21, 2013.

109. Nolwenn Le Blevennec, "À Paray-Le-Monial, étrange séminaire plutôt que grand complot," *Rue89*, January 13, 2013, http://www.rue89.com/2013/01/13/paray-le-monial-etrange-seminaire-plutot-que-grand-complot-238553.

110. "Le député UMP Christian Vanneste condamné en appel pour homophobie," *Le Monde*, January 26, 2007.

111. Nicolas Sarkozy extensively borrowed this rhetoric during his 2014 campaign to regain the leadership of the UMP. First explaining that "'marriage for all' has humiliated the family," he went on to say he would not "use families against homosexuals the way homosexuals were used against families," thereby rejecting the very possibility that homosexual families might be considered as such. Television interview, France 2, September 21, 2014.

112. "Manif pour Tous: 'Le gouvernement ne nous entend pas, ne nous voit pas et ne nous compte pas," *Libération*, February 2, 2014.

113. Lindell, *Les Veilleurs*, 22.

114. "Interpellations et gardes à vues abusives: la réaction des portes paroles et des avocats de LMPT," La Manif pour Tous, June 4, 2013, http://www.lamanifpourtous.fr/actualites/interpellations-et-gardes-a-vues-abusives-la-reaction-des-portes-paroles-et-des-avocats-de-lmpt.

115. Liberté pour Tous, accessed February 7, 2015, http://www.libertepourtous.fr/.

116. "Débordements à la fin de la Manif pour Tous," *Le Huffington Post*, April 24, 2013, http://www.huffingtonpost.fr/2013/04/23/mariage-gay-debordements-fin-manif-pour-tous_n_3142181.html.

117. "La Manif pour Tous déboutée ce matin au tribunal," *L'Écho Républicain*, February 17, 2014. See also "Les anti-mariage gay qui poursuivaient l'État déboutés," *Le Parisien*, July 25, 2014.

118. Such is the case concerning essayist Jean-Yves le Gallou, who came up with the theory of "national preference" for the Front National and was formerly an activist in the Parti Républicain. He promotes the struggle against "the dictatorship of minorities" that "cling to and prop up one another," that is, "sexual minorities," "grant-aided associations," "ethnic and religious" minorities, and "media [and] parliamentary" minorities.

Jean-Yves Le Gallou, "La radicalité contre la dictature des minorités," *Polemia*, April 14, 2013, http://www.polemia.com/la-radicalite-contre-la-dictature-des-minorites.

119. "'On ne lâche rien!' Manifeste du Printemps Français."

120. Michel Boyancé et al., eds., *L'Éducation à l'âge du "gender"* (Paris: Salvator, 2013), 8.

121. Les Veilleurs de Reims, Facebook, January 17, 2014, https://www.facebook.com/permalink.php?id=445705972186971&story_fbid=568176276606606.

122. Quoted in Lindell, *Les Veilleurs*, 39.

123. Parité dans le mariage, Facebook, accessed July 10, 2015, https://www.facebook.com/Parit%C3%A9-dans-le-mariage-489045111119950/.

124. Françoise Gaspard, Claude Servan-Schreiber, and Anne Le Gall, *Au Pouvoir citoyennes! Liberté, égalité, parité* (Paris: Seuil, 1992).

125. On this issue, see Joan Wallach Scott, *Parité! Sexual Equality and the Crisis of French Universalism* (Chicago: University of Chicago Press, 2005).

126. Sylviane Agacinski, *Corps en miettes* (Paris: Flammarion, 2009). For further analysis, see Chapter 4, "The Specter of Queer Theatricality."

127. "Élections européennes 2014: La Manif pour Tous lance l'opération Europe for Family . . . ," La Manif pour Tous, April 28, 2014, http://www.lamanifpourtous.fr/actualites/elections-europeennes-2014-la-manif-pour-tous-lance-l-operation-europe-for-family-pour-une-europe-au-service-de-la-famille.

128. "Élections internes des partis: choisissez le bon candidat!," La Manif pour Tous, June 24, 2014, http://www.lamanifpourtous.fr/c25-du-cote-des-elus/elections-internes-des-partis-choisissez-le-bon-candidat.

129. "Charte des municipales," accessed February 18, 2015, http://www.chartedesmunicipales.fr/.

130. Manif pour Tous, Twitter, December 13, 2015, 4 :00 p.m., https://twitter.com/LaManifPourTous.

131. "Comment la Manif pour Tous veut faire plier Sarkozy et l'UMP," *L'Obs*, October 5, 2014.

132. Jack A. Goldstone, "Bridging Institutionalized and Noninstitutionalized Politics," in *States, Parties, and Social Movements*, ed. Jack A. Goldstone (Cambridge: Cambridge University Press, 2003), 1–24.

133. Nina Eliasoph and Paul Lichterman, "Culture in Interaction," *American Journal of Sociology* 108, no. 4 (January 2003): 735–94.

134. "Une antenne de la Manif pour Tous à l'UMP," *Le Figaro*, April 29, 2014.

135. "La Manif pour Tous–Paris," YouTube, March 24, 2013, https://www.youtube.com/watch?v=VlA6skcWZqI&feature=youtube_gdata_player.

136. "Les Gays, à l'extrême-droite, toute?," *Têtu*, January 2015, 48–51.

137. Le Petit Journal, Canal Plus, June 4, 2015, http://www.canalplus.fr/c-divertissement/c-le-petit-journal/pid6515-emission.html?vid=1272938.

138. Alain Degenne, "Un langage pour l'analyse des réseaux sociaux," in *L'Esprit des lieux. Localité et changement social en France* (Paris: Éditions du CNRS, 1986), 291–312.

139. "Sens Commun lance son manifeste: la droite que nous voulons!," Sens Com-

mun, April 30, 2014, http://senscommun.fr/sens-commun-lance-son-manifeste-la-droite-que-nous-voulons/.

140. "Une militante de la Manif pour Tous nommée secrétaire nationale à l'UMP," *Le Monde*, December 12, 2014.

141. Camping pour Tous, inspired by the conservative Scout movement and religious pilgrimages, organized camp outings on the fringes of Manif pour Tous. The association is noteworthy for its rhetorical vehemence (racist insinuations on its Facebook page, support for Jacques Bompard, a former founding member of the Front National). Accessed February 17, 2015, https://www.facebook.com/CampingPourTous2.

142. See "La Manif pour Tous devient un parti politique," *Le Monde*, April 24, 2015.

143. François Hollande, press conference, November 14, 2012.

144. The hearings are available on the Assemblée Nationale website, accessed February 7, 2015, http://www.assemblee-nationale.fr/14/dossiers/mariage_personnes_meme_sexe.asp; "Hollande reçoit les associations opposées au mariage gay," *L'Express*, January 25, 2013.

145. On the media as an interface where social movements and institutions can clash and simultaneously recognize one another, see Steven F. Cohn and James E. Gallagher, "Gay Movements and Legal Change: Some Aspects of the Dynamics of a Social Problem," *Social Problems* 32, no. 1 (October 1, 1984): 72–86.

146. "Mariage gay: Ségolène Royal aurait préféré une 'union civile' sans le mot 'mariage,'" *Le Huffington Post*, May 25, 2013, http://www.huffingtonpost.fr/2013/05/25/mariage-gay-segolene-royal-prefere-union-civile-sans-mot-mariage_n_3336473.html.

147. Quoted in "Mariage pour tous, les députés socialistes veulent revenir aux 'vrais sujets,'" *Le Figaro*, April 23, 2013.

148. "Patrick Mennucci: 'Le mariage pour tous nous a coûté des voix,'" *Le Monde*, April 1, 2014.

149. Éric Fassin, *L'Inversion de la question homosexuelle* (Paris: Éditions Amsterdam, 2005). See Chapter 4, "The Specter of 'Sameness.'"

150. No. 344, Assemblée Nationale, Accessed January 5, 2016, http://www.assemblee-nationale.fr/14/projets/pl0344.asp.

151. Christiane Taubira resigned on January 27, 2015, to express her disagreement with the restrictions to civil liberties enforced by the Valls government following the Paris attacks in November 2015.

152. *Bulletin officiel du ministère de la justice*, no. 2013-05, May 31, 2013. http://www.textes.justice.gouv.fr/art_pix/JUSC1312445C.pdf.

153. Declaration by President Hollande on May 28, 2013. Referral of the question to the Comité Consultatif National d'Éthique effectively killed extension of MAP. Since it was founded in 1983, the National Ethics Commission has tended to restrict use of procreative techniques to situations of medical infertility that presuppose the "potential fertility" of the couple. Thus, the relevant French law of 1994, which is the direct result of the commission's deliberations, excludes recourse to MAP by single people and homosexual couples. In 2005, in Opinion 90, the commission stated that "the deliberately asexual term 'homoparenthood' denies any significant difference between the sexes.

What is at stake here are the paternal and maternal roles and their complementarity in nurturing kinship relations that are humanly edifying [*sic*]." See "Comité National d'Éthique, gardien de la famille?," *Libération*, February 6, 2013.

154. See the statement made by Sergio Coronado, a legislator for the green coalition Europe Ecologie–Les Verts, from the podium of the Assemblée Nationale on the first day of public debate, January 29, 2013. See http://www.assemblee-nationale.fr/14/cri /2012-2013/20130119.asp.

155. Bruno Perreau, "The Political Economy of 'Marriage for All,'" *Contemporary French Civilization* 39, no. 3 (2014): 351–67.

156. "Jean-Marc Ayrault: 'Je ne veux pas réformer en passant en force,'" *20 Minutes*, April 25, 2013.

157. Quoted in "Mariage pour tous, les députés socialistes veulent revenir aux 'vrais sujets.'"

158. "Entretien avec Philippe Meunier, député UMP du Rhône: 'Le mariage pour tous est un caprice de bobo,'" *Minutes*, September 19, 2012.

159. Nico Sifra Quintana, Josh Rosenthal, and Jeff Krehely, "On the Streets: The Federal Response to Gay and Transgender Homeless Youth," June 21, 2013, https://www .americanprogress.org/issues/lgbt/report/2010/06/21/7983/on-the-streets/. See also M. V. Lee Badgett, Laura E. Durso, and Alyssa Schneebaum, "New Patterns of Poverty in the Lesbian, Gay, and Bisexual Community," June 2013, http://williamsinstitute.law .ucla.edu/wp-content/uploads/LGB-Poverty-Update-Jun-2013.pdf.

160. Marie-Thérèse Lanquetin, Marie-Thérèse Letablier, and Hélène Périvier, "Acquisition des droits sociaux et égalité entre les femmes et les hommes," *Revue de l'OFCE* 90, no. 3 (2004): 461–88.

161. Once again this reading of *Les Misérables* is a little hasty, since Javert ultimately realizes that Jean Valjean is a good man. Wracked with remorse for having wrongly persecuted him, Javert commits suicide.

162. "Manif pour Tous: des enfants bouclier contre les CRS," YouTube, March 26, 2013, https://www.youtube.com/watch?v=dfsn-F5LoSo&feature=youtube_gdata_player.

163. Bruno Perreau, *The Politics of Adoption: Gender and the Making of French Citizenship*, trans. Deke Dusinberre (Cambridge, MA: MIT Press, 2014). I return to this point, notably on the role played by expertise, in Chapter 4.

164. Daniel Borrillo, "Biologie et filiation: les habits neufs de l'ordre naturel," *Contemporary French Civilization* 39, no. 3 (2014): 303–19.

165. "Zapping TV du 28 mai 2013 . . . ," Dailymotion, May 28, 2013, http://www.daily motion.com/video/x10am3u_zapping-tv-du-28-mai-2013-le-derapage-d-une-manifes tante-anti-mariage-gay-au-petit-journal_news.

166. "Circulaire du 25 janvier 2013 relative à la délivrance des certificats de nationalité française," January 25, 2013, http://www.textes.justice.gouv.fr/art_pix/JUSC1301528C.pdf.

167. Conseil d'État, decision "Association Juristes pour l'Enfance et Autres," December 12, 2014, http://www.conseil-etat.fr/Decisions-Avis-Publications/Decisions /Selection-des-decisions-faisant-l-objet-d-une-communication-particuliere/CE -12-decembre-2014-Association-Juristes-pour-l-enfance-et-autres.

168. "Circulaire Taubira: Un passeport pour la GPA," La Manif pour Tous, December 12, 2014, http://www.lamanifpourtous.fr/actualites/circulaire-taubira-un-passeport-pour-la-gpa/ (emphasis added).

169. Cour de Cassation, decision 619, July 3, 2015, https://www.courdecassation.fr/jurisprudence_2/assemblee_pleniere_22/619_3_32230.html.

170. "GPA: les enfants nés à l'étranger pourront être inscrits à l'état civil," Le Monde, July 3, 2015.

171. "GPA: la Manif pour Tous écrit à Manuel Valls," Le Figaro, October 8, 2014.

172. In relation to Germany, see Sabine Hark and Paula-Irene Villa, eds., (Anti-)Genderismus: Sexualität Und Geschlecht Als Schauplätze Aktueller Politischer Auseinandersetzungen (Bielefeld: Transcript, 2015); in relation to Poland, see Magdalena Grabowska, "Between Gender Studies and 'Gender Ideology': Gender Education in Post-1989 Poland," in Materials of the Second International Gender Workshop "Overcoming Gender Backlash: Experiences of Ukraine, Belarus, Russia, Georgia, Armenia and Poland" (Warsaw: Heinrich Böll Stiftung, 2013), 43–50.

173. Paternotte, "Habemus Gender!," 12–13.

174. David Paternotte, "Blessing the Crowds: Catholic Mobilisations against Gender in Europe," in Hark and Villa, (Anti-)Genderismus, 129–47.

175. Sara Garbagnoli, "Le Vatican contre la dénaturalisation de l'ordre sexuel: structure et enjeux d'un discours institutionnel réactionnaire," Synergies Italie 10 (2014): 145–67.

176. "Ludovine de La Rochère—Demo Für Alle—Stuttgart," YouTube, March 23, 2015, https://www.youtube.com/watch?v=nHNQDopl858&feature=youtube_gdata_player.

177. Phillip M. Ayoub, "With Arms Wide Shut: Threat Perception, Norm Reception, and Mobilized Resistance to LGBT Rights," Journal of Human Rights 13, no. 3 (2014): 337–62.

178. René Poujol, "Reçue à Moscou, la Manif pour Tous en voie de poutinisation," Rue89, March 29, 2014, http://rue89.nouvelobs.com/2014/03/29/manif-tous-voie-poutinisation-251066.

179. Ludovine de la Rochère, "La Manif pour Tous et Poutine: droit de réponse de Ludovine de La Rochère," Rue89, April 1, 2014, http://rue89.nouvelobs.com/2014/04/01/manif-tous-poutine-droit-reponse-ludovine-rochere-251157.

180. "Russia Flies 'Straight Flag' to Combat 'Gay Fever,'" Huffington Post UK, July 9, 2015, http://www.huffingtonpost.co.uk/2015/07/09/russia-flies-straight-flag-to-combat-gay-fever_n_7760252.html.

181. For example, see the comments by far-right pundit Alain Soral in a videotaped discussion of "activist minorities" (minorités agissantes), "Les minorités agissantes expliquées par Alain Soral," YouTube, July 2, 2013, https://www.youtube.com/watch?v=V4a4RR3ngGM.

182. Florence Tamagne, "Caricatures homophobes et stéréotypes de genre en France et en Allemagne: la presse satirique, de 1900 au milieu des années 1930," Le Temps des Médias, no. 1 (2003): 42–53.

183. Chapter 4 places the fantasy of betrayal and gender deviation in a historical perspective.

184. Marina Allal, "Antisémitisme, hiérarchies nationales et de genre. Reproduction et réinterprétation des rapports de pouvoir," *Raisons Politiques* 24 (2006): 135.

185. "Théorie du genre: Judith Butler répond à ses détracteurs," *L'Obs*, December 15, 2013.

186. See comments made by Claude Timmerman, a lecturer linked to far-right and royalist groups, at a symposium organized by the Centre d'Études et de Prospectives sur la Science (an organization that seeks to reconcile "faith" and "science"), hosted by the convent of Saint-Gildard in Nevers on October 1–2, 2011. Timmerman stated that "gender theory is an ethnic theory that is trying to legitimize homosexuality. Period. It is the product, exclusively the product, of American Jewish lesbians." "Théorie du genre, théorie de lesbiennes juives américaines," YouTube, February 2, 2014, http://www.you tube.com/watch?v=w8esfEoqLkE.

187. "Marriage March 2014 in Washington DC," YouTube, June 19, 2014, http://www .youtube.com/watch?v=gKqhCluosHE#t=4517.

188. See Pierre Birnbaum, *Sur un Nouveau Moment antisémite: "Jour de colère"* (Paris: Fayard, 2015).

189. See "Dieudonné: énorme quenelle à la théorie du genre," YouTube, May 10, 2014, http://www.youtube.com/watch?v=CsmF3CQHMWQ.

190. Natacha Chetcuti, "Quand les questions de genre et d'homosexualités deviennent un enjeu républicain," *Les Temps Modernes* 678, no. 2 (2014): 249.

191. There are many videos that rail against gender theory, including Berny Marrakchy, "La théorie du genre par Belkacem (arabe ou juive?) des africains et LGBT," YouTube, February 3, 2014, http://www.youtube.com/watch?v=hazDGdBlOmA.

192. Pursuing the "human ecology" theme, Pope Benedict XVI explained in 2008 that the family called for protection just as "rain forests" do. See "Address of His Holiness Benedict XVI to the Members of the Roman Curia," December 22, 2008, http:// w2.vatican.va/content/benedict-xvi/en/speeches/2008/december/documents/hf_ben -xvi_spe_20081222_curia-romana.html.

193. "Petit journal Civitas: y'a bon banania, y'a pas bon Taubira," YouTube, October 30, 2013, https://www.youtube.com/watch?v=gVqTcwLYjkM.

194. Melissa Nobles, *The Politics of Official Apologies* (New York: Cambridge University Press, 2008), x.

195. UMP senator Colette Giudicelli argued before the Sénat on April 9, 2013, that marriage for all "would open the way for other demands that are totally eccentric yet already exist, such as marriage with an object. In the United States an American woman married the Eiffel Tower; someone married himself, again in the U.S.; in Brazil three people got married; in Australia, they marry an animal." See "Mariage gay: la sénatrice UMP Colette Giudicelli lie mariage pour tous et mariage avec des objets," *Huffington Post*, April 10, 2013, http://www.huffingtonpost.fr/2013/04/10/colette-giudicelli-mariage -gay-mariage-objets_n_3053728.html.

196. Christopher Peterson refers to a "disavowal of human animality" in *Bestial Traces: Race, Sexuality, Animality* (New York: Fordham University Press, 2012), 7.

197. Richard Poirot, "Taubira traitée de 'guenon': la vidéo qui le prouve," *Liberation.fr*, November 2, 2013, http://www.liberation.fr/societe/2013/11/02/taubira-traitee-de -guenon-la-video-qui-le-prouve_944083.

198. "Taubira comparée à un singe: la condamnation annulée," *Liberation*, June 22, 2015.

199. "La Manif pour Tous 'horrifiée' par la nomination de Najat Vallaud-Belkacem," *Le Figaro*, August 26, 2014.

200. "Najat Vallaud-Belkacem, 'l'ayatollah,'" *Valeurs Actuelles*, September 4–10, 2014.

201. Mary Douglas, *Purity and Danger: An Analysis of Concepts of Pollution and Taboo* (London: Routledge, 1966), 3–4.

202. Kathryn Bond Stockton, *The Queer Child, or Growing Sideways in the Twentieth Century* (Durham, NC: Duke University Press, 2009), 17–27.

203. See the warning against gender theory issued by the Associations Familiales Catholiques: "Le Genre à l'école: parents, êtes-vous informés?," 2013, http://www.afc -france.org/attachments/article/1630/Tract%20AFC%20Genre%20rentr%C3%A9e%20 2013.pdf. See also an interview published by *La Croix* with Pascal Balmand, former education director of the diocese of Seine Saint-Denis and general secretary of the Catholic school system since 2013: "Les priorités de Pascal Balmand, nouveau patron de l'enseignement catholique," *La Croix*, August 25, 2013.

204. Quoted in "La Manif pour Tous, acte II," *Le Monde*, October 2, 2014.

205. Michel Onfray, "Chronique mensuelle no. 106," *Michel Onfray* (blog), March 2014, http://mo.michelonfray.fr/chroniques/la-chronique-mensuelle-de-michel -onfray-n-106-mar-2014/.

206. Luc Cédelle, "Le catéchisme 'antipédago,' le 'gender' et la nouvelle extrême droite soralo-dieudonniste," *Interro Écrite* (blog), January 24, 2014, http://education. blog.lemonde.fr/2014/01/24/le-catechisme-antipedago-le-gender-et-la-nouvelle-ex treme-droite-soralo-dieudonniste/.

207. "Cinq intox sur la 'théorie du genre,'" *Le Monde*, January 28, 2014.

208. "'Théorie du genre': l'appel au boycott qui alarme l'école," *Le Monde*, January 29, 2014.

209. Vigi Gender, accessed February 2, 2015, http://www.vigi-gender.fr.

210. "Les religions entendent calmer le jeu," *Le Figaro*, January 30, 2014.

211. "'Théorie' du genre: Aurélie Filippetti dénonce les pressions contre des bibliothèques," *Le Monde*, February 10, 2014.

212. "À Nantes, la Manif pour Tous scande son opposition à la 'Journée de la jupe,'" *Le Figaro*, May 15, 2014.

213. See the interview with the film's lead actress: "Isabelle Adjani: 'La journée de la jupe,'" YouTube, November 28, 2011, https://www.youtube.com/watch?v=A0xenDz9aOo.

214. Christine Bard, *Ce que soulève la jupe: identités, transgressions, résistances* (Paris: Autrement, 2010).

215. See, for example, "Les hommes sont-ils encore virils? Ce que veulent les femmes," *Psychologies Magazine*, November 2007.

216. Thibaud Collin, "La théorie du *genre*, une lecture critique," in *L'Éducation à l'âge du "gender"*, 26.

217. Ibid., 32–33.

218. Ibid., 33–34.

219. Working as a trainer in an underprivileged middle school, Natacha Chetcuti has analyzed the impact of opposition to "the primer on equality" program in training sessions on how to deal with sexist abuse. Natacha Chetcuti, "'Théorie du genre' et normes sexuelles. L'écho d'une polémique en milieu scolaire," *Politique de l'image* 9 (2014): 91–97.

220. Ted Brader, "Striking a Responsive Chord: How Political Ads Motivate and Persuade Voters by Appealing to Emotions," *American Journal of Political Science* 49, no. 2 (April 1, 2005): 388–405.

221. Bénédicte Mathieu, "'Le Petit Journal' s'offre Christine Boutin," *Yagg*, March 26, 2013, http://yagg.com/2013/03/26/le-petit-journal-soffre-christine-boutin/.

222. Chapter 2 focuses on queer movements themselves and discusses their reactions to Manif pour Tous.

223. "Manifestation pour le mariage gay et pour l'égalité de tous," YouTube, April 10, 2013, https://www.youtube.com/watch?v=jzhxFCRYGPs&feature=youtube_gdata_player.

224. Ouiouioui collective, accessed February 26, 2015, http://ouiouioui.org.

225. "Lesbian Kiss Steals Spotlight at French Anti-gay Parenting Protest," *France 24*, October 25, 2012, http://www.france24.com/en/20121024-lesbian-kiss-steals-spotlight-gay-parenting-protest-marseille-lgbt-marriage-france.

226. "Kiss-in contre l'homophobie devant l'Hôtel de Ville de Paris," YouTube, November 15, 2012, https://www.youtube.com/watch?v=8AQTX0uD5rU&feature=youtube_gdata_player.

227. "Kiss-in contre la Manif pour Tous," YouTube, October 6, 2014, https://www.youtube.com/watch?v=zmDmrUygknQ&feature=youtube_gdata_player.

228. Roman Kuhar and David Paternotte have reviewed efforts deployed in several European countries to come up with alternatives and/or reappropriate the rhetoric of gender theory. See Roman Kuhar and David Paternotte, *Gender Ideology: Mobilization of Conservative Groups against Gender Equality and Sexual Citizenship* (Budapest: Friedrich Ebert Stiftung, 2015).

229. "Mariage gay: après le kiss-in pour, au tour des manifs contre," *Atlantico*, November 16, 2012, http://www.atlantico.fr/pepitesvideo/mariage-gay-apres-kiss-pour-au-tour-manifs-contre-547135.html.

230. Petra Meier and David Paternotte, "Mouvements sociaux et action publique entre dynamiques transnationales et multi-niveaux," in *Au-delà et en deçà de l'État. Le genre entre dynamiques transnationales et multi-niveaux*, ed. Bérengère Marques Pereira, Petra Meier, and David Paternotte (Louvain-la-Neuve: Academia Bruylant, 2010), 13–33.

231. Phillip M. Ayoub, "Cooperative Transnationalism in Contemporary Europe: Europeanization and Political Opportunities for LGBT Mobilization in the European Union," *European Political Science Review* 5, no. 2 (2013): 279–310.

232. Élisabeth Zucker-Rouvillois, "Éléments pour une chronologie scientifique, juridique et politique: l'expertise familiale," in *Au-delà du PaCS. L'expertise familiale à l'épreuve de l'homosexualité*, ed. Daniel Borrillo, Éric Fassin, and Marcela Iacub (Paris: La Découverte, 1999), 130–44.

233. Daniel Borrillo and Pierre Lascoumes, *Amours égales? Le Pacs, les homosexuels et la gauche* (Paris: La Découverte, 2002)

234. David Paternotte and Kelly Kollman, "Regulating Intimate Relationships in the European Polity: Same-Sex Unions and Policy Convergence," *Social Politics* 20, no. 4 (2013): 510–33.

235. Paternotte, *Revendiquer le "mariage gay,"* 136.

236. Sylvain Gatelais, "La 'Manif pour Tous' ou le trolling rose fuchsia," *L'Obs*, March 28, 2013.

237. Murray Pratt, "Post-queer and beyond the PaCS: Contextualising French Responses to the Civil Solidarity Pact," in *In a Queer Place: Sexuality and Belonging in British and European Contexts*, ed. Kate Chedgzoy, Emma Francis, and Murray Pratt (Aldershot, UK: Ashgate, 2002), 177–206.

238. "Marie-Jo Bonnet, lesbienne, féministe, de gauche et opposée à la PMA et à la GPA," *Le Figaro*, July 18, 2014. See also a text by Lesbiennes of Colors, part of the coordinated lesbian movement: "Mariage pour tous: quelle égalité?," Coordination Lesbienne en France, January 24, 2013, http://www.coordinationlesbienne.org/spip.php?article245.

239. "Réflexions d'un Afro-descendant," *Le Blog de João*, Facebook, accessed March 15, 2015, https://www.facebook.com/pages/Les-Chronik-du-N%C3%A8gre-Inverti/1820 42851899167.

240. Karen Zivi has noted the same tendency in the American context. See "Performing the Nation: Contesting Same-Sex Marriage Rights in the United States," *Journal of Human Rights* 13, no. 3 (2014): 290–306.

241. "Bertinotti: 'La procréation médicalement assistée (PMA) ne figurera pas dans la loi famille,'" *Le Journal du Dimanche*, January 3, 2014.

242. Perreau, "The Jurisprudential Forum," in Perreau, *The Politics of Adoption*, 47–72.

CHAPTER 2: THE MANY MEANINGS OF QUEER

1. Alain de Benoist, *Non à la théorie du genre!* (Paris: Mordicus, 2014), 10.

2. Ibid., 21.

3. Ibid., 28; Bérénice Levet, *La Théorie du genre ou le Monde rêvé des anges* (Paris: Grasset, 2014), Kindle, 1204 of 2894.

4. Peeters, *Le Gender, une norme mondiale?*, 50–53.

5. "Le Livre polémique: que font les petits garçons? En images," *Le Salon Beige* (blog), September 18, 2014, http://lesalonbeige.blogs.com/my_weblog/2014/09/le-livre -polémique-que-font-les-petits-garçons-en-images.html.

6. Levet, *La Théorie du genre*, 744 of 2894. See also Peeters, *Le Gender, une norme mondiale?*, 35.

7. Interview, July 1, 2015.

8. Personal notes from attendance at the event.

9. Leopold Lippert, "Writing Transnational Queer Histories, or Stonewall in Wien," in *Import-Export-Transport: Queer Theory, Queer Critique and Activism in Motion*, ed. Sushila Mesquita, Maria Katharina Wiedlack, and Katrin Lasthofer (Vienna: Zaglossus, 2012), 247–59.

10. The story of the origins of the article was described by Eribon in his blog, *Site personnel de Didier Eribon* (blog), August 31, 2012, http://didiereribon.blogspot.com /2012/08/eve-kosofsky-sedgwick-et-le-temps-quil.html.

11. Eve Kosofsky Sedgwick, "Construire des significations queer," in *Les Études gay et lesbiennes. Colloque du Centre Georges Pompidou 23 et 27 Juin 1997*, ed. Didier Eribon (Paris: Éditions du Centre Pompidou, 1998), 109–16.

12. Eve Kosofsky Sedgwick, "Making Gay Meanings," in *The Weather in Proust*, ed. Jonathan Goldberg (Durham, NC: Duke University Press, 2011), 183–89.

13. John Money, "Hermaphrodism, Gender and Precocity in Hyperardrenocorticism: Psychologic Findings," *Bulletin of the John Hopkins Hospital* 96 (1955): 253–64.

14. Vincent Bourseul, *Le Genre et le Psychanalyste* (Paris: Eres, 2016), 14.

15. Robert J. Stoller, *Sex and Gender: On the Development of Masculinity and Femininity* (New York: Science House, 1968); Ann Oakley, *Sex, Gender and Society* (London: Maurice Temple Smith, 1972).

16. Judith Butler, *Gender Trouble: Feminism and the Subversion of Identity* (London: Routledge, 1990), vii.

17. Joan W. Scott, "Gender, a Useful Category of Historical Analysis," *American Historical Review* 91, no. 5 (1986): 1053–75; Denise Riley, *Am I That Name? Feminism and the Category of Women in History* (London: Macmillan, 1988).

18. In her introduction to the 1990 edition of *Gender Trouble*, Judith Butler explained that her book was largely written in 1987–88 at the Institute for Advanced Study in Princeton, where Joan W. Scott ran a seminar on gender. Butler also stated that Denise Riley's deconstruction of the "I" was crucial to her own analyses.

19. Paola Bacchetta and Jules Falquet introduced this aspect of queer studies in France in a special issue of *Cahiers du CEDREF*, published in 2011. See Paola Bacchetta and Jules Falquet, "Introduction," *Les Cahiers du CEDREF: Centre d'Enseignement, d'Études et de Recherches pour les Études Féministes*, no. 18 (December 1, 2011): 7–40.

20. Gloria Anzaldúa, *Borderlands—La Frontera: The New Mestiza* (San Francisco: Aunt Lute Books, 1999), 106, 142.

21. David M. Halperin, *Saint Foucault: Towards a Gay Hagiography* (Oxford: Oxford University Press, 1995), 122.

22. David M. Halperin, *How to Do the History of Male Homosexuality* (Chicago: University of Chicago Press, 2004); and *How to Be Gay* (Cambridge, MA: Harvard University Press, 2014).

23. Butler, *Gender Trouble*; Eve Kosofsky Sedgwick, *Epistemology of the Closet* (Berke-

ley: University of California Press, 1990). Teresa de Lauretis used the term "queer theory" during a conference at the University of Santa Cruz in February 1990. See "Queer Theory: Lesbian and Gay Sexualities," *Differences: A Journal of Feminist Cultural Studies* 3, no. 2 (1991): iii–xviii.

24. Lisa Duggan described that approach as a critique of identities that remained "'essential,' residing clearly, intelligibly and unalterably in the body or psyche, and fixing desire in a gendered direction." See Lisa Duggan, "Making It Perfectly Queer," in *Sex Wars: Sexual Dissent and Political Culture*, ed. Lisa Duggan and Nan D. Hunter (New York: Taylor and Francis, 2006), 155.

25. Linda B. Glaser, "The College Years of Eve Kosofsky Sedgwick, a Founder of Queer Theory," CornellArts&Sciences, *Medium*, May 12, 2015, https://medium.com/@cornellcas/the-college-years-of-eve-kosofsky-sedgwick-founder-of-queer-theory-f86c52b9fbd7.

26. Michael Piore, "Economic Identity / Sexual Identity," in *A Queer World*, ed. Martin Duberman (New York: NYU Press, 1997), 502–7.

27. Leslie Feinberg, *Transgender Warriors: Making History from Joan of Arc to Dennis Rodman* (Boston: Beacon Press, 1997), 10.

28. Jack Halberstam, *Female Masculinity* (Durham, NC: Duke University Press, 1998), 268–69.

29. Such work is being done by Chandan Reddy when she employs a queer epistemology to explore the law as an identitarian archive to which homosexual Pakistani immigrants are confronted when they arrive in the United States. See Chandan Reddy, "Asian Diasporas, Neoliberalism, and Family: Reviewing the Case for Homosexual Asylum in the Context of Family Rights," *Social Text* 23, no. 3–4 (Fall–Winter 2005): 101–19.

30. The title of this section ("Queer 'sans le savoir'") is a nod to Philippe Mangeot, a former president of ACT UP Paris, who unironically titled one of his presentations "Foucault sans le savoir" (a pun on "Foucault without knowing it" and "Foucault minus the knowledge"). See Philippe Mangeot, "Foucault sans le savoir," in *L'Infréquentable Michel Foucault: renouveaux de la pensée critique*, ed. Didier Eribon (Paris: EPEL, 2001), 89–100.

31. Interview, July 9, 2013.

32. *Androzine*, no. 15 (1992), 36.

33. QRD mailing list archives, March 7, 1995, http://www.qrd.org/qrd/media/print/1995/androzine-03.07.95.

34. David Michels, "La Croisière: une expérience de gays libertaires," *Clio: Femmes, Genre, Histoire*, no. 22 (2005): 157–66.

35. Interview, September 19, 2013.

36. See excerpts from *Bangbang* now archived on the Internet, accessed August 12, 2015, http://bangbang1969.free.fr/pageshtml/bangbang1/La%20Croisi%E8rejetexplique.htm.

37. Minutes of the 2002 UEEH, internal document, personal archives of Christian de Leusse, loaned to the author.

38. Interview, June 17, 2015.

39. The same was true of Les Panthères Roses, a group that arose from several stu-

dent organizations and far-left political parties, notably the Ligue Communiste Révolutionnaire. Although they employ methods perceived as queer (sequins, staged actions, ironic slogans), members of Les Panthères Roses identify themselves only as feminist. Interview with Panthères Roses activist Rosa Deluxe, September 24, 2013.

40. Philippe Mangeot, "Pour en finir . . . ," *Action* 63 (October 1999): 6.

41. Christophe Broqua, *Agir pour ne pas mourir! Act up, les homosexuels et le sida* (Paris: Les Presses de Sciences Po, 2006), 380–82.

42. Quoted in ibid., 382.

43. For a detailed analysis of the moral registers distinguishing a sense of community from free will in debate over bareback sex in France, see Gabriel Girard, "HIV Risk and Sense of Community: French Gay Men Discourses on Barebacking," *Culture, Health & Sexuality: An International Journal for Research, Intervention and Care* 18, no. 1 (2016), http://www.tandfonline.com/doi/full/10.1080/13691058.2015.1063813#.VdNG_yx_Oko.

44. See especially Michel Feher, "Identités en évolution: individu, famille, communauté aux États-Unis," *Esprit*, no. 6 (June 1995): 114–31.

45. Éric Fassin, "Pouvoirs sexuels: le juge Thomas, la cour suprême et la société américaine," *Esprit*, no. 12 (December 1991): 102–30.

46. Interview with Michel Feher, April 7, 2015.

47. Judith Butler, *Trouble dans le genre*, trans. Cynthia Kraus (Paris: La Découverte, 2005).

48. Camille Robcis, *The Law of Kinship: Anthropology, Psychoanalysis, and the Family in France* (Ithaca, NY: Cornell University Press, 2013).

49. Daniel Borrillo, Éric Fassin, and Marcela Iacub, eds., *Au-delà du PaCS*.

50. Zoo, *Q comme Queer. Les séminaires Q du zoo (1996–1997)* (Lille: Question de Genre, 1998), 7.

51. Ibid., 10.

52. Ibid., 11.

53. "Q comme questions," in ibid., 84–86.

54. Paul B. Preciado, *Manifeste contra-sexuel* (Paris: Balland, 2000), 67.

55. Judith Butler, "Les genres en athlétisme: hyperbole ou dépassement de la dualité sexuelle?," *Cahiers du Genre*, no. 29 (2000): 21–36. Originally published in English as "Athletic Genders: Hyperbolic Instance and/or the Overcoming of Sexual Binarism," *Stanford Humanities Review* 6, no. 2 (1995): 103–11.

56. Archiveshomo.info, 2001–16, http://www.archiveshomo.info/.

57. Samuel Zralos, "Archives LGBT: où sont nos mémoires?," *Yagg*, July 10, 2013, http://yagg.com/2013/07/10/lgbt-ou-sont-nos-memoires.

58. Interview with Marco Dell'Omodarme, July 11, 2013.

59. See Zoo, *Q comme Queer*, 94: "zoo = queer = nonassimilation."

60. Sabine Prokhoris, *L'Insaisissable Histoire de la psychanalyse* (Paris: Presses universitaires de France, 2014), 162.

61. Didier Eribon analyzes the feeling of exclusion that Roland Barthes felt while passing by the Saint-Sulpice church, where a marriage was being celebrated. Didier Eribon, *Sur Cet Instant fragile . . . Carnets, janvier–août 2004* (Paris: Fayard, 2004), 84–88.

62. Eribon, *Les Études gay et lesbiennes*.

63. Frédéric Martel, *Le Rose et le Noir. Les homosexuels en France depuis 1968* (Paris: Seuil, 1996).

64. Frédéric Martel, "Dans la solitude des bibliothèques gay," *Le Monde*, June 27, 1997.

65. "Sur les études gays et lesbiennes: une lettre de Pierre Bourdieu au '*Monde*' (11 juillet 1997)," *Site personnel de Didier Eribon* (blog), February 2, 2014, http://didiereribon .blogspot.com/2014/02/sur-les-etudes-gays-et-lesbiennes-une.html.

66. Marie-Hélène/Sam Bourcier, *Queer Zones. Politique des identités sexuelles, des représentations et des savoir* (Paris: Balland, 2001), 192; and Marie-Hélène/Sam Bourcier, *Sexpolitiques: Queer Zones 2* (Paris: La Fabrique, 2005), 115–20.

67. Françoise Gaspard recounted the history of the seminar in "'Les Homosexualités': un 'objet' de recherche légitime?," in *Le Choix de l'homosexualité: recherches inédites sur la question gay et lesbienne*, ed. Bruno Perreau (Paris: EPEL, 2007), 235–41.

68. Personal notes from attendance at the seminar, January 21, 2003.

69. George Chauncey, *Gay New York. 1840–1940* (Paris: Fayard, 2003); Michael Lucey, *Les Ratés de la famille: Balzac et les formes sociales de la sexualité* (Paris: Fayard, 2008).

70. Perreau, *Le Choix de l'homosexualité*.

71. Interview with Marco Dell'Omodarme, July 11, 2013.

72. Personal archives from attendance at the event.

73. Document collected from personal attendance at the event.

74. Marie-Hélène/Sam Bourcier, "Théorie queer de la première vague et politique du disempowerment: la seconde Butler," in *Queer Zones 3. Identités, cultures, politiques* (Paris: Éditions Amsterdam, 2011), 326.

75. Jérôme Vidal, the head of Les Éditions Amsterdam, discussed the stages in the controversy triggered by the translation of Butler's books. See Jérôme Vidal, "À propos du Féminisme, Judith Butler en France. Trouble dans la réception," *Mouvements*, no. 47–48 (2006): 229–39.

76. Judith Butler, *Défaire le genre*, trans. Maxime Cervulle (Paris: Éditions Amsterdam, 2006).

77. "Hélène Hazéra répond à Marie-Hélène Bourcier," *Têtu*, July 31, 2009, http:// www.tetu.com/2009/07/31/news/france/helene-hazera-repond-a-marie-helene-bourcier (site discontinued).

78. "Queer Theory in France," Warwick University, October 2012, http://www2.war wick.ac.uk/fac/arts/modernlanguages/research/french/currentprojects/queertheory.

79. Marie-Hélène/Sam Bourcier, "'F***' the Politics of Disempowerment in the Second Butler," *Paragraph: A Journal of Critical Theory* 35, no. 2 (June 2012): 233–53.

80. Régis Révenin, "A Preliminary Assessment of the First Four Decades of LGBTQ Studies in France (1970–2010)," *Paragraph: A Journal of Critical Theory* 35, no. 2 (June 2012): 164–80.

81. Adrian Rifkin, "Does Gay Sex Need Queer Theory?," *Paragraph: A Journal of Critical Theory* 35, no. 2 (June 2012): 202.

82. Claire Boyle, "Post-Queer (Un)Made in France?," *Paragraph: A Journal of Critical Theory* 35, no. 2 (June 2012): 265–80; Lisa Downing, "Interdisciplinarity, Cultural

Studies, Queer: Historical Contexts and Contemporary Contentions in France," *Paragraph: A Journal of Critical Theory* 35, no. 2 (June 2012): 215–32.

83. Oliver Davis, "Didier Eribon, Restive Rationalist: The Limits of Sociological Self-Understanding in *Retour à Reims*," *French Cultural Studies* 23, no. 2 (2012): 124.

84. Bourcier completed his secondary schooling at the Maison d'Éducation de la Légion d'Honneur and attended college at the École Normale Supérieur in Saint-Cloud. He was awarded a PhD for a dissertation on television coverage of the war in Iraq, supervised by Dominique Wolton and Alain Touraine, at which point he was accredited to teach at the university level by the Conseil National des Universités. He was immediately hired as an assistant professor by the communication and information sciences department at the Université de Lille III. Eribon was born into a working-class family in Reims but left his family to earn a master's degree in philosophy. He began a career as a journalist rather than pursue a PhD. He was accredited to supervise doctoral research only some thirty years later, becoming a professor at the Université d'Amiens, even though the Conseil National des Universités initially refused to accredit him for that post.

85. For a detailed discussion of this subject, see Michel Tort, *Fin du dogme paternel* (Paris: Aubier, 2005). On the question of marriage, see Vincent Bourseul, "Les normes sexuelles, la psychanalyse et le 'mariage pour tous,'" *Cahiers de Psychologie Clinique*, no. 45 (2015): 97–109.

86. The École lacanienne de psychanalyse was founded in 1985 after Jacques Lacan dissolved the École freudienne de Paris.

87. Jean Allouch, "Accueillir les *gays and lesbian studies*," *L'Unebévue*, no. 11 (Fall 1998): 145–54.

88. Interview, April 20, 2015.

89. Butler had very old ties with France. While still a doctoral candidate she developed an interest in women's writing and the way that Luce Irigaray interpreted the work of Lacan. At that time Butler also attended seminars run by Hélène Cixous. Interview, July 1, 2015.

90. Interview with Laurie Laufer, June 2, 2015.

91. Vincent Bourseul, "L'expérience queer et l'inquiétant," *Recherches en Psychanalyse*, no. 10 (2010): 242–50.

92. "Usages des théories queer: normes, sexualités, pouvoir," *EHESS. Séminaires et enseignements*, 2013–14, http://www.ehess.fr/fr/enseignement/enseignements/2013/ue/293.

93. Luca Greco, "Exhumer le corps du placard: pour une linguistique *queer* du corps *king*," in *Écritures du corps: nouvelles perspectives*, ed. Pierre Zoberman, Anne Tomiche, and William J. Spurlin (Paris: Garnier Flammarion, 2013), 269–89.

94. Jean Zaganiaris, *Queer Maroc: sexualités, genres et (trans)identités dans la littérature marocaine* (Paris: Lulu.com, 2014).

95. "Oyé oyé! Avis à la population: la décadence enseignée à Paris-IV-Sorbonne. Fiiiiiiiiiiiiiii! Rhabille-toi!," *Diatala*, July 4, 2013, http://www.diatala.org/article-paris-iv-sorbonne-vous-propose-des-ateliers-de-bondage-de-porno-gender-d-ejaculation-lgtb-de-po-118891234.html.

96. France first aired the British version of *Queer as Folk*. The American version was broadcast by another cable channel, Jimmy, from 2002 onward. The audience for the series had therefore been very limited when *Queer, cinq experts dans le vent* was aired on France's largest television station during prime time, drawing millions of viewers.

97. See Chapter 4 for an analysis of how this relationship has been described in literature and philosophy as the archetype of an impossible community.

98. Although the link between the word "queer" and homosexuality is sufficiently suggestive in today's English, uses of the term are multiple and remain unstable in an anglophone context, particularly a literary one. See David Harvey, "L'étrange mot d' . . . queer," *Rue Descartes*, no. 40 (May 2003): 27–35.

99. Eve Sedgwick proposed the idea of "the spectacle of the closet" in the chapter on Proust in her *Epistemology of the Closet*, 213 ff.

100. Denis Provencher came to the same conclusion in *Queer French*, where he analyzed the sources of coming-out television in the French context. He based his examples on *Loft Story*, the first French reality show, broadcast for the first time on channel M6 on April 26, 2001. The show aimed to create a "perfect couple" by eliminating one participant each week. During the first season, the homosexual candidate, Steevy, was shown simply as someone youthful and exuberant—his homosexuality was never mentioned. During the second season, the gay candidate, Thomas, was chosen for his reserve. He came out, implicitly, in front of the TV cameras. However, in a nod to the title of a book by Michael Lucey, *Never Say I*, Provencher shows that, unlike what happened in American programs, the coming out occurred without Thomas ever saying "I." See Denis M. Provencher, *Queer French* (Burlington, VT: Ashgate, 2007), 144.

101. Édouard Launet, "'Queer,' marque déposée par Ardisson," *Libération*, March 4, 1999.

102. One of the TV show's experts, Gilles Tessier, published a how-to book aimed at straight couples. Gilles Tessier, *La Méthode queer: on va booster votre couple!* (Paris: Ramsay, 2006).

103. "La télé parie sur les homos," *Le Parisien*, January 30, 2004.

104. Stéphanie Kunert, *Publicité, Genre et Stéréotypes* (Fontenay-le-Comte: Éditions Lussaud, 2013), 39–48.

105. Rosemary Hennessy, "Queer Visibility in Commodity Culture," *Cultural Critique*, no. 29 (1994): 31–76.

106. Quoted by Arnaud Lerch in "Des usages de l'ambivalence sexuelle," *Rue Descartes*, no. 20 (2003): 76.

107. Wittig, *The Straight Mind*, 68–75, 76–89.

108. Judith Butler, *Gender Trouble*, 151–74. See also Judith Butler, "Wittig's Material Practice: Universalizing a Minority Point of View," *GLQ: A Journal of Lesbian and Gay Studies* 13, no. 4 (2007): 519–33.

109. Nicole-Claude Mathieu, "Dérive du genre / stabilité des sexes," in *Lesbianisme et Féminisme: histoires politiques*, ed. Natacha Chetcuti and Claire Michard (Paris: L'Harmattan, 2003), 291–311.

110. "Un entretien avec Christine Delphy," *Politis*, September 28, 2013, republished

on "*Le blog de Christine Delphy* (blog)," November 14, 2013, https://delphysyllepse.word press.com/2013/11/14/un-entretien-avec-christine-delphy-politis.

111. Christine Delphy, *L'Ennemi principal 2. Penser le genre* (Paris: Syllepses, 2001), 257.

112. Louise Turcotte, "Queer Theory: Transgression and/or Regression," *Canadian Woman Studies* 16, no. 2 (1996): 118–21.

113. Interview, October 10, 2013.

114. Interview, February 7, 2014.

115. Elsa Dorlin, "Le queer est un matérialisme: entretien avec Gabriel Girard," in *Les Cahiers de Critique Communiste*, ed. Sandrine Bourret et al. (Paris: Syllepse, 2007), 47–58.

116. Kevin Floyd, *The Reification of Desire: Toward a Queer Marxism* (Minneapolis: University of Minnesota Press, 2009).

117. Sophie Noyé, "Pour un féminisme matérialiste et queer," *Contretemps*, April 17, 2014, http://www.contretemps.eu/interventions/f%C3%A9minisme-mat%C3%A9ria liste-queer.

118. Charlotte Prieur and Bruno Laprade, "Les dimensions francofolles des politiques féministes queers: autocritique d'une gestation," *Revue PolitiQueer*, June 2014, http://politiqueer.info/numeros/rpqfrancofolles/introductionauxdimensionsfrancofolles.

119. Mathieu Hauchecorne, "Le polycentrisme des marges: les 'filières' belge et québécoise d'importation de la philosophie politique étasunienne contemporaine en France," *Histoire@Politique* 15, no. 3 (2011): 90–109.

120. Maite Escudero-Alias, "Transatlantic Dialogues and Identity Politics: Theorising Bilateral Silences in the Genesis and Future of Queer Studies," *Journal of Transatlantic Studies* 7, no. 4 (Winter 2009): 389–98.

121. Cornelia Möser, "Translating Queer Theory to France and Germany: Tickets and Boundaries for a Traveling Theory," in Mesquita, Wiedlack, and Lasthofer, *Import-Export-Transport*, 150. For further details, see Cornelia Möser, *Féminismes en traductions: théories voyageuses et traductions culturelles* (Paris: Éditions des Archives Contemporaines, 2013), 131–41, 152–59.

122. Robert Kulpa, Joanna Mizielinska, and Agata Stasiska, "(Un)translatable Queer?, or What Is Lost and Can Be Found in Translation . . . ," in Mesquita, Wiedlack, and Lasthofer, *Import-Export-Transport*, 117.

123. Vendula (Esteban) Wiesnerová, "LGBTQ Activism and the Appropriation of Queer Theory in Spain," in Mesquita, Wiedlack, and Lasthofer, *Import-Export-Transport*, 163–78.

124. Konstantinos Eleftheriadis, "Organizational Practices and Prefigurative Spaces in European Queer Festivals," *Social Movement Studies* 14, no. 6 (April 2015): 1–17.

125. Konstantinos Eleftheriadis, "Queer Activism and the Idea of 'Practicing Europe,'" in *LGBT Activism and the Making of Europe: A Rainbow Europe?*, ed. Phillip M. Ayoub and David Paternotte (London: Palgrave Macmillan, 2014), 154, 155.

126. Michel Foucault, "Of Other Spaces, Heterotopias," a transcription of "Les Hétérotopies," *Conférences radiophoniques de France Culture* (1966), accessed July 24, 2015, http://foucault.info/doc/documents/heterotopia/foucault-heterotopia-en-html.

127. Charlotte Prieur, "Des géographies queers au-delà des genres et des sexualités?," EspacesTemps.net, April 20, 2015, http://www.espacestemps.net/articles/des-geog raphies-queers-au-dela-des-genres-et-des-sexualites. Charlotte Prieur is thus following in the footsteps of Marianne Blidon, who pioneered the introduction into France of many Anglo-American studies that themselves established a bridge with queer theory. For example, in 2010 she organized a symposium for the fifteenth anniversary of the publication of David Bell and Gill Valentine's classic *Mapping Desire: Geographies of Sexualities*, as well as a seminar on the "Geography of Sexualities" at the Université de Paris I (Sorbonne-Panthéon) that discussed the work of Katherine Browne and Catherine J. Nash, Andrew Tucker, and Scott Herring.

128. Charlotte Prieur, "Du quartier gay aux lieux queers parisiens: reproduction des rapports de domination et stratégies spatiales de résistance," *Actes du colloque "Espaces et rapports de domination"* (forthcoming).

129. Interview, February 8, 2014.

130. "Too Much Pussy!," Émilie Jouvet, 2009, http://www.emiliejouvet.com/#!too -much-pussy-film-jouvet/c24qw.

131. See also Pierre Zoberman, "Introduction," in *Queer. Écritures de la différence?*, vol. 1, *Autres temps, autres lieux* (Paris: L'Harmattan, 2008), 16–17.

132. Interview with Elisabeth Lebovici, November 25, 2013.

133. Donna Haraway, *Manifeste cyborg et autres essais. Sciences—fictions—féminismes*, trans. Laurence Allard, Delphine Gardey, and Nathalie Magnan (Paris: Exils éditeurs, 2007).

134. Eunice Lipton, *Alias Olympia: A Woman's Search for Manet's Notorious Model and Her Own Desire* (Ithaca, NY: Cornell University Press, 1999).

135. "Let's Queer Art History!," Centre Pompidou, May 21, 2011, https://www.centre pompidou.fr/cpv/resource/cnyxb44/razMKjo.

136. "Loud & Proud," *La Gaîté lyrique*, March 23, 2015, http://gaite-lyrique.net/loud -proud. See also https://www.facebook.com/pages/Loud-Proud-festival/456886237799341.

137. Personal archives, document collected from the Pink Panthers.

138. Personal archives, from mailing list of Les Tordu(e)s, June 2015.

139. Quotation from Gay Shame San Francisco (site discontinued).

140. "Deux hommes, une femme, une possibilité," Rainbow Attitude press release, personal archives, October 18, 2003.

141. Collectif de la marche de nuit 2008, accessed February 25, 2015, https:// marchedenuit2008paris.wordpress.com/2008/07/18/slogans-de-la-marche-de-nuit-du-14062008 -paris/.

142. "Marche de nuit non-mixte pour l'appropriation de l'espace public par les femmes," October 8, 2012, http://hypathie.blogspot.com/2012/10/marche-de-nuit-non -mixte-pour.html.

143. Interview, October 18, 2012.

144. "Le 'nous' du zoo," in Zoo, *Q comme Queer*, 94–98.

145. Although some members of Les Panthères Roses participated in the march organized by Les Tordu(e)s and adopted the term *transpdgouine*, the word is not pro-

36. Daniels, "Judith Butler Refuses Award."

37. See Palestinian Queers for BDS, https://pqbds.wordpress.com/.

38. "Résister au pinkwashing—au cœur du mouvement queer arabe: rencontre-débat avec Haneen Maikey et Ramzy Kumsieh," Vimeo, March 20, 2012, https://vimeo.com/46453856.

39. The Indivisibles is an organization that fights the racist strategies behind a widespread acceptance of a "racialized other," especially through its annual "Y'a Bon" Prize, awarded to public figures who have made racist comments. See Les Indivisibles, http://www.lesindivisibles.fr/.

40. Les Mots Sont Importants was founded by sociologist Sylvie Tissot and philosopher Pierre Tevanian to shed light on the stereotypes that lay the groundwork for law-and-order policies. See Les Mots Sont Importants, http://lmsi.net/.

41. Personal archives, prospectus collected by the author.

42. With regard to the Taubira Act, Mayanthi Fernando has shown that Christianity was presented as being capable of change, while Islam was alleged to be incapable of such a move. Mayanthi L. Fernando, *The Republic Unsettled: Muslim French and the Contradictions of Secularism* (Durham, NC: Duke University Press, 2014), 249.

43. An attentiveness to such complexity informed publication of a special issue of *Raisons Politiques*. The introduction to the review perfectly summed up those issues: "National identities, like sexual identities, appear to be interlinked objects whose modes of production are related to the consubstantial nature of social relationships." Alexandre Jaunait, Amélie Le Renard, and Élisabeth Marteu, "Nationalismes sexuels? Reconfigurations contemporaines des sexualités et des nationalismes," *Raisons Politiques* 49, no. 1 (2013): 5.

44. "Conference: Sexual Nationalisms: Gender, Sexuality, and the Politics of Belonging in the New Europe," Amsterdam Institute for Social Science Research, January 27–28, 2011, http://aissr.uva.nl/events/content/conferences/2011/01/conference-sexual-nationalisms-gender-sexuality-and-the-politics-of-belonging-in-the-new-europe.html.

45. Alexandre Jaunait wrote a thorough summary of the event: "Retours sur les nationalismes sexuels," *Genre, Sexualité & Société*, no. 5 (June 1, 2011), http://gss.revues.org/1957?lang=en#ftn7.

46. On this point I disagree with Alexandre Jaunait, who tends to exonerate individuals of their moral responsibility in academic self-reproduction in order to shed greater light on structural effects. See ibid.

47. Didier Eribon, "Borders, Politics and Temporality," *Site personnel de Didier Eribon* (blog), March 1, 2011, http://didiereribon.blogspot.fr/2011/02/politics-and-temporality.html.

48. Ibid.

49. Jasbir Puar, *Terrorist Assemblages: Homonationalism in Queer Times* (Durham, NC: Duke University Press, 2007), 125.

50. When Fatima El-Tayeb discussed Judith Butler's analysis in her article "Imitation and Gender Subordination," she explained that some subjects are discursively defined as being "opposite of the norm" because those subjects, which may be the explicit object of discourse or present in its silences, establish the lines of the norm through their

oppositeness, but El-Tayeb does not conclude that those subjects are therefore nonnormative. See Fatima El-Tayeb, *European Others: Queering Ethnicity in Postnational Europe* (Minneapolis: University of Minnesota Press, 2011), 169.

51. Janet E. Halley, "Reasoning about Sodomy: Act and Identity in and after *Bowers v. Hardwick*," *Virginia Law Review* 79, no. 7 (October 1, 1993): 1721–80.

52. Michael Warner, *The Trouble with Normal: Sex, Politics, and the Ethics of Queer Life* (Cambridge, MA: Harvard University Press, 2000).

53. Puar, *Terrorist Assemblages*, 130, 136, 131.

54. John Edgar Wideman, *Brothers and Keepers: A Memoir* (1984; repr., New York: Mariner Books, 2005).

55. Puar, *Terrorist Assemblages*, 137.

56. Ibid., 137–38.

57. Ibid., 140.

58. Amy Lutz, "Who Joins the Military? A Look at Race, Class, and Immigration Status," *Journal of Political and Military Sociology* 36, no. 2 (January 1, 2008): 167–88.

59. See Geoffroy de Lagasnerie, "Simplette s'en va-t-en guerre," *Le Site de Geoffroy de Lagasnerie* (blog), June 28, 2013, http://geoffroydelagasnerie.com/2013/06/28/simplette-sen-va-ten-guerre/.

60. Eribon, "Borders, Politics, and Temporality."

61. Éric Fassin, "Same-Sex Marriage, Nation, and Race: French Political Logics and Rhetorics," *Contemporary French Civilization* 39, no. 3 (January 2014): 294.

62. "Des juristes font le scénario de l'abrogation de la Loi Taubira," *Le Figaro*, September 24, 2014.

63. Gianmaria Colpani and Adriano José Habed, "'In Europe It's Different': Homonationalism and Peripheral Desires for Europe," in *LGBT Activism and the Making of Europe: A Rainbow Europe?*, ed. Phillip M. Ayoub and David Paternotte (London: Palgrave Macmillan, 2014), 73–93.

64. Robert Kulpa, "Nations and Sexualities—'East' and 'West,'" in *De-centering Western Sexualities: Central and Eastern European Perspectives*, ed. Robert Kulpa and Joanna Mizielinska (Farnham, UK: Ashgate, 2011), 56.

65. Félix Boggio Éwanjé-Épée and Stella Magliani-Belkacem, *Les Féministes blanches et l'Empire* (Paris: La Fabrique, 2012).

66. Ibid., 77–78.

67. Ibid., 78.

68. Franck Chaumont, *Homo-ghetto. Gays et lesbiennes dans les cités: les clandestins de la République* (Paris: Le Cherche-Midi, 2009).

69. See especially the following *Pédérama* radio stories: "Moi, Nicolas, 29 ans, pédé libanais," July 2003, Audio file 7:50; and "Moi, Léo, 27 ans, pédé, antillais," Audio File 8:07, November 2003, broadcast on *Radio Libertaire*, http://pederama.free.fr/audio.html.

70. Éwanjé-Épée and Magliani-Belkacem, *Les Féministes blanches et l'Empire*, 87–88.

71. David Halperin, "Homosexualité," in *Dictionnaire des cultures gays et lesbiennes*, ed. Didier Eribon (Paris: Larousse, 2003), 257.

72. Valerie Traub, "The Past Is a Foreign Country? The Times and Spaces of Islami-

cate Sexuality Studies," in *Islamicate Sexualities: Translations across Temporal Geographies of Desire*, ed. Kathryn Babayan and Afsaneh Najmabadi (Cambridge, MA: Harvard University Press, 2008), 12.

73. Joseph Allen Boone, *The Homoerotics of Orientalism* (New York: Columbia University Press, 2014), 53.

74. Ibid., xxxi.

75. "The Empire of Sexuality: An Interview with Joseph Massad," *Jadaliyya*, March 5, 2013, http://www.jadaliyya.com/pages/index/10461/the-empire-of-sexuality_an-interview-with-joseph-m.

76. David Paternotte and Hakan Seckinelgin, "'Lesbian and Gay Rights Are Human Rights': Multiple Globalizations and LGBT Activism," in *The Ashgate Research Companion to Lesbian and Gay Activism*, ed. David Paternotte and Manon Tremblay, (Farnham, UK: Ashgate, 2015), 218ff.

77. Joseph A. Massad, *Desiring Arabs* (Chicago: University of Chicago Press, 2008), 188–89.

78. Ibid., 189.

79. Wahid Al Farchichi and Nizar Saghiyeh, "Homosexual Relations in the Penal Codes: General Study regarding the Laws in the Arab Countries with a Report on Lebanon and Tunisia," Helem, 2012, http://daleel-madani.org/sites/default/files/HelemStudy.pdf, 44.

80. Traub, "The Past Is a Foreign Country?"

81. Interview, July 21, 2013.

82. Maxime Cervulle, "French Homonormativity and the Commodification of the Arab Body," *Radical History Review*, no. 100 (2008): 176.

83. Nacira Guénif-Souilamas, "Fanon. Et après?," Johannesburg Workshop in Theory and Criticism, 2012, http://jwtc.org.za/salon_volume_5/nacira_gu_nif_souilamas.htm.

84. Nacira Guénif-Souilamas, "La fin de l'intégration, la preuve par les femmes," *Mouvements* 39–40, no. 3 (2005): 152.

85. Ibid. See also Nacira Guénif-Souilamas and Éric Macé, *Les Féministes et le Garçon arabe* (La Tour-d'Aigues: Éditions de l'Aube, 2004).

86. In 2005, several leftist activists issued a call: "We are the indigenous of the republic." Five years later, they created the Party of the Indigenous of the Republic. Their goal was to offer new concepts such as "indigenous" and "white political field" to transform mainstream political practices. The party immediately attracted mass-media attention but proved to be highly controversial because of its rather essentialist understanding of race, as well as the sympathy of its spokesperson, Houria Bouteldja, for the anti-Semitic stand-up comedian Dieudonné. See Clemens Zobel, "The 'Indigènes de la République' and Political Mobilization Strategies in Postcolonial France," *e-cadernos CES*, no. 7 (2010), http://eces.revues.org/390; and Houria Bouteldja, "Party of the Indigenous of the Republic (PIR) Key Concepts," trans. Paola Bacchetta, *Critical Ethnic Studies* 1, no. 1 (Spring 2015), 27–32.

87. Oral comments taken from a television broadcast, *Ce soir ou jamais*, November 6, 2012, quoted by Bouteldja in Houria Bouteldja, "Universalisme gay, homoracialisme

et 'mariage pour tous,'" Les Indigènes de la République, February 12, 2013, http://indi
genes-republique.fr/universalisme-gay-homoracialisme-et-mariage-pour-tous-2.

88. Abdellah Taïa, "Non, l'homosexualité n'est pas imposée aux Arabes par
l'Occident," *Rue89*, August 2, 2013, http://www.rue89.com/2013/02/08/non-lhomo
sexualite-nest-pas-imposee-aux-arabes-par-loccident-239439.

89. Tassadit Yacine, "Dire ou ne pas dire les homosexualités: de quelques exemples
en Afrique du Nord et au-delà," *Tumultes* 41, no. 2 (2013): 49–59; Sofiane Merabet, "Se
dire 'gay': entre la (ré)appropriation d'un espace queer et la formation de nouvelles identités dans le Liban d'aujourd'hui," *Tumultes* 41, no. 2 (2013): 131–40.

90. Christophe Broqua, "Les Formes sociales de l'homosexualité masculine à Ba-
mako dans une perspective comparée: entre tactiques et mobilisations collectives," *Politique et Sociétés* 31, no. 2 (2012): 113–44.

91. "In Iran, We Don't Have Homosexuals," YouTube, September 24, 2007, https://
www.youtube.com/watch?v=U-sC26wpUGQ.

92. Both boys were minors at the time of the acts, which means that Iran broke its
international commitments, having signed two UN conventions that prohibit the death
sentence for minors, the International Covenant on Civil and Political Rights and the
Convention on the Rights of the Child. Iran expressly ratified both conventions, which
became part of its substantive law on June 24, 1975, and July 13, 1994, respectively.

93. See Iranian Queer Organization, http://www.irqo.net.

94. See Ian Buruma and Avishai Margalit, *Occidentalism: The West in the Eyes of
Its Enemies* (New York: Penguin Books, 2005), 147–48. Petrus Liu has shown that when
"Chinese sexuality" is constructed as opposite or exterior to Western sexuality, the paradoxical effect is to render the West uniform, thereby keeping us blind to the ways that
so-called non-Western sexualities themselves produce a certain imaginative construct
of the West. Petrus Liu, "Why Does Queer Theory Need China?," *Positions* 18, no. 2
(September 21, 2010): 298–99.

95. As a counterpart, see Gayatri Gopinath, *Impossible Desire: Queer Diasporas and
South Asian Public Cultures* (Durham, NC: Duke University Press, 2005) ; and Bobby
Benedicto, *Under Bright Lights: Gay Manila and the Global Scene* (Minneapolis: Univer-
sity of Minnesota Press, 2014).

96. Binnie, *The Globalization of Sexuality*, 134–36.

97. Marianne Blidon and France Guérin-Pace, "Un rêve urbain? La diversité des
parcours migratoires des gays," *Sociologie* 4, no. 2 (2013): 119–38.

98. Sébastien Roux, "On m'a expliqué que je suis 'gay,'" *Autrepart* 49, no. 1 (March
1, 2009): 33–34, 37.

99. John Treat has shown that "the lesson for those of us interested in pink-washing
and homonationalism around the world will be that these are ad hoc strategies borne
less from any conviction in favor of human rights than from an intent to contain and
limit them." John W. Treat, "The Rise and Fall of Homonationalism in Singapore," *Positions: East Asia Cultures Critique* 23, no. 2 (2015): 352.

100. Salima Amari has interviewed Algerian, Moroccan, and French women of Algerian or Moroccan background who live in France and identify themselves as female

homosexuals or lesbians. Amari found that "a 'direct, Western-style coming out' is often related to the production of oral discourse. But when the language of self-definition based on a positive discourse on homosexuality is French, whereas the everyday language of communication between the women interviewed and their parents is usually Arabic or Berber, tacitness becomes a real option. The parlance employed can be renegotiated according to context. This discrepancy between discourses in Arabic or Berber and French was recounted by Kadera, who could not invite her parents to celebrate her civil union and could not recount the event to them because she did not know how to express it in Arabic." Salima Amari, "Sujets tacites: le cas de lesbiennes d'origine maghrébine," *Tumultes* 41, no. 2 (2013): 216.

101. Valérie Pouzol, "Dire la différence sexuelle: stratégies, discours et mise en scène des militantismes LGBTQ en Israël et en Palestine," *Tumultes* 41, no. 2 (2013): 174.

102. Ibid., 171.

103. Peter Hitchcock, *Imaginary States: Studies in Cultural Transnationalism* (Urbana: University of Illinois Press, 2003), 185.

104. Interview, July 21, 2013.

105. Ibid.

106. Bourcier, "Théorie queer," 306.

107. Marie-Hélène/Sam Bourcier, "Homosadomaso: Leo Bersani lecteur de Foucault," in *Queer Zone 1* (Paris: Éditions Amsterdam, 2001), 64–74.

108. Bourcier, "'F***' the Politics of Disempowerment in the Second Butler," 246.

109. Marie-Hélène/Sam Bourcier, "Politique et Théorie queer: la seconde vague," Nonfiction.fr, March 28, 2011, http://www.nonfiction.fr/article-4344-p2-politique_et _theorie _queer__la_seconde_vague.htm.

110. Judith Butler, "Endangered/Endangering: Schematic Racism and White Paranoia," in *Reading Rodney King / Reading Urban Uprising*, ed. Robert Gooding-Williams (New York: Routledge, 1993), 15–22.

111. Judith Butler, *Bodies That Matter: On the Discursive Limits of Sex* (1993; repr., New York: Routledge, 2011), 81–98.

112. Marie-Hélène/Sam Bourcier, "Post-gay, la politique queer débarque: entretien avec la sociologue Marie-Héléne Bourcier," *Les Lettres Françaises*, 2010, http://www. les-lettres -francaises.fr/2010/10/post-gay-politique-queer/. On the pitfalls of this non-normative viewpoint, already expressed during the debate over civil unions, see Lucille Cairns, "Queer, Republican France, and Its Euro-American 'Others,'" in *What's Queer about Europe? Productive Encounters and Re-enchanting Paradigms*, ed. Mireille Rosello and Sudeep Dasgupta (New York: Fordham University Press, 2014), 96–100.

113. Bouteldja, "Universalisme gay."

114. Perreau, "The Political Economy of 'Marriage for All,'" 356.

115. Virginie Descoutures et al., eds., *Mariages et Homosexualités dans le monde: l'arrangement des normes familiales* (Paris: Éditions Autrement, 2008).

116. Kimberlé Crenshaw, "Cartographies des marges: intersectionnalité, politique de l'identité et violences contre les femmes de couleur," trans. Oristelle Bonis, *Cahiers du genre* 39, no. 2 (2005): 51–82.

117. See Danièle Kergoat, "Dynamique et consubstantialité des rapports sociaux," in *Sexe, Race, Classe. Pour une épistémologie de la domination*, ed. Elsa Dorlin (Paris: Presses universitaires de France, 2009), 111–25.

118. Sirma Bilge, "Théorisations féministes de l'intersectionnalité," *Diogène*, no. 225 (2009): 70–88.

119. Kimberlé Crenshaw, "Mapping the Margins: Intersectionality, Identity Politics, and Violence against Women of Color," *Stanford Law Review* 43, no. 6 (July 1991): 1244.

120. Ibid., 1246.

121. Jasbir K. Puar, "'I Would Rather Be a Cyborg Than a Goddess': Becoming-Intersectional in Assemblage Theory," *philoSOPHIA* 2, no. 1 (2012): 52, 53, 59.

122. Ibid., 55–56.

123. Puar, *Terrorist Assemblages*, 206.

124. Puar, "I Would Rather Be a Cyborg Than a Goddess," 57. Paola Bacchetta has pointed out that "assemblage" is also often used in the United States as a translation of Foucault's concept of *dispositif* (interview, December 9, 2013). The problem of translation is patent here: *dispositif* is usually something mechanical and dynamic, whereas an assemblage is a collage, a layer of several distinct, inert components.

125. Brian Massumi, translator of Deleuze and Guattari's *Thousand Plateaus* (Minneapolis: University of Minnesota Press, 2005), renders *le devenir minoritaire* somewhat differently as "becoming-minority." See 105–6.

126. Ibid., 63.

127. To avoid confusion, in this book I respect the terms people use to identify themselves and do not use "queer" as a synonym for "gay," "lesbian," "bi," or "trans."

128. Marie-Hélène/Sam Bourcier, *Sexpolitiques: Queer Zones 2* (Paris: La Fabrique, 2005), 30.

129. The English translation of the last sentence loses a significant part of the original meaning. François Cusset wrote in French: "De même que nous *en* serions tous, tous les textes littéraires *en* seraient." The expression *en être* (to be one) is a veiled reference to the category of perverts, or homosexuals. This inference seeks to establish an epistemological complicity among those who know, without others knowing that they know (sometimes including the person so labeled). Furthermore, the personal pronoun *en* links individual identity to collective identity (being one "of them") in such a way that *en être tous* stretches the idea of "being [one] of them" to the brink of nonsense. François Cusset, *The Inverted Gaze: Queering the French Literary Classics in America*, trans. David Homel (Vancouver: Arsenal Pulp Press, 2011), 16–17. For the French version, see François Cusset, *Queer Critics: la littérature française déshabillée par ses homo-lecteurs* (Paris: Presses universitaires de France, 2002), 10.

130. Robert Payne and Cristyn Davies, "Introduction to the Special Section: Citizenship and Queer Critique," *Sexualities* 15, no. 3–4 (June 1, 2012): 254–55.

131. Biddy Martin, "Extraordinary Homosexuals and the Fear of Being Ordinary," in *Feminism Meets Queer Theory*, ed. Elizabeth Weed and Naomi Schor (Indianapolis: Indiana University Press, 1997), 101, 103, 123.

132. Marie-Hélène/Sam Bourcier and Suzette Robichon, eds., *Parce que les lesbiennes*

ne sont pas des femmes . . . Autour de l'œuvre politique, théorique et littéraire de Monique Wittig. Actes du colloque des 16–17 juin 2001 (Paris: Éditions Gaies et Lesbiennes, 2002), 178.

133. Judith Butler, *Precarious Life: The Powers of Mourning and Violence* (New York: Verso, 2004), 44–45.

134. Martin, "Extraordinary Homosexuals," 133.

135. Personal notes, from participation in the conference.

136. Teresa de Lauretis, "Queer Theory: Lesbian and Gay Sexualities, an Introduction," *Differences* 3, no. 2 (1991): iii.

137. Annamarie Jagose, "The Trouble with Antinormativity," *Differences* 26, no. 1 (May 1, 2015): 30.

138. Judith Butler, "Critically Queer," *GLQ: A Journal of Lesbian and Gay Studies* 1, no. 1 (November 1, 1993): 20.

139. Elizabeth A. Armstrong, *Forging Gay Identities: Organizing Sexuality in San Francisco, 1950–1994* (Chicago: University of Chicago Press, 2002), 178–84.

140. Héctor Carrillo, *The Night Is Young: Sexuality in Mexico in the Time of AIDS* (Chicago: University of Chicago Press, 2001), 117–28.

141. Butler, "Critically Queer," 20.

142. Leo Bersani has made this point in reference to *Moby-Dick* in America: "Mass borrowing from other cultures is identical to a self-distancing from other cultures. Sense is borrowed without being subscribed to, and the very indiscriminacy of the borrowing should produce a society without debts, one that never holds what it nonetheless greedily takes." Leo Bersani, "Incomparable America," in *The Culture of Redemption* (Cambridge, MA: Harvard University Press, 1992), 153.

143. This is what Elizabeth Povinelli and George Chauncey ask in their introduction to a special issue of *GLQ: A Journal of Lesbian and Gay Studies*. They state that "post-colonial nations are witnessing the emergence of sex-based social movements whose political rhetoric and tactics seemed to mimic or reproduce Euro-American forms of sexual identity, subjectivity, and citizenship and, at the same time, to challenge fundamental Western notions of the erotic, the individual, and the universal rights attached to this fictive 'subject.'" George Chauncey and Elizabeth A. Povinelli, "Thinking Sexuality Transnationally: An Introduction," *GLQ: A Journal of Lesbian and Gay Studies* 5, no. 4 (1999): 439.

144. Chauncey and Povinelli first proposed the notion of "traffic in cultural representations" as a way of jointly grasping the effects of hegemony and multiple identitarian recompositions. Ibid., 441.

145. Deleuze and Guattari, *A Thousand Plateaus*, 322.

146. Michael Warner, ed., *Fear of a Queer Planet: Queer Politics and Social Theory* (Minneapolis: University of Minnesota Press, 1993), xii.

CHAPTER 4: THE SPECTER OF QUEER POLITICS

1. On this point see Paul Lichterman, "Talking Identity in the Public Sphere: Broad Visions and Small Spaces in Sexual Identity Politics," *Theory and Society* 28, no. 1 (1999): 101–41.

2. Sedgwick, *Epistemology of the Closet*, 1.

3. Michel Foucault, *Discipline and Punish: The Birth of the Prison*, trans. Alan Sheridan (New York: Vintage Books, 1995), 193.

4. See Janine Mossuz-Lavau, *Les Lois de l'amour: les politiques de la sexualité en France, de 1950 à nos jours* (Paris: Payot, 2002).

5. Éric Fassin, "The Purloined Gender: American Feminism in a French Mirror," *French Historical Studies* 22, no. 1 (1999): 113–38.

6. Éric Fassin, Nicolas Ferran, and Serge Slama, "'Mariages gris' et matins bruns," *Le Monde*, December 8, 2009. For a complete analysis, see Judith Surkis, "Hymenal Politics: Marriage, Secularism, and French Sovereignty," *Public Culture* 22, no. 3 (2010): 531–56. See also Hélène Neveu Kringelbach, "'Mixed Marriages,' Citizenship and the Policing of Intimacy in Contemporary France," Oxford International Migration Institute Working Papers, no. 77 (2013).

7. Sedgwick, *Epistemology of the Closet*, 61.

8. Ibid., 11.

9. André Glucksmann, *Le Discours de la haine* (Paris: Plon, 2004).

10. Interview, April 6, 2015.

11. See Laurent Chambon, "Le Placard universaliste. Quand la République se fait particulariste contre les gays," *Mouvements* 38 (March–April 2005): 34–40.

12. Recently, Luc Carvounas publicly announced his homosexuality on the occasion of his marriage in July 2015; he is currently the only openly gay member of the Socialist Party sitting in the French parliament. See Florian Bardou, "Luc Carvounas, sénateur PS, premier parlementaire à épouser une personne du même sexe," *Yagg*, June 24, 2015, http://yagg.com/?post_type=post&p=91954.

13. Aron Rodrigue, "The Jew as the Original 'Other': Difference, Antisemitism, and Race," in *Doing Race: 21 Essays for the 21st Century*, ed. Hazel Rose Markus and Paula Moya (New York: W. W. Norton, 2010), 187.

14. See Timothy Tackett, *Becoming a Revolutionary: The Deputies of the French National Assembly and the Emergence of a Revolutionary Culture, 1789–1790* (Philadelphia: Pennsylvania State University Press, 1996).

15. Foucault, "Of Other Spaces, Heterotopias."

16. David K. Johnson, *The Lavender Scare: The Cold War Persecution of Gays and Lesbians in the Federal Government* (Chicago: University of Chicago Press, 2004), 16.

17. Michael S. Sherry, *Gay Artists in Modern American Culture: An Imagined Conspiracy* (Chapel Hill: University of North Carolina Press, 2007).

18. Carolyn J. Dean, "The 'Open Secret,' Affect, and the History of Sexuality," in *Sexuality at the Fin de Siècle: The Making of a 'Central Problem,'* ed. Peter Maxwell Cryle and Christopher E. Forth (Newark: University of Delaware Press, 2008), 160.

19. Leslie Choquette, "Homosexuals in the City: Representations of Lesbian and Gay Space in Nineteenth-Century Paris," *Journal of Homosexuality* 41, no. 3–4 (2002): 149–67.

20. See Régis Révenin, *Homosexualité et Prostitution masculines à Paris, 1870–1918* (Paris: L'Harmattan, 2005).

21. Laure Murat, "La tante et le policier," in *La Loi du genre. Une histoire culturelle du troisième sexe* (Paris: Fayard, 2006), 27–65.

22. Foucault, *History of Sexuality*, 43.

23. Jean Danet has uncovered several trials for pederasty at the time, including a case in the Cour d'Appel in Paris, October 11, 1930 (GP 1930, 2nd sem., 886), and another at Tribunal de Grande Instance de la Seine, February 26, 1932 (GP 1932, 1st sem., 778). See Jean Danet, *Discours juridique et Perversions sexuelles (XIXe–XXe siècles)* (Nantes: Presses de l'Université de Nantes, 1977).

24. Among late nineteenth-century publications, John Addington Symonds's *A Problem in Greek Ethics* became a key reference work for French upper-class homosexual circles of the 1920s. See Florence Tamagne, *Histoire de l'homosexualité en Europe: Berlin, Londres, Paris: 1919–1939* (Paris: Seuil, 2000), 238–39.

25. See Gilles Barbedette and Michel Carassou, *Paris gay 1925* (Paris: Presses de la Renaissance, 1981), 269.

26. See Olivier Jablonski, "The Birth of a French Homosexual Press in the 1950s," *Journal of Homosexuality* 41, no. 3–4 (2002): 233–48.

27. Marc Boninchi, *Vichy et l'Ordre moral* (Paris: Presses universitaires de France, 2005), 143–93.

28. Jean Le Bitoux was a journalist with *Libération* and a leader of revolutionary homosexual movements in the 1970s. See Jean Le Bitoux, "Notes," in *Moi, Pierre Seel, déporté homosexuel*, by Pierre Seel (Paris: Calmann-Lévy, 1994), 130; also quoted in Boninchi, *Vichy et l'Ordre moral*, 145.

29. Homosexual relations with a "minor" between thirteen and twenty-one was punishable by six months to three years in prison and a fine of two hundred to sixty thousand francs. An average of three hundred successful prosecutions of male homosexuals were carried out in French courts every year. Data published by Claude Courouve in *Le Bulletin de l'Association pour la Liberté d'Expression des Pédérastes et Homosexuels*, quoted in Jean-Louis Bory and Guy Hocquenghem, *Comment nous appelez-vous déjà? Ces hommes que l'on dit homosexuels* (Paris: Calmann-Lévy, 1977), 220.

30. See Badinter's speech before the Assemblée Nationale on December 20, 1981, published in Bruno Perreau, *Homosexualité: dix clés pour comprendre, vingt textes à découvrir* (Paris: Librio, 2005), 62–63.

31. The partial failure of Vichy's policies with respect to sexuality and gender was also reflected in the participation of women in the Resistance. See Miranda Pollard, *The Reign of Virtue: Mobilizing Gender in Vichy France* (Chicago: University of Chicago Press, 1998), 71.

32. See Cyril Olivier, *Le Vice ou la Vertu: Vichy et les politiques de la sexualité* (Toulouse: Presses universitaires du Mirail, 2005).

33. Fabrice Virgili has shown that shaving women's heads was directly linked to a reassertion of virile male bonding based on a rejection of homosexuality. Fabrice Virgili, *La France virile. Des femmes tondues à la Libération* (Paris: Payot, 2000), 264.

34. See Judith Surkis, "Enemies Within: Venereal Disease and the Defense of French Masculinity between the Wars," in *French Masculinities: History, Culture, and*

Politics, ed. Christopher E. Forth and Bertrand Taithe (New York: Palgrave Macmillan, 2007), 103–22.

35. See Julian Jackson, "Le Mouvement Arcadie (1954–1982)," *Revue d'Histoire Moderne et Contemporaine* 53, no. 4 (2006): 150–74.

36. See Julian Jackson, "Sex, Politics and Morality in France, 1954–1982," *History Workshop Journal*, no. 61 (2006): 77–102.

37. See Tamagne, "Le 'Crime du Palace,'" 128–49.

38. These lampooning songs emerged from the Eulenburg affair, involving the scandal of a presumed homosexual relationship in Kaiser Willem II's entourage between Prince Philip of Eulenburg and General Kuno von Moltke. See Norman Domeier, *The Eulenburg Affair: A Cultural History of Politics in the German Empire* (Rochester, NY: Camden House, 2015). It is interesting to note Dreyfus's accusers also played on his links to non-Jewish homosexuals. See Pierre Gervais, Romain Huret, and Pauline Peretz, "Une relecture du 'dossier secret': homosexualité et antisémitisme dans l'affaire Dreyfus," *Revue d'Histoire Moderne et Contemporaine* 55, no. 1 (January–March 2008): 125–60.

39. Carolyn J. Dean, "The 'Open Secret,'" 162. There is a vast literature on the topic of "contaminating agents." It shows that the figure of the disloyal Jew is meant to exemplify multiple forms of sexual perversion and gender trouble (weak masculinity, inversion, sexual predator, and so on). This discourse was thus used widely, including by antifascist movements (see Mark Meyers, "Feminizing Fascist Men: Crowd Psychology, Gender, and Sexuality in French Antifascism, 1929–1945," *French Historical Studies* 29, no. 1 [2006], 109–42) and beyond World War II, when it became an instrument for denouncing a "deficit in heterosexual attraction." See Dagmar Herzog, *Sex after Fascism: Memory and Morality in Twentieth-Century Germany* (Princeton, NJ: Princeton University Press, 2007), 95.

40. Jérémy Guedj, "La figure du juif efféminé: genre, homophobie et antisémitisme dans la France des années 30 à travers les discours d'extrême-droite," in *Hommes et Masculinités de 1789 à nos jours*, ed. Régis Révenin (Paris: Autrement, 2007), 227.

41. Carolyn J. Dean, *The Frail Social Body: Pornography, Homosexuality, and Other Fantasies in Interwar France* (Berkeley: University of California Press, 2000), 88 ff.

42. Jean-Paul Sartre, "Qu'est ce qu'un collaborateur?," in *Situations III* (Paris: Gallimard, 1949), 43–61.

43. George Mosse also mentions a 1942 article by Jean Guéhénno, "Problème sociologique: pourquoi tant de pédérastes parmi les collaborateurs?" See Mosse, *Nationalism and Sexuality*, 176.

44. For a historiographic discussion on fascism and sexual practices, see Sandrine Sanos, *The Aesthetics of Hate: Far-Right Intellectuals, Antisemitism, and Gender in 1930s France* (Stanford, CA: Stanford University Press, 2013), 202–4.

45. *L'Amour qui n'ose pas dire son nom* (The Love That Dare Not Speak Its Name) was a 1927 novel by Francis Porcher devoted to homosexual romance, alluding to the 1896 poem by Lord Alfred Douglas, "I Am the Love That Dare Not Speak Its Name." Oscar Wilde, when questioned during his own trial, was asked to explain the line by

Douglas, his lover; he claimed it was a reference to a spiritual bond between an older and a younger man, in reference to Plato and Shakespeare.

46. Alice Kaplan, *The Collaborator: The Trial and Execution of Robert Brasillach* (Chicago: University of Chicago Press, 2000), 162.

47. Didier Eribon, *Hérésies. Essais sur la théorie de la sexualité* (Paris: Fayard, 2003), 199.

48. Jean-Paul Sartre, *Being and Nothingness*, trans. Hazel E. Barnes (New York: Routledge, 1989), 107–8.

49. Benstock, "Paris Lesbianism and the Politics of Reaction."

50. Eribon, *Hérésies*, 201.

51. Sanos, *The Aesthetics of Hate*, 124 ff.

52. In *Aujourd'hui en France*, September 4, 1995.

53. This represents one of the main contradictions of contemporary neoliberal thought according to philosopher Wendy Brown. See *Regulating Aversion: Tolerance in the Age of Identity and Empire* (Princeton, NJ: Princeton University Press, 2006), 168.

54. Laurent Bouvet, "Contre le (faux) débat identitaire qui vient," *L(B)LOG* (blog), May 19, 2012, http://laurentbouvet.net/2012/05/19/contre-le-faux-debat-identitaire-qui-vient.

55. Ibid.

56. Serge Berstein et al., eds., *Le Parti socialiste entre résistance et République* (Paris: Publications de la Sorbonne, 2001).

57. Noëlline Castagnez, "La notabilisation du PS-SFIO sous la Quatrième République," *Vingtième Siècle* 4, no. 87 (2007), 35–46.

58. Olivier Duhamel, *La Gauche et la Ve République* (Paris: Presses universitaires de France, 1980).

59. Laurent Kestel, *La Conversion politique: Doriot, le PPF et la question du fascisme français* (Paris: Seuil, 2012).

60. Didier Eribon discusses in particular the path followed by the magazines *Esprit*, *Commentaires*, and *Le Débat*. See Didier Eribon, *D'une Révolution conservatrice et de ses effets sur la gauche française* (Paris: Leo Scheer, 2007), 93–131.

61. Claude Nicolet, *L'Idée républicaine en France (1789–1924)* (Paris: Gallimard, 1994), 9–10.

62. *Archives parlementaires de 1787 à 1860* (Paris: Librairie administrative de Paul Dupont, 1878), 756.

63. Quoted in Serge Audier, *Les Théories de la République* (Paris: La Découverte, 2007), 37.

64. Pierre Bourdieu, *Sur l'État. Cours au Collège de France. 1989–1992* (Paris: Seuil, 2012), 486–90.

65. The professionalization of these public health roles was an integral part of the young Third Republic, legitimizing it through practice. See Andrew E. Aisenberg, *Contagion: Disease, Government, and the "Social Question" in Nineteenth-Century France* (Stanford, CA: Stanford University Press, 1999), 111–12.

66. Perreau, *The Politics of Adoption*, 113.

67. Robcis, *The Law of Kinship*, 213–61.

68. Ibid., 29 ff.

69. Andrew Knapp and Vincent Wright, *The Government and Politics of France* (London: Routledge, 2006), 368.

70. Steven Seidman, *Difference Troubles: Queering Social Theory and Sexual Politics* (Cambridge: Cambridge University Press, 1997), 253.

71. Camille Robcis, "Liberté, Égalité, Hétérosexualité: Race and Reproduction in the French Gay Marriage Debates," *Constellations* 22, no. 3 (2015): 458.

72. Rémi Lefebvre and Frédéric Sawicki, *La Société des socialistes. Le PS aujourd'hui* (Bellecombe-en-Bauges: Croquant, 2006), 231.

73. "Comité National d'Éthique, gardien de la famille?"

74. Irène Théry, *Le Contrat d'union sociale en question* (Paris: Fondation Saint-Simon, 1997). Republished in *Esprit*, no. 236 (1997): 159–87.

75. Françoise Dekeuwer-Défossez will later play a key role in bringing together legal experts and Catholic activists against gay marriage. For a study of how these networks entangle, see Céline Béraud and Philippe Portier, *Métamorphoses catholiques. Acteurs, enjeux et mobilisations depuis le mariage pour tous* (Paris: Éditions de la Maison des sciences de l'homme), 73–74.

76. Assemblée Nationale, October 9, 1998.

77. Théry, *Le Contrat d'union sociale en question*, 26.

78. Irène Théry and Anne-Marie Leroyer, *Filiation, Origines, Parentalité. Le droit face aux nouvelles valeurs de responsabilité générationnelle*, Report from the Committee on "Filiation, Origines, Parentalité" (Paris: Ministère des Affaires Sociales et de la Santé, 2014), 199 ff., http://www.justice.gouv.fr/include_htm/etat_des_savoirs/eds_thery-rapport-filiation-origines-parentalite-2014.pdf.

79. Françoise Héritier, "Aucune société n'admet de parenté homosexuelle," *La Croix*, September 11, 1998.

80. Other well-known anthropologists have refuted the fantasy of invariants. See Jeanne Favret-Saada, "La pensée Lévi-Strauss: anthropologie des sexualités," *Journal des Anthropologues*, no. 82–83 (2000): 53–70.

81. For a deconstruction of this theoretical and legal fantasy, see Sabine Prokhoris, *Le Sexe prescrit* (Paris: Aubier, 2000).

82. For example, sociologist Nathalie Heinich wrote of a "perverse system" that produced guilt ("L'extension du domaine de l'égalité," *Le Débat* 180, no. 3 [2014]: 128); Maurice Berger compared the situation of children in homoparental families to transgenic corn, requiring the implementation of a principle of precaution ("Homoparentalité et développement affectif de l'enfant," *Le Débat* 180, no. 3 [2014]: 145).

83. François-Xavier Bellamy, *Les Déshérités ou l'Urgence de transmettre* (Paris: Plon, 2014), 166.

84. A few pages after the previous quotation, Bellamy cites enology as an example of a language that uses physical experience to assign wines their qualities. Ibid., 169.

85. Ibid., 166.

86. Commission Nationale Consultative des Droits de l'Homme, Assemblée Plénière, *Avis sur l'identité de genre et sur le changement de la mention de sexe à l'état civil*,

June 27, 2013, http://www.cncdh.fr/sites/default/files/27.06.13_avis_sur_lidentite_de_genre_et_sur_le_changement_de_la_mention_de_sexe_a_letat_civil.pdf, 3.

87. Thomas Hammarberg, *Human Rights and Gender Identity*, CommDH/IssuePaper, Council of Europe, Commissioner for Human Rights, July 29, 2009, https://wcd.coe.int/ViewDoc.jsp?id=1476365.

88. Delphine Philbert, "Du paternalisme d'HES à la soumission de l'Existrans," *Yagg*, October 24, 2014, http://yagg.com/?post_type=post&p=81269.

89. Tom Reucher, "Quand les trans deviennent experts: le devenir trans de l'expertise," *Multitudes* 1, no. 20 (2005): 163.

90. "Projet de loi de modernisation de la justice du XXIc siècle," Assemblée Nationale, June 29, 2016, http://www.assemblee-nationale.fr/14/textes/3906.asp#D_Article_18_quater.

91. Chaynesse Khirouni, "Lettre à la Garde des Sceaux," Assemblée Nationale, May 6, 2015, http://www.ant-france.eu/int-doc/deputee_khirouni-ministre_de_la_justice.pdf.

92. Comité Consultatif National d'Éthique, Opinion no. 90, § V-6, 2005, http://www.ccne-ethique.fr/sites/default/files/publications/avis090.pdf.

93. Lefebvre and Sawicki, *La Société des socialistes*, 141.

94. For a description of the political and social context surrounding this discourse, see Scott Gunther, *The Elastic Closet: A History of Homosexuality in France, 1942–Present* (New York: Palgrave Macmillan, 2008), 81 ff.

95. "Didier Eribon à propos de la communauté gay et du livre de Frédéric Martel 'Le Rose et le Noir . . . ,'" *Le Cercle de Minuit*, Ina video, televised May 6, 1996, http://www.ina.fr/video/I12243837.

96. On the notion of a French model of society, see Jean-Philippe Mathy, *Extreme-Occident: French Intellectuals and America* (Chicago: University of Chicago Press, 1993), 253.

97. Secrétariat national aux problèmes de société, Parti socialiste, "Des droits nouveaux pour les couples hors mariages. Le contrat d'union sociale," May 1996, 10.

98. Lesbian & Gay Pride Île de France, *Livre Blanc 2000*, May 18, 2000, http://www.inter-lgbt.org/IMG/pdf/livreblanc2000.pdf, 18.

99. Inter-LGBT, "Press Release on the Contrat d'Union Civile," September 22, 2007, http://www.inter-lgbt.org/spip.php?article784.

100. Massimo Prearo, *Le Moment politique de l'homosexualité. Mouvements, identités et communautés en France* (Lyon: Presses universitaires de Lyon, 2014), 236–38.

101. William Poulin-Deltour has stressed that when it opened in 1994, the Centre Gay et Lesbien de Paris, home to many political, social, and athletic clubs, sought to "valorize a community identity and culture," reflecting the influence of ACT UP Paris. Fifteen years later, when ACT UP Paris leaders were no longer an active part of the center (which became the Centre Lesbien, Gai, Bi & Trans in 2002), it claimed that it followed a "civic, non-communitarian approach." See Poulin-Deltour, "Le militantisme homosexuel," 148–49.

102. Philippe Mangeot, "Foucault sans le savoir," 89.

103. Didier Lestrade, *ACT UP. Une histoire* (Paris: Denoël, 2000), 49.

104. Foucault's doctors did not inform him of the cause of the sudden deterioration

in his health. His partner, Daniel Defert, learned the reason only after Foucault's death. As Georges Dumézil and Paul Veynehave reported, Foucault nevertheless knew he was infected with HIV, even if his health had briefly improved. See Didier Eribon, *Michel Foucault* (Paris: Flammarion, 2011), 530–32.

105. Daniel Defert, *Une Vie politique: entretiens avec Philippe Artières et Éric Favereau, avec la collaboration de Joséphine Gross* (Paris: Seuil, 2014), 100 ff.

106. Philippe Mangeot, "Communautés et communautarisme," Les Mots Sont Importants, May 26, 2004, http://lmsi.net/Communautes-et-communautarisme.

107. Marianne Constable, "The Rhetoric of Community: Civil Society and the Legal Order," in *Looking Back at Law's Century: Time, Memory, Change*, ed. Bryant Garth, Robert Kagan, and Austin Sarat (Ithaca, NY: Cornell University Press, 2001), 225.

108. Ronald Dworkin referred to the liberal community as a "super-person." See Ronald Dworkin, "Liberal Community," *California Law Review* 77, no. 3 (May 1989): 495.

109. Béatrice Fracchiolla, "Violence verbale dans le discours des mouvements antagonistes: le cas de 'mariage pour tous' et 'Manif pour Tous,'" *Argumentation et Analyse du Discours*, no. 14 (2015), http://aad.revues.org/1940.

110. "I will probably be criticized for considering this mutual dependence [between men and women] to be natural, thereby implicitly admitting that humanity is naturally 'heterosexual.' I take this point of departure to be an obvious fact." Sylviane Agacinski, *Politique des sexes* (Paris: Seuil, 1998), 107–8. In a more recent newspaper column, Agacinski explained that this heterosexual nature is characterized by the "finiteness and incompleteness of each of the sexes," *Le Monde*, February 3, 2013.

111. I have analyzed Legendre's dogmatic argument elsewhere. See Bruno Perreau, "Faut-il brûler Legendre? La fable du péril symbolique et de la police familiale," *Vacarme*, no. 23 (2003): 62–68.

112. Tort, "Le père du nouveau testament lacanien," in *Fin du dogme paternel*, 123–84.

113. Jacqueline Stevens, *Reproducing the State* (Princeton, NJ: Princeton University Press, 1999), 226.

114. Ibid., 105.

115. Elisa Camiscioli analyzed this imaginative construct in terms of racial fantasies of assimilation, association, and education. Elisa Camiscioli, *Reproducing the French Race: Immigration, Intimacy, and Embodiment in the Early Twentieth Century* (Durham, NC: Duke University Press, 2009), 156–58.

116. Mona Ozouf, *Women's Words*, trans. Jane Marie Todd (Chicago: University of Chicago Press, 1997). Éric Fassin, in "The Purloined Gender," has analyzed Ozouf's fantasies of Americanization and how they sustained the idea of French singularity.

117. Éric Zemmour, *Le Premier Sexe* (Paris: J'ai Lu, 2007).

118. Anne Emmanuelle Berger, *The Queer Turn in Feminism: Identities, Sexualities, and the Theater of Gender*, trans. Catherine Porter (New York: Fordham University Press, 2013), 75–76.

119. Ibid., 76.

120. Ibid.

121. Ibid., 75–76, 76, 80.

122. Quoted in ibid., 80.

123. Ibid., 81, 81–82.

124. Ibid., 124.

125. Using the example of a couple composed of a gay man and a trans man, Gayle Salamon points out that acknowledging that their sexual difference informs their relationship avoids reducing all males to a single undifferentiated category, even while recognizing that the two individuals are men. Salamon suggests that "it may in fact be true that there is a certain ineffable power, some enthralling and catalyzing force, in sexual difference. . . . Sexual undecidability does not condemn the subject to placelessness, but rather locates difference at the heart of both subjectivity and relation." Gayle Salamon, *Assuming a Body: Transgender and Rhetorics of Materiality* (New York: Columbia University Press, 2010), 144.

126. This exclusiveness was challenged as early as 1884 by the novelist Rachilde in *Monsieur Vénus*, where the lovers switch gender roles and invent a new kind of couple. In a similar vein, Michel Journiac's photographs interrogated the exclusiveness of male/female identities by taking mimicry of the family to an extreme. Rachilde, *Monsieur Vénus* (Paris: Flammarion, 1977); Michel Journiac, *Exposition au musée de Strasbourg* (Paris: Éditions de l'École Nationale Supérieure des Beaux Arts, 2004).

127. The empire of faithfulness also extends to civil unions (PACS), even though the law does not impose it on couples within those unions. See Blandine Grosjean, "Dépacsés pour adultère," *Libération*, February 20, 2003.

128. Kristin Elizabeth Gager, *Blood Ties and Fictive Ties: Adoption and Family Life in Early Modern France* (Princeton NJ: Princeton University Press, 1996), 42.

129. Albert Hirschman, *The Passions and the Interests: Political Arguments for Capitalism before Its Triumph* (Princeton, NJ: Princeton University Press, 1977), 63–66.

130. Charles Fourier, *The Theory of the Four Movements*, trans. Ian Patterson (Cambridge: Cambridge University Press, 1996), 143.

131. Perreau, *The Politics of Adoption*, 21–31.

132. Jan Willem Duyvendak, *The Politics of Home: Belonging and Nostalgia in Western Europe and the United States* (New York: Palgrave McMillan, 2011), 39 ff.

133. Judith Halberstam, *The Queer Art of Failure* (Durham, NC: Duke University Press, 2011), 72.

134. George Chauncey, *Gay New York: Gender, Urban Culture, and the Making of the Gay Male World, 1890–1940* (New York: Basic Books, 1994).

135. John D'Emilio and Estelle B. Freedman, *Intimate Matters: A History of Sexuality in America* (New York: Harper and Row, 1988).

136. Dianne Chisholm, *Queer Constellations: Subcultural Space in the Wake of the City* (Minneapolis: University of Minnesota Press, 2004).

137. Nathaniel M. Lewis, Greta R. Bauer, Todd A. Coleman, Soraya Blot, Daniel Pugh, Meredith Fraser, and Leanne Powell, "Community Cleavages: Gay and Bisexual Men's Perceptions of Gay and Mainstream Community Acceptance in the Post-AIDS, Post-Rights Era," *Journal of Homosexuality* 62 (2015): 1201–27.

138. Denis Altman, *The End of the Homosexual?* (Manchester, NH: University of Queensland Press, 2013).

139. Didier Eribon has proposed a Sartrean reading of the relationship to identity and the group via the notion of serial collectives. He showed that gay mobilization is "the taking up on a conscious level and in a deliberate fashion of a preexisting collective which unites gay people whether they will or not." Eribon, *Insult and the Making of the Gay Self*, trans. Michael Lucey (Durham, NC: Duke University Press, 2004), 132.

140. In South Africa, where LGBT persons enjoy legal equality on the constitutional level, Andrew Tucker has documented the persistence of many forms of invisibility and the strategic importance of the multipositioning of queer lives. Andrew Tucker, *Queer Visibilities. Space, Identity, and Interaction in Cape Town* (London: Wiley-Blackwell 2009), 187 ff.

141. Sylvie Tissot, *Good Neighbors: Gentrifying Diversity in Boston's South End*, trans. David Broder with Catherine Romatowski (New York: Verso, 2015), Kindle, 2084 of 6094.

142. Gilles Barbedette and Michel Carassou, *Paris Gay 1925* (Paris: Éd. Non Lieu, 2008).

143. Antoine Idier, *Dissidance rose: fragments de vies homosexuelles à Lyon dans les années 70* (Lyon: Éd. Michel Chomarat, 2012).

144. See Kath Weston, *Families We Choose: Lesbians, Gays, Kinship* (New York: Columbia University Press, 1991).

145. The French text reads *bonheur de femme mariée*, which Bernard Flechtman's English translation renders as "marital happiness." Cf. Jean Genet, *Notre-Dame-des-Fleurs* (Décines: L'Arbalète, 1948), 45, and *Our Lady of the Flowers*, trans. Bernard Flechtman (New York: Grove, 1987), 94.

146. Marina Tsvetaeva, *Mon Frère féminin* (Paris: Mercure de France, 1979), 17. My thanks to Natacha Chetcuti for bringing this passage to my attention.

147. Suzette Robichon, preface to Rosa Bonheur, *Ceci est mon testament . . .* (Paris: La petite iXe, 2012), 9.

148. Sharon Marcus offers a detailed analysis of the symbolic role of dolls—and the Rosa Bonheur doll in particular—among female couples. See Sharon Marcus, *Between Women: Friendship, Desire, and Marriage in Victorian England* (Princeton, NJ: Princeton University Press, 2007), 149 ff.

149. Wendy Brown, "Suffering the Paradoxes of Rights," in *Left Legalism / Left Critique*, ed. Wendy Brown and Janet Halley (Durham, NC: Duke University Press, 2002), 428.

150. This is the argument developed by George Chauncey in *Why Marriage? The History Shaping Today's Debate over Gay Equality* (New York: Basic Books, 2005), Kindle, 163 of 205.

151. Elizabeth Povinelli points out that this marking reduces forms of life to metabolic life forms and overlooks a potentiality specific to the environment and the relationships we weave into it. She bases her analysis of this interweaving on the notion of substance. See Elizabeth A. Povinelli, *Economies of Abandonment: Social Belonging and Endurance in Late Liberalism* (Durham, NC: Duke University Press, 2011), 107–8.

152. Elizabeth Freeman, *Time Binds: Queer Temporalities, Queer Histories* (Durham,

NC: Duke University Press, 2010), 12–13. This hypothesis of a passionate relationship to the past must also be correlated to the rejection of the future, as discussed in the final paragraphs of this chapter. On this point, see Lippert, "Writing Transnational Queer Histories," 251.

153. This is what Ann Cvetkovich calls "the everyday life of queer trauma," in *An Archive of Feelings: Trauma, Sexuality, and Lesbian Public Cultures* (Durham, NC: Duke University Press, 2003), 15 ff.

154. It is important to distinguish "shared memory" from "common memory," for the latter does not imply that lives that had something in common ever encountered one another. See Avishai Margalit, *The Ethics of Memory* (Cambridge, MA: Harvard University Press, 2004), 51.

155. Alan Hollinghurst's novels offer a particularly rich panorama of these configurations of everyday affections, especially *The Swimming Pool Library* (London: Vintage International, 1988).

156. Sedgwick, *Epistemology of the Closet*, 91 ff.

157. Eribon, *Insult and the Making of the Gay Self*, 132.

158. Diana Fuss, "Freud's Fallen Woman," in Warner, *Fear of a Queer Planet*, 42–68.

159. Murray Pratt discusses the way philosopher Jean Baudrillard played on the poetic irony of the epidemic, scarcely taking its real impact into consideration. See Murray Pratt, "Getting It from Noise and Other Myths: AIDS and Intellectuals in France," *Paragraph* 35, no. 2 (2012): 188.

160. Jeff Nunokawa, "'All the Sad Young Men': AIDS and the Work of Mourning," in *Inside / Out: Lesbian Theories, Gay Theories*, ed. Diana Fuss (New York: Routledge, 1991), 312.

161. See Dominique Mehl, *La Bonne Parole. Quand les psys plaident dans les médias* (Paris: La Martinière, 2003).

162. Family sociology shows that the Western nuclear family, rather than generating heterogeneity tends to reproduce social homogeneity. See Franz Schulteis, "The Family's Contribution to Social Reproduction: A State Concern," in *The European Family: The Family Question in the European Community*, ed. Jacques Commaille and François de Singly (Dordrecht, Netherlands: Kluwer Academic Publishers, 1997), 181–94.

163. At the time, comparisons were made between homosexuality and Nazism, for example, in articles by jurist Pierre Legendre during the debate over parenthood following the implementation of civil unions. "Conferring a family status on homosexuality," he wrote, "means using the democratic principle to foster a fantasy. It is fatal insofar as the law, based on the genealogical principle, gives way to a hedonistic system descended from Nazism" (Pierre Legendre, "Entretien avec Antoine Spire," *Le Monde*, October 23, 2001). Such was also the discourse of philosopher Alain Badiou in 1997: "Instances of identitarian politics, such as Nazism, are bellicose and criminal. . . . Lastly, in the case of love, there will be the complementary demands, either for the genetic right to have such and such a form of specialized sexual behavior recognized as a minoritarian identity; or, for the return, pure and simple, to archaic, culturally established conceptions, such as of strict conjugality, the confinement of women, and so forth. It is

perfectly possible to combine the two, as becomes apparent when homosexual protest concerns the right to be reincluded in the grand traditionalism of marriage and the family" (Alain Badiou, *Saint Paul: The Foundation of Universalism*, trans. Ray Brassier [Stanford, CA: Stanford University Press, 2003], 12–13).

164. Perreau, *The Politics of Adoption*, 119–21.

165. Jeffrey Bennett has analyzed what he calls a "state of non becoming" in the context of the fantasized expression of AIDS and homosexuality. He argues that "AIDS has signaled the loss of the body, the implosion of identity, and the stagnation of development." Jeffrey A. Bennett, *Banning Queer Blood: Rhetorics of Citizenship, Contagion, and Resistance* (Tuscaloosa: University of Alabama Press, 2014), 43.

166. Tim Dean argues that, paradoxically, the spread of HIV created a counter-community linked by blood. See Tim Dean, *Unlimited Intimacy: Reflections on the Subculture of Barebacking* (Chicago: University of Chicago Press, 2009), 90–91.

167. Dean states that barebackers are guided by a life-affirming instinct within a culture of "breeding." Ibid., 93.

168. See Christophe Broqua, "Le fantasme de l'homosexuel meurtrier," and "Le séropositif comme modèle," in *Agir pour ne pas mourir!*, 384–89, 389–98.

169. David Caron, *The Nearness of Others: Searching for Tact and Contact in the Age of HIV* (Minneapolis: University of Minnesota Press, 2014), 198–99.

170. Ibid., 80–86. The prevalence of HIV resulting from homosexual practices bears no comparison with its prevalence resulting from heterosexual practices—new contaminations in France in 2008 were two hundred times more frequent in cases of homosexual practices. "Infection à VIH et SIDA," InVS, June 10, 2013, http://www.invs.sante.fr /Dossiers-thematiques/Maladies-infectieuses/VIH-sida-IST/Infection-a-VIH-et-sida/ Incidence-de-l-infection-par-le-VIH.

171. For an analysis of the notion of community within ACT UP, particularly the impact of the international spread of discussion of barebacking, see Gabriel Girard, *Les Homosexuels et le Risque du SIDA* (Rennes: Presses universitaires de Rennes, 2013), 117–35.

172. Leo Bersani, "Is Rectum a Grave?," in "AIDS: Cultural Analysis/Cultural Activism," special issue, *October* 43 (Winter 1987): 222.

173. Lee Edelman, *No Future: Queer Theory and the Death Drive* (Durham, NC: Duke University Press, 2004), 47–48.

174. This is true even if Edelman is a perhaps indulging in a measure of irony, as suggested by his expression, "We the *sintho*mosexual." Ibid., 153.

175. See José Esteban Muñoz, *Cruising Utopia: The Then and There of Queer Futurity* (Durham, NC: Duke University Press, 2009), 91–96.

176. Peeters, *Le Gender, une norme mondiale?*, 18.

177. Ibid., 19.

178. Ibid., 39.

179. Ibid., 57.

180. Jean-Luc Nancy, *L'Il y a du rapport sexuel* (Paris: Galilée, 2001), 28.

181. In the context of the emergence of reflections on community, Jean-Luc Nancy

219. Didier Eribon, *De la Subversion. Droit, norme et politique* (Paris: Cartouche, 2010), 19ff.

220. Gayatri Chakravorty Spivak, "Can the Subaltern Speak?," in *Marxism and the Interpretation of Culture*, ed. Cary Nelson and Lawrence Grossberg (Urbana: University of Illinois Press, 1988), 274.

221. Ibid., 279. Here she invokes *The Eighteenth Brumaire of Louis Bonaparte*, but whereas Marx separated these two dimensions, Spivak links them.

222. Asserting that the subject is not indivisible does not, however, make it a "dividual," that is, the simple sum of the lives inhabiting it. That interpretation would suggest that each life is infinitely reproducible in identical conditions. The materiality of the body contradicts this idea. Each life, by its very presence in the world, is an event.

223. In psychoanalytic theory, scopic usually refers to the drive associated with watching and being watched, the drive through which the self is defined. I use it to describe the ambivalent relation between possession and dispossession within a community. Homi Bhabha makes a similar use of the term in *The Location of Culture* (London: Routledge, 1994), 76.

224. As Mary Douglas has aptly pointed out, this process of embodiment compensates for the fact that "institutions cannot have minds," even while masking this embodiment behind the rational notion of the "thought collective," as Ludwik Fleck's concept has come to be known. Douglas, *How Institutions Think*, 8, 16.

225. Suzy Killmister, "Resolving the Dilemma of Group Membership," in *How Groups Matter: Challenges of Toleration in Pluralistic Societies*, ed. Gideon Calder, Magali Bessone, and Federico Zuolo (London: Routledge, 2014), 89–108.

CONCLUSION

1. It is interesting to note that the discussion between Gayatri Chakravorty Spivak and Judith Butler, *Who Sings the Nation-State?*, was translated into French as *L'État global* (The Global State). Gayatri Chakravorty Spivak and Judith Butler, *Who Sings the Nation-State? Language, Politics, Belonging* (New York: Seagull Books, 2007); Spivak and Butler, *L'État global*, trans. Françoise Bouillot (Paris: Payot, 2009).

2. Judith Butler and Athena Athanasiou, *Dispossession: The Performative in the Political* (Boston: Polity, 2013), 3.

3. Michel Foucault, *The Politics of Truth*, ed. Sylvère Lotringer, trans. Lisa Hochroth and Catherine Porter (Cambridge, MA: MIT Press/Semiotext(e), 2007), 45.

4. For a critical analysis of this debate, see Evelyne Pisier, "Sexes et sexualités: bonnes et mauvaises différences," *Les Temps Modernes*, no. 609 (2000): 156–75.

5. Eribon, *D'une Révolution conservatrice*, 114–21.

6. Wilfried Rault, *L'Invention du PACS. Pratiques et symboliques d'une nouvelle forme d'union* (Paris: Presses de Sciences Po, 2009).

7. Mathieu Trachman, "Genre: état des lieux. Entretien avec Laure Bereni," *La Vie des Idées*, October 5, 2011, http://www.laviedesidees.fr/Genre-etat-des-lieux.html.

8. Joan W. Scott, *Only Paradoxes to Offer: French Feminists and the Rights of Man* (Cambridge, MA: Harvard University Press, 1997).

9. "Alain Juppé: l'invité de Ruth Elkrief," BFM TV video, September 23, 2014, http://www.bfmtv.com/mediaplayer/video/alain-juppe-l-invite-de-ruth-elkrief-2309-22 -319857.html.

10. Philippe Raynaud, "De la tyrannie de la majorité à la tyrannie des minorités," *Le Débat* 69, no. 2 (1992): 48–56.

11. Nicolas de Condorcet, *Condorcet: Political Writings*, ed. Steven Lukes and Nadia Urbinati (Cambridge: Cambridge University Press, 2012), 184–86.

12. On "good" values, see Carlos A. Ball, *The Morality of Gay Rights: An Exploration in Political Philosophy* (New York: Routledge, 2003), 206–14. On "bad" values, see Badiou, *Saint Paul*. According to philosopher Alain Badiou, "What inexhaustible potential for mercantile investments in this upsurge—taking the form of communities demanding recognition and so-called cultural singularities—of women, homosexuals, the disabled, Arabs! And these infinite combinations of predicative traits, what a god-send! Black homosexuals, disabled Serbs, Catholic pedophiles, moderate Muslims, married priests, ecologist yuppies, the submissive unemployed, prematurely aged youth!" (10).

13. Joan W. Scott, "The Evidence of Experience," *Critical Inquiry* 17, no. 4 (July 1, 1991): 773–97.

14. Michel Foucault, *"Society Must Be Defended": Lectures at the Collège de France, 1975–1976*, trans. David Macey (New York: Picador, 2003), 164.

15. Wendy Brown, "Configurations contemporaines de la domination et des résistances: un regard transnational," *Cahiers du Genre* 1, no. 50 (2011): 159.

16. Stephen Macedo advocates a cumulative approach to rights based on the institution of marriage. At the same time, in regard to polygamy, he reveals the porousness of the boundary line between behavior recognized within marriage and behavior accepted only outside it. See Stephen Macedo, *Just Married: Same-Sex Couples, Monogamy, and the Future of Marriage* (Princeton, NJ: Princeton University Press, 2015), 179–203, 208.

17. See Wendy Brown, "Educating Human Capital," in *Undoing the Demos: Neoliberalism's Stealth Revolution* (New York: Zone Books, 2015), 175–200.

18. Douglas, *How Institutions Think*, 55.

19. Lauren Berlant and Elizabeth Freeman, "Queer Nationality," *boundary 2* 19, no. 1 (1992): 180.

INDEX

Page numbers in italics refer to figures.

abortion, 17, 146. *See also* anti-abortion
movement
Abu Ghraib, readings of, 123
academicism, 86, 139
academic/scholarly events. *See* seminars;
symposiums
academic self-reproductive mechanisms, 120
Action Française, 36–37, 154, 198–99n85
ACT UP New York, 79
ACT UP Paris, 83, 85, 86, 110, 117, 130,
210n30; and Les Tordu(e)s, 101, 102,
103, 105, 106, 107; notion of community
within, 163, 172, 233n101, 238n171; and
queer theory, 12, 77, 83–84
adoption: according parenthood through,
as a stated purpose, 47; Catholic Church
on, 167; certifying parental candidates
for, 167; court rulings on, 4, 73; forestalling on reform of, 159; inequalities
involving, 4, 47, 189; successful and un-
successful, tale involving, 51–52. *See also*
gay adoption
affirmative action, 42, 217n152
Agacinski, Sylviane, 42–43, 164, 201n126,
234n110
Ahmadinejad, Mahmoud, 132
AIDES organization, 72, 158, 163, 176
AIDS. *See* HIV/AIDS

Aisenberg, Andrew E., 231n65
Alduy, Cécile, 220n32
Alessandrin, Arnaud, 92
Al Farchichi, Wahid, 223n79
Algeria, criminalization of homosexuality
in, 131
Allal, Marina, 205n184
Allègre, Claude, 88
Alliance Vita (anti-abortion group), 26, 56
Allouch, Jean, 77, 91, 92, 213n87
Al-Qaws (Palestinian association), queer
activism by, 119, 133–34
Altman, Denis, 168, 235n138
Amara, Fadela, 126
Amari, Salima, 224–25n100
Americanization, 10, 87, 149, 162, 234n116.
See also anti-Americanism
Amsterdam Research Center for Gender
and Sexuality, 120
anarchist movements, 102, 107
anatomical difference, desire and, 175
anatomical sex, 23
Anatrella, Tony, 23, 195n35
Andréa, Yann, 174, 175
androgyny, 10, 11, 62
anti-abortion movement, 1, 25, 26, 37, 56,
196n44
anti-Americanism, 20, 57, 113, 143, 184,
218n2
anticapitalism, 56, 108

anticommunitarianism: archaeological analysis of, task in, 9; article espousing, 87; deconstruction of, 163; fear leading to, 147, 155, 185; and fixation on the notion of sexual difference, 164–65; indivisibility underpinning, 116–17; LGBT associations and, 162, 163; sexuality as an important vector of, 146, 148; Socialist Party and, 15, 156, 157–59, 162; solidifying of, 113, 172; threat to, 111

anti-gay-marriage movement: claims in, 1–2, 185; fear at the heart of, 10, 15; heterogeneous, 31–37; key issue behind, 6; overview of, 11; politicized, 43–46; reactionary, 40–43; religious convictions in, 37–40; rise of, 27; traditional, 27–31, 125. See also specific manifestations of the anti-gay-marriage movement

antinormativity, 81, 86, 141

antiracist activism, 126

anti-Semitism, 58, 59, 152, 153, 154, 199n85, 205n186, 220n30, 223n86

Anzaldúa, Gloria, 134, 209n20; Borderlands —La Frontera: The New Mestiza, 79

Apollinaire, Guillaume, 41

apologies, purpose of, 62

Arab homoeroticism, 127–30, 131

Arabic language, 133–34, 225n100

Aragon, Louis, 41

Arcadie (homophile association), 151

archaeological approach, 9

ArchiQ, 86

Ardisson, Thierry, 94

Armstrong, Elizabeth, 142, 227n139

artwork: analysis of, in the "Sociology of Homosexualities" seminar, 88–89; destruction of, by gay-marriage opponents, 6–7; at Queer Week, 110; street prayers organized against, 27

assemblage, notion of, 121, 138, 226n124

Assemblée des Évêques Orthodoxes (Assembly of Orthodox Bishops), 38

Assemblée Nationale, 2, 26, 30, 39, 41, 44, 46, 151, 158, 217n151

assimilation, 130, 188

Associations Familiales Catholiques (AFC), 67, 206n203

Aswat (Palestinian group), queer activism by, 133–34

Athanasiou, Athena, 241n2

Aubry, Martine, 87

Au Diable Vauvert (publishing house), 106

Audier, Serge, 231n63

Augustine, Saint, 195n26

authenticity: fantasy of, 128; principle of, 113

autonomy, achieving, 106

Ayeva, Abdel Fahd, 217n155

Ayoub, Phillip M., 204n177, 208n231

Ayrault, Jean-Marc, 48, 160, 161, 203n156

Bacchetta, Paola, 110, 209n19, 226n124

Badgett, M. V. Lee, 203n159

Badinter, Robert, 150, 229n30

Badiou, Alain, 237–38n163, 242n12

Baldwin, James, 240n210

Balibar, Étienne, 89

Ball, Carlos A., 242n12

Balland (publishing house), 86

Balmand, Pascal, 206n203

Barbarin, Philippe, 27

Barbedette, Gilles, 229n25, 236n142

Bard, Christine, 206n214

Bardèche, Maurice, 153

Bardou, Florian, 217n149, 220n23, 228n12

bareback sex, 84, 172, 211n43, 238n167, 238n171

Barjot, Frigide, 19, 27, 29, 30–31, 39, 40, 71, 197n62, 197n65

Barney, Natalie, 154

Barré, Camille, 3–4

Barthes, Roland, 211n61

Bartolone, Claude, 30

Baudrillard, Jean, 8, 165, 237n159

Bauer, Greta R., 235n137

Bauman, Zygmunt, 41

Bazin de Jessey, Madeleine, 45, 194n10

Beauvoir, Simone de, 70, 76, 135

Beck, Ulrich, 195n25

Belghoul, Farida, 66–67

Belgium: gay anarchist event in, 82; and marriage laws, 3, 56–57, 72; opposition to gender theory in, 57; queer theory initiatives undertaken in, 98; workshop on "Gender(s) and Sexuality(ies)" in, 98

Bellamy, François-Xavier, 43, 159–60, 232nn83–85

belonging, sense of: boundaries in, disruption of, 113; and citizenship, 2, 115,

145, 189; destabilizing, 112, 144; greater reflection on, encouraging, 140; individual relationships to, cultural influences on, seminar dissecting, 88; introducing a criterion of immunity into, 172; issue of, basis of, 10, 115; language and, 107, 166; links between sexuality and, 115, 123; queer theory and, 168, 178, 183; reconceptualizing, 15–16, 181, 189; and representation, 179–80, 181–82

Benedicto, Bobby, 224n95

Benedict XVI, 20, 21, 22, 23, 24, 27, 205n192

Bennett, Jeffrey, 238n165

Benoist, Alain de, 75, 208nn1–3

Benstock, Shari, 10, 193n34, 231n49

Béraud, Céline, 38, 199n98, 232n75

Berber language, 225n100

Berger, Anne Emmanuelle, 165–66, 234–35nn118–24

Berger, Maurice, 232n82

Berl, Emmanuel, 152

Berlant, Lauren, 242n19

Berliner, David, 98

Bernheim, Gilles, 38, 39

Berry, David, 220n31

Bersani, Leo, 88, 193n35, 227n142, 238n172; *Is the Rectum a Grave?* 91

Berstein, Serge, 231n56

bestiality, 62–63, 123, 132, 195n26, 206n196

betrayal, fear of, 10, 14, 58–59, 96, 100, 146, 147, 148–57

Beyer, Caroline, 218n164

Bhabha, Homi, 241n223

Bigot, Chantal, 89

bilateral conventions on marriage laws, 4–5, 73

Bilge, Sirma, 137, 226n118

binary choice, removal of, 186–87

Binnie, Jon, 115, 219n14, 224n96

bioethics law, 4, 161, 167

biological determinism, 21–22, 23

biological sex: Catholic views on, 22, 23; change of, and precondition for change of legal status, 5, 160; establishing legal kinship increasingly based on, 52–53; and grammatical sex, 166; presentation of, in school curricula, 25, 70

Birkin, Jane, 3, 70

Birnbaum, Pierre, 205n188

birth rates, 151, 156

bisexuality, 110, 142

Black Panthers, 130

Blanchot, Maurice, 15, 175, 180, 186, 239n182, 239n184, 239n186, 239n190, 239n194; *The Unavowable Community*, 174

Blidon, Marianne, 89, 133, 216n127, 224n97

Bloche, Patrick, 158

Bloc Identitaire (Identity Block), 36, 59

blogs: *Comité Urgence Pape* (Pope Relief Committee), 19; *Le Blog de João*, 73; *Le Salon Beige* (Beige Salon), 26, 76

Blot, Soraya, 235n137

Blum, Léon, 58, 152

Boehringer, Sandra, 89

Bompard, Jacques, 26, 202n141

Bongibault, Xavier, 28, 197n54

Bonheur, Rosa, 169–70, 236n147

Bonikowski, Bart, 219n6

Boninchi, Marc, 150, 229n27

Bonis, Oristelle, 137

Bonnard, Abel, 118, 153

Bonnet, Marie-Jo, 73

books/articles. *See specific authors*

Boone, Joseph Allen, 223nn73–74; *The Homoerotics of Orientalism*, 127–28

borders: defining, by leaving, 177; LGBT movements and, 99; obsession over, 14; oscillating, 143–44; redrawing, of national community, 172

Borghi, Rachele, 92–93

Boris, Lorraine, 217–18n155

Borrillo, Daniel, 3, 85, 89, 176, 195n26, 203n164, 208n233, 211n48

Bory, Jean-Louis, 229n29

Bosia, Michael J., 219n11

Boswell, John, 195n26

Boulevard Hitler, 64

Bourcier, Marie-Hélène/Sam, 212n66, 212n74, 212n79, 225nn106–9, 225n112, 226n128, 226n132; background on, 213n84; Belgian workshop host, 98; criticisms of Butler's works, 89–90, 135; vs. Eribon, 91; on Fassin's translation of *Gender Trouble*, 89; "Fuck My Brain" workshop launched by, 90; on gay and lesbian studies, 139; on gay marriage, 136; and his attacks on Gaspard and Eribon's seminar, 89; international symposium organized by Robichon and, 96; involvement of, with Pink TV and *Le Set*, 94; and performativity, 140; pioneering role of, 12, 77; queer scholars associated with, race issue raised by, 134; on queer theory, 139; and Queer Week at Sciences Po, 110; *Queer Zones*, 86; *Queer Zones 3*, 90; radical stance of, examining, 140–41; "Screw Your Gender" workshop run by, 82–83; on sexual-political roots, 140; "Transgenders: New Identities and Visibilities" seminar, 90; translations done by, 86; and Zoo working group, 85, 86, 88, 99, 106, 139

Bourdieu, Pierre, 34, 87–88, 178, 198n81, 231n64, 240n213

Bourges, Béatrice, 25, 27, 30, 111, 194n9, 197n59

Bourseul, Vincent, 83, 92, 209n14, 213n91

Boussemart, Marie-Stella, 39

Bouteldja, Houria, 131, 136, 137, 223n86, 225n113

Boutin, Christine, 25, 26, 27, 45, 70, 71

Bouvet, Laurent, 154, 155, 231nn54–55

Bowers v. Hardwick, 121–22, 123

Boyancé, Michel, 201n120

Boyle, Claire, 91, 212n82

Brader, Ted, 207n220

"Brand Israel" policy, 119

Brasillach, Robert, *Présence de Virgile*, 153

Briand, Aristide, 152

Bright, Damien, 218n155

Briois, Steeve, 118

Broqua, Christophe, 132, 211nn41–42, 224n90, 238n168

Brown, Wendy, 236n149, 240n216, 242n15, 242n17

Browne, Katherine, 216n127

Brustier, Gaël, 37, 199n86, 199n91, 199n93, 200n107

Buddhism, position of, on marriage, 39

Burger, Warren, 123

Burggraf, Jutta, 23, 195n34

burlesque performance, 110

Buruma, Ian, 224n94

Buss, Doris, 23, 195nn31–32

Butler, Judith, 12, 86, 209n16, 209n23, 211n47, 211n55, 212nn75–76, 214n108, 221n50, 225nn110–11, 227n133, 227n138, 227n141, 240n218, 241nn1–2; *Antigone's Claim* translated as *Antigone*, 92, 135, 168; Belgian workshop host, 98; *Bodies That Matter*, 98, 135; criticism of works by, 1, 23, 69, 75, 76, 134–35, 136; and deconstruction of categories, 80; *Excitable Speech*, 135; *Gender Trouble*, 23, 85, 89, 90, 97, 98, 135; "Imitation and Gender Insubordination," 91–92; influences on, 96, 209n18, 213n89; initial invitation to France, purpose of, 92; interview with, 91; on mourning, 135, 180, 181; origin of ideologies attributed to, 1–2, 111; personal attacks on, 14, 24, 58, 76; *Precarious Life*, 135; in protest of racism in Berlin Pride, 115, 118–19; *The Psychic Life of Power*, 135; at Sciences Po, 217n154; seminar attended by, 88; on the term "queer," 142; *Undoing Gender*, 90, 135

Cadinot, Jean-Daniel, 129–30

Cairns, Lucille, 225n112

Calame, Claude, 91

camp humor, 83, 171

Camping pour Tous (Camping for All), 45, 202n141

Camus, Albert, 41

capitalism, 147, 187

Carassou, Michel, 229n25, 236n142

Caresche, Christophe, 46

Carmiscioli, Elisa, 234n115

Caron, David, 172, 238nn169–70; *My Father and I*, 92

Carrillo, Héctor, 227n140

Cartesian "I think," reading of, offsetting, 135

Carvounas, Luc, 228n12

Case, Mary Anne, 195n30

Casini, Annalisa, 98

Castagnez, Noëlline, 231n57

castration, fear of, 76

categorical boundaries, crossing of, attentiveness to, 80

categories: analytical and political, 124; globalization of, rejection of, 183; meaning of, swings in, 7; use of, as identities, queer theory on, 142

categorization: double deconstruction of, 79; political history as an operation of, 148

Catholic Charismatic Renewal movement, 39

Catholic Church/Vatican, 199n85, 199n90, 206n203; on adoption, 167; on family, 21, 22, 205n192; and gender-monitoring projects, 21, 22, 23–24; on homosexuality, 24, 38; on the human body, 22, 23, 56; and human ecology, 11, 20–21, 22, 173, 205n192; influence of, on schools, through intermediaries, 25–26; *Lexicon: Ambiguous and Debatable Terms regarding Family Life and Ethical Questions*, 22, 23; on male/female equality, 20, 21–22; on marriage, 11, 21, 167; and medically assisted procreation, 18, 37; news of, blog containing, 26; opposition to gay marriage supported by, 2, 17, 27, 38, 39, 124, 125, 196n44; positive image of, mobilization concerned with creating, 28; on queer studies, 11; on reproductive technique, 21; on sexuality, 20, 21, 22; theology of natural law, 20, 21–22, 33, 39, 52–53; and Vatican II, 21; on women's rights, 23; and the World Conference on Women, 11, 20

Catholic family associations, 27, 67, 206n203

Catholicism, 69, 125, 156, 199n85

Catholic martyr ethic, 41

Catholic movements, 11, 17, 37, 125. *See also specific people and groups*

Catholic networks forming, 232n75

Catholic parent-teacher associations, 11, 66

Catholic Pride, 32

Catholic schools: opposition to textbooks at, 26; state supervision of, public demonstrations over, 1, 66

Cédelle, Luc, 206n206

censorship, period of, 150

Centre d'Analyse et d'Intervention Sociologiques (CADIS), 90

Centre d'Études et de Prospectives sur la Science, 205n186

Centre Freudien de Formation et de Recherches Psychanalytiques, 92

Centre Gai et Lesbien de Paris, 85, 99, 233n101

Cervulle, Maxime, 90, 129–30, 134, 223n82

Césaire, Aimé, 47

Chambon, Laurent, 130, 228n11

charismatic communities, 39–40

Chatel, Luc, 26

Chaumont, Franck, 222n68; *Homo-Ghetto*, 126

Chauncey, George, 88, 212n69, 227nn143–44, 235n134, 236n150; *Gay New York, 1840–1940*, 89

Chauvin, Sébastien, 14, 89

Chazal, Claire, 94

Chenu, Sébastien, 117

Chetcuti, Natacha, 89, 110, 205n190, 207n219

Chevènement, Jean-Pierre, 161

Chicana studies, 79

childhood: impact of poverty during, effect of marriage on, 48; obsession with passing homosexuality on during, 40; orphaned during, 4, 167; perceived threat of the queer child during, 65–66; and the sacredness of the body, 52–56; wretched, linking, with adoption, 51, 167. *See also* adoption; schools; youth corruption

children's rights: as full citizens, perceived threat from, 173; protection of, 55; rhetorical issues involving, 19

Chisholm, Dianne, 235n136

Chodorow, Nancy, 78

Choquette, Leslie, 228n19

Christian humanism, 21

Christianity, 119, 221n42

Christian networks, meeting seeking to politically unite, 40

Chrysostom, John, 195n26

Cineffable, 110

citizenship, 227n143; abstract notions of, power of, belief in, 57; challenge to, 144; and conceptualization of citizenship, 6; denaturalization of, rights perceived to imply, 23; entitlement to, 54; foundation of, 2, 189; "good," perceived threat to, 10, 60–61; Judaism and, 156; majority conceptualization of, 6; and "marriage of contrivance," 146; moored in sexual difference, 156, 164; multitiered systems of, 177; and performativity, 98; and the principle of exclusiveness, rethinking, 13, 145; queer theory and, 183, 185; refashioned, 120; and sense of belonging,

2, 115, 145; sexual, 123; surrogate, 123; via
nationality, 130, 145
civic purity, 12, 65
civic rights, 23
civilization, perceived threat to, 159–60,
173, 184
civil law, reforms in, 76
civil rights, 55
civil unions (PACS): acceptance of, 30; and
adoption, 158–59, 189; attention to gay
consumers during debate over, 95; as a
concession, 5; and faithfulness, 235n127;
first in, between gay men, 111; gay marketing following legalization of, 103–4;
homophobia during debate over, 23;
inception of, idea reinforced following,
93; legal recognition through, effect of,
176, 185; majority preference for, 46; opposition to, 1, 27, 53, 92, 162, 184; passage
of law authorizing, 176, 191n7; promotion of, 72; sabotaging first attempt at
passage of, 158; Socialist Party and, 3;
and ties of kinship, 30, 40, 158–59
Civitas (far-right group), 27, 28, 36, 40, 44,
59, 60
Cixous, Hélène, 8, 213n89
class: accusation involving, in critique of
queer theory, 84; communism and,
186; criticism of Sciences Po involving,
217n152; and Gay Pride events, 104; and
homonormativity, 121, 124; and intersectionality, 130, 136, 137; multipositionality
as a question of, 188–89; and nationalism, 124; preeminence of, as a political
campaign issue, 118; specter of, 176–79;
stigmatization based on, 168; use of, by
opponents of gay marriage, 11, 30, 37,
40, 48, 49, 125, 154, 155
classification, gender as a system of, 78
classism, 178
class racism, 79
class revenge, 118
class stereotypes, 79, 93–94
Clermont Tonnerre, Stanislas de, 156
Coad, David, 90
Cohn, Steven F., 202n145
Colas, Dominique, 195n26
Coleman, Todd A., 235n137
collage: assemblage as, 226n124; practices
of, seminar's analysis of, 88–89

Collard, Gilbert, 30, 44
Collectif pour l'Enfant (Collective for the
Child), 25, 30
collective good, 47
collective memory, 61, 86, 170, 177, 237n154
Collective National des Musulmans de
France (National Collective of French
Muslims), 39
collective rights, 189
Collège International de Philosophie, 92
Collin, Thibaud, 69
Colombani, Mathieu, 45
colonialism, 60, 127, 132
colonial law, 129
Colpani, Gianmaria, 222n63
Columbia University: in New York, 84; in
Paris, 96
coming out, 117, 118, 133, 147, 214n100,
220n35, 225n100, 228n12
Comité Consultatif National d'Éthique
(National Ethics Commission), 47, 158,
161, 202n153
commercialization, 103, 104, 108
Commission Nationale Consultative
des Droits de l'Homme (National
Consultative Commission on Human
Rights), 160
commodification: of Arab boys, 129–30; of
children, 56, 70; of the human body, 54
Communauté de l'Emmanuel at Paray-le-
Monial, 39–40
communism, 23, 149, 174, 239n181
communitarianism: as a perceived
threat, 145, 172, 176; of the United
States, view of, 57, 87, 162. See also
anticommunitarianism
community: alternative model of, 172; attachment to, 180; bareback sex and creation of, 172, 211n43, 238n171; comprised
solely of family and nation, 14; desire
for, 107; gay, idea of, 162, 163, 169, 184,
187; "good" and "bad," notion of, 187,
242n12; impossible, myth of, 147, 148,
174–75, 180–81, 239n186; interpretive,
basis of, 77; interwoven with sexuality and nation, 9, 13, 145–46; liberal,
notion of, 234n108; notion of "common" and, 15–16, 174, 186, 238–39n181;
political, membership in, 62, 164; from
a queer perspective, 148, 183, 184, 185,

186; questioning what makes, 13, 145; reconceiving, need for, 61–62; specter of "sameness" and, 157–63; united, principle of, 158; US model of, view of, 14, 77

Company of Jesus, 22

comparative cultural sociology, critique of, 9

complementarity of the sexes: challenge to, 21–22, 161, 202–3n153; idea of parity becoming synonymous with, 42; parenthood and, 52; promotion of, 21

Condorcet, Nicolas de, 186–87, 242n11

Confédération Nationale du Travail, 102

Conference of Bishops, 27

Confraternity of Saint Pius X, 27

conjugal tie, 169

Conseil Constitutionnel (Constitutional Court), 2–3, 197n64

Conseil de la Fédération Protestante de France (Council of the French Protestant Federation; CFPF), 38

Conseil d'État (Council of State), 55, 56, 67

Conseil Français du Culte Musulman (French Council of Muslim Cult; CFCM), 38

Conseil National des Universités (CNU), 213n84

conservatism, 6–7, 12, 58, 91, 117, 120, 129

conservative movements, 11, 17, 147. See also specific people and groups

conspiracy, idea of, 13, 14, 20, 24, 41, 58, 65, 70, 78, 88, 110–11, 173, 185

Constable, Marianne, 163, 234n107

consumerism, 12, 57, 103–4

contamination: fear of, 145, 152, 170, 171–72; as a layer of discourse, defined, 10; post-independent states and, 132; through "sameness," 147

contraception, 24, 146, 173

conversion: fear of, 40; Francis warning of, 22; as a layer of discourse, defined, 10; and the notion of reeducation, 65, 70, 73

Copé, Jean-François, 71

corruption: of culture, linking, to individualism, 159, 160; of democracy, perceived, 145; as a layer of discourse, defined, 10; moral, 40, 110–11, 118. See also youth corruption

cosmopolitanism, 2, 114, 146

Cosse, Emmanuelle, 83

Council of Europe, 13, 125, 160

Cour d'Appel, 3, 229n23

Cour de Cassation (highest judiciary court), 4, 5, 56, 73

Courouve, Claude, 229n29

court rulings: on adoption, 4, 73; on age of consent for homosexuality, 150–51; on arrests of Manif pour Tous demonstrators, 41; on change of gender marker, 5, 160; on marriage, 3, 4, 5, 73; on pederasty, 229n23; on sodomy, 121–22, 123; on surrogate pregnancy, 55

creationism, 62

Crenshaw, Kimberlé, 225n116, 226nn119–20; "Mapping the Margins," 137

Crouch, Gregory, 219n17

Crowley, Martin, 239n192

cruising, police investigations of, 149, 150

cultural flows, history of, 115

cultural insecurity, 154–55

culturalism, 2

cultural studies, 79

cultural translation, insistence on, 143, 227n142

cultural transmission, 159–60

cultural voyaging, 219n4

Currah, Paisley, 192n14

Cusset, François, 139–40, 218n3, 226n129

Cvetkovich, Ann, 237n153

Daladier, Édouard, 37, 151

Damas, Léon-Gontran, 47

Danet, Jean, 229n23

Daniel-Ange, Father, 32

Daniels, Jessie, 219n15, 221n36

Darlan, François, 150

Darling, Cherry Lyly, 110

Davies, Cristyn, 226n130

Davis, Oliver, 90, 91, 213n83

Dean, Carolyn, 88, 153, 228n18, 230n39, 230n41

Dean, Tim, 238nn166–67

death: anonymous, 180; commonality of, 186; specter of, 173–76, 180

death drive, 15, 76, 175–76

death wish, 75

Debout Étudiants Gays et Lesbiennes (DEGEL), 102, 105

decentralization, 157

decolonization, 117, 136

Defert, Daniel, 163, 234nn104–5
de Gaulle, Charles, 151
Degenne, Alain, 201n138
Dekeuwer-Défossez, Françoise, 158, 232n75
Delaire, Franck, 162
Delanoë, Bertrand, 70
de la Rochère, Ludovine, 27, 31, 43, 56, 57, 59, 65, 197n67, 198n83, 204n179
de Lauretis, Teresa, 80, 95, 134, 141–42, 210n23, 227n136; *Théorie queer et Cultures populaires*, 86
Deleuze, Gilles, 8, 84, 138, 143, 226nn125–26, 227n145
Dell'Omodarme, Marco, 85, 86, 89, 99
Delorme, Wendy (Stéphanie Kunert), 100, 105–6, 165–66
Delors, Jacques, 156
Delphy, Christine, 215n111; *L'Ennemi principal*, 97
D'Emilio, John, 235n135
democracy: corruption of, perceived, 145; and meritocracy, 178; minority, plea for, 186–89; new, wariness of, 180; secular, and religion, 37; sexual, 115–16
demonstrations: anti-Semitic, 59; against consumerism, 103, 104; to counter Gay Pride event, 13, 78, 101, 103, 104, 105, 107–8; and "The Day of Wrath," 59; in defense of gay marriage and adoption, 70–72; against gay marriage, 1, 6, 10, 14, 19, 20, 27–31, 34, 38, 39, 40, 41, 44, 54, 124, 197n58; of Gay Pride, 82, 101, 104–5; against gender theory, 20, 67; history of, 1; nationalist, 59; over state supervision of Catholic schools, 1, 66; symbolic-style, emergence of, against gay marriage, 31–37, 51, 52
Denizeaux, Paul, 109
Derrida, Jacques, 3, 8, 41, 86, 111, 219n5
Derville, Tugdual, 26, 27, 39
Deschamps, Catherine, 85, 99
Descoings, Richard, 109, 110–11, 217n152
Descoutures, Virginie, 225n115
Deslandes, Mathieu, 196n53
Desprez, Victoire, 218n155
Deville, Louise, 110
Di Bella, Giuseppe, 197n54
Didier, Geoffroy, 44
Dieudonné (stand-up comic), 59, 66, 223n86

difference: critique of, as a system of thought, linking analysis of performativity to, 79–80; hierarchical systems and the notion of, 79; manufacturing, 139; notion of, as crucial to sex, fixation on, 164; recognizing, in the "other," essentialness of, 147; zone of, between original and translation, 166
difference between the sexes. *See* sexual difference
Dinechin, Bénédicte de, 45
disciplinary regimes, nature of, 146
disintegration, 145, 156
disorder, politics of, group wanting to give weight to, 101
distinctions, loss of: gay adoption and, 52; as a layer of discourse, defined, 10; between the sexes, anxiety over, 65–66, 69, 110, 160, 164, 165
diversity: approach to, in TV shows, 77–78, 93, 94–95; avoiding conflict over, 160; domination in the name of, reinforcing other forms of, 109, 120, 123; promotion of, in Palestine, 119
dolls, symbolic, 170
Domeier, Norman, 230n38
Dorlin, Elsa, 98, 215n115
Doucet, Philippe, 48, 49
Douchy-Oudot, Mélina, 240n200
Douglas, Alfred, 230–31n45
Douglas, Mary, 9, 192n26, 206n201, 241n224, 242n18
Downing, Lisa, 91
drag king performance, 92, 105, 110
drag performance, 83
Dreyfus affair, 198–99n85, 230n38
Drieu la Rochelle, Pierre, *Gilles*, 152
Dudink, Stefan, 220n29
Duflot, Cécile, 70
Duggan, Lisa, 120, 210n24
Duhamel, Olivier, 231n58
Dumézil, Georges, 87, 154
Duquesne University, 39
Duras, Marguerite, 239n183, 239n185, 239n187, 239n189; *La Vie matérielle* (Material Life), 175; *Les Yeux bleus, Cheveux noirs*, 175; *The Malady of Death*, 174, 175
Durso, Laura E., 203n159
Dustan, Guillaume, 84, 86, 172

Duyvendak, Jan Willem, 235n132
Dworkin, Ronald, 234n108
dystopia, 95, 96, 100

echo, meaning of, 8
École des Hautes Études en Sciences
    Sociales (EHESS): academic unit of,
    90; research unit at, 120; seminars at, 3,
    88–89, 90, 92, 106
École Normale Supérieure (ENS), 84, 85,
    89, 178
ecology party (Europe Écologie–Les Verts),
    18, 83, 145, 203n154
economic issues: dominance of neoliber-
    alism over, 80; failing to present the
    Taubira Act in terms of, effect of, 11, 48,
    49, 50, 72, 146; race and, 122, 123; as "the
    real issues," calling for a return to, effect
    of, 49, 146–47, 186
economic scarcity, principle of, 167
Edelman, Lee, 238nn173–74; L'Impossible
    Homosexuel, 92; No Future, 173
Éditions et Publications de l'École
    Lacanienne (EPEL), 12, 91–92
Einstein, Albert, 41
Eleftheriadis, Konstantinos, 99,
    215nn124–25
Eliasoph, Nina, 201n133
elitism, claims of, 11, 30, 37, 40, 84, 217n152
El-Tayeb, Fatima, 120, 221–22n50
enemies: collaboration with, perceived, 14,
    37, 134, 151; designated, by opponents
    of gay marriage and gender theory, 37;
    former, becoming standard-bearers for
    the French nation against foreigners,
    146; horizontal collaboration with, pe-
    nalizing, 151
enemy within: fear of, 11, 23, 58, 146, 152–53;
    idea of, 10, 59, 151
English language: combining with French,
    106; as the main tool for queer interac-
    tion, 99; meaning of "queer" in, 95,
    214n98; and the pronoun "I," 96; and
    translation, 107, 166; of the Web, 165–66
equality: primer on, (Les ABCD de
    l'Égalité), opposition to, 17–18, 66–67,
    207n219; principle of, assertion of,
    Taubira Act and, 47; uniform, 12. See
    also gender equality; male/female
    equality

Eribon, Didier, 178, 209n10, 211n61, 212n62,
    220n30, 221nn47–48, 222n60, 231n47,
    231n50, 231n60, 236n139, 237n157,
    239n188, 239n197, 240n204, 241n5,
    241n219; accusing, of promoting
    Americanization, 162; background on,
    87, 213n84; Belgian workshop host, 98; vs.
    Bourcier, 91; Bourcier's criticism of, 89;
    on community, 15–16; on homonational-
    ism, 121; on male bonding, 154; media
    attack on, 87; petition launched by, 3;
    pioneering role of, 12, 77; "Queer . . . and
    After?—a Future for Subversion," 109; at
    Queer Week, 109, 110; Réflexions sur la
    question gay, 88; Returning to Reims, 177;
    seminar run by Gaspard and, 3, 88–89,
    90, 101, 105–6, 212n67; symposium orga-
    nized by, 77, 87, 90; on where his work is
    located, 139
Ernaux, Annie, 178
erotic difference, notion of, 165
eroticism: legitimizing heterosexual, 172;
    potential for, alterity and, 148; question
    of, attention to, 85, 91; student publica-
    tion of, 109; theatricality and, 147, 164,
    165, 166. See also homoeroticism
Escada, Alain, 27, 44
Escudero-Alias, Maite, 215n120
Espace Analytique, 92
Espineira, Karine, 85, 92, 99, 110
Esposito, Roberto, 239n196
essentialization, 155, 210n24; community
    free from, 186; in gender studies, 78; of
    minority experiences, 187–88; and na-
    tionalism, 124; of the Oedipal triangle,
    159; of the opposite, avoiding, question
    of, 143, 227n143; and race, 223n86; of
    sexual categories, 14, 106, 124, 137, 185
ethnocentrism, 187
Etiemble, René, 153
eugenist theology, 24
Eulenburg affair, 230n38
Europe, 90, 207n228; activist ideas and
    practices in, circulation of, effect of,
    100; gay identity in, 131; and gentrifica-
    tion, 168; and homonationalism, 120;
    legal recognition of homosexuality in,
    effect of, 115–16; nationalism in, rise of,
    10, 183; queer theory in, networks of, 13,
    98; reformation of marriage laws in, 3,

47, 72, 185, 191n6; socialist parties in, 3; spread of queer theory in, 98–99

European Convention on Human Rights, 55, 56, 125

European Court of Human Rights, 72

European queer database, 81

European Union, 13, 72

evangelization, 21, 22, 28, 40

evolutionary theory, using, to condemn gender theory, 62–63

Éwanjé-Épée, Félix Boggio, 222nn65–67, 222n70; *White Feminists and Empire*, 125–27, 128

exclusiveness, principle of: challenge to, 166–67, 186, 235n126; rethinking, 13, 145

Existrans (march), 116–17

Facebook, 64, 100, 119, 202n141

Falguières, Patricia, 101

Fallières, Armand, 152

Falquet, Jules, 209n19

familial triangulation, 136

family: belonging to, immunological conception of, 13; Catholic Church/Vatican on, 21, 22, 205n192; challenge to the complementarity of the sexes within the, 21–22; and multiple identities, 168, 169; and the politics of marriage, 136; as a republican value, 14; and tax reform, 37. *See also* traditional family

family expertise: contemporary, emerging critique of, 85; networks of, links between, 156; Socialist Party's reliance on, for consultation, 158–61

family-planning structures, 156

family welfare policies, 44

fantasy, meaning of, 8

fantasy echo, and formation of identity, described, 8–9

fanzines: *Bangbang*, 82; *Queer Terrorist/ Queer Tapette*, 81; *Star*, 82

far-right movements, 10, 154; and anti-Semitism, 59, 152; appropriation of anti-homophobia, 117, 126; and Christian blogs, 26; joining Manif pour Tous, 34, 36; and nationalism, 59; newspaper of, 48, 63, 65; and opposition to gay marriage, 34, 36, 37, 40, 41; in opposition to gender theory, 62; rise of, 14, 15, 157; websites, 111. *See also specific people and groups*

Fassin, Éric, 194n22, 202n149, 211n45, 219n16, 219n19, 220n25, 222n61, 228nn5–6, 234n116; Bourcier's criticism of translation by, 89; feminist critique of, 97; pioneering role of, 12, 77; seminar run by Feher, Tort, and, 84, 85, 89, 90; on sexual democracy, 115, 116; symposium organized by Chauvin and, 14; translation by, of Butler's work, 85, 89; on the Vatican's natural law, 21

Favier, Anthony, 24, 195n37

Favret-Saada, Jeanne, 232n80

Fayard (publishing house), 12, 89

Feher, Michel, 211n44; background on, 84–85; "The Betwixt," 84; *Fragments for a History of the Human Body*, 85; pioneering role of, 77; seminar run by Fassin, Tort, and, 84, 85, 89, 90

Feinberg, Leslie, 80, 210n27

Femen (feminist group), 11, 33, 34

femininity: altered standards of, among leaders of anti-gay-marriage movement, 198n83; and gay identity in Thailand, 133; group advocating for, to oppose feminism, 33; masculinity expressed by women not adhering to, 80; national ideal of, gender deviance at odds with, 58

feminism: contemporary, critique of, 125–26; expression of, attack on, 11; group advocating for femininity to oppose, 33; instrumentalization of, opposing, 119; and intersectionality, 137–38; paradigm shift in academic, 98; as threat to heterosexual romantic relationships, 68–69, 165

feminist movements, 32, 70, 75, 165. *See also specific people and groups*

feminist studies, 75, 98, 109, 140

feminist theory, convergence of queer theory and, 96–98, 100

feminization, 68–69, 118

Femmes en Luttes 93, 107

Fernando, Mayanthi L., 221n42

Ferran, Nicolas, 228n6

Ferry, Jules, 179

Fifth Republic: constitution of, 3, 116; founding of, change in Socialist Party since, 14–15, 156, 157; ideal of, attachment to, 46; left-wing ideals underpinning, 14

Fillod, Odile, 195n34, 196n46, 196n49
Fillon, François, 71
films: *Harem* (pornographic), 129–30; *La Journée de la jupe* (Skirt Day), 69; *Le Baiser de la lune* (The Moon's Kiss), 25; *Les Contes de Queer Factory* (Tales from Queer Factory), 100; *L'Ordre des mots* (documentary on trans persons), 110; *Paris is Burning* (documentary), 135; Queer Week collaborating with Cineffable to show, 110; *Race d'Ep* and *Ire* (experimental films by Soukaz), 88; *Tomboy* (drama by Sciamma), 11, 65–66, 110; *Too Much Pussy!* (Jouvet's documentary on *Queer X Show*), 100
Finkielkraut, Alain, 192n19
first queer wave, 134, 135
Flechtman, Bernard, 236n145
Fleck, Ludwick, 241n224
Fleckinger, Hélène, 89
Floyd, Kevin, 215n116; *The Reification of Desire*, 98
Fondation de Service Politique (Foundation for Political Service), 69
Force Vive (Vital Force), 45
Fortin, Jacques, 163
Foucault, Michel, 16, 193nn29–30, 193n36, 215n126, 226n124, 228n3, 228n15, 229n22, 241n3, 242n14; on archaeological analysis, 9; biographer of, 87; Bourcier on Butler and, 135; death of, 72, 234n104; Delphy on, 97; on disciplinary regime, 146; Halperin on, 79, 91; on heterotopia, 149; and HIV/AIDS, 72, 163, 233–34n104; label identified with, 8; on labeling homosexuals as a category, 150; *The Order of Things*, 41; and the origin of gender studies, 111; presentations titled after, 210n30
Fourier, Charles, 167, 235n130
Fourth Republic, 156
Fracchiolla, Béatrice, 234n109
Français de Souche (Those of French Extraction), 111, 119
France Queer Resource Directory, 81
Francis, 22
Franco-American relationship: intellectual history in, 96, 98; interface in, 13, 85; networks in, 13
Fraser, Meredith, 235n137

Freedman, Estelle B., 235n135
Freeman, Elizabeth, 236–37n152, 242n19
French language: and coming out, 225n100; discriminatory labels in, 82, 106; double transformation of, 106; gendered, 98, 106, 166; lack of pejorative connotation for "queer" in, 93; as the official language, 179; and the pronoun "I," 96; and translation, 83, 107, 166; unclear meaning of "queer" in, 95
French Republic: Fifth Republic, 3, 14–15, 46, 116, 156, 157; Fourth Republic, 156; symbol of, 49, 116; Third Republic, 150–51, 156, 231n65
French Revolution, 15, 68
French State (during WWII). *See* Vichy regime
French theory: new, association with, 15; representatives of, 8; return home of, 2, 7, 8, 13, 113, 143; use of the term, clarifying, 8
Freud, Sigmund, 135, 171
friendship, 153, 163, 168
Front du 20 Mars, 119
Front Homosexuel d'Action Révolutionnaire (Homosexual Front for Revolutionary Action, FHAR), 73, 96, 107, 126, 188, 217n151
Front National (FN), 26, 30, 44, 63–64, 117–18, 154, 157, 200n118, 202n141
Fuss, Diana, 237n158
future: projection into the, 15, 19, 52, 142, 171, 172, 173, 180; rejection of the, 148, 171–72, 237n152

Gager, Kristin Elizabeth, 235n128
Gaîté Lyrique theater, 101
Gallagher, James E., 202n145
Gandhi, Mahatma, 41
Garbagnoli, Sara, 204n175
Garner, Tyron, 122, 123
Garréta, Anne F., *Pas un Jour* (Not a Single Day), 88
Gaspard, Françoise, 201n124; Bourcier's criticisms of, 89; marginalization of, 158; parity concept proposed by, purpose of, 42, 89; petition launched by, 3; pioneering role of, 12, 77; at Sciences Po, 217n154; seminar run by Eribon and, 3, 88–89, 90, 101, 105–6, 212n67

Gatelais, Sylvain, 208n236
Gauchet, Marcel, 159
Gavroche (street urchin character/symbol), 11, 49, 51, 52
Gaxotte, Pierre, 154
"gay": interchanging "queer" with, 81; and "lesbian" as overly essentialist, seeking alternative to, 106; vs. "queer," 77, 139
gay adoption: and civil unions, 158–59, 189; legalizing, 4, 46, 48; and medically assisted procreation, 4, 73, 155; opposition to, 1, 25, 30, 40, 42–43, 51, 52, 70, 92, 155, 158, 167, 176; seen as a "slippery slope," 42–43; stated purpose of legalizing, 47
gay and lesbian studies: conservative critique of, 12; examining queer theory/studies in relation to, 12, 86, 139–40, 141–42; first major symposium on, 77, 87; incorporating performativity into, 98; as minoritarian, 139; as a self-evident concept, criticism of, 87
gay commercial zone (Marais neighborhood), 103, 104
gay community, idea of, 162, 163, 169, 184, 187
gay consumerism, 103–4
gay culture, 79, 85–86
gay identity, 131, 133, 136, 139
gay imperialism, 13, 124, 126, 128, 185; defined, 14
gay international, 114, 125–34
Gay Internationalist organizations, 128
GayLib, 73, 117, 161
gay libraries, establishment of, opposition to, 87
gay marketing strategy, 94–95, 103
gay marriage: binational, 4, 5, 73; cast as not a "real issue," 49, 146–47, 186; concern for, as situational, 136; early petition for, 3, 176; era ushered in by, 2; key factors in the emergence of, 13, 125; lack of clarity in regard to, 5–6; parental tie and, 4; and the question of gender, 3–6; second queer wave and views on, 136; Socialist Party committing to, 3, 72, 158; and ties of kinship, 4, 159. See also anti-gay-marriage movement; Taubira Act
gay parenthood: demands for, rise of, 172; normativity of, Boucier's denunciation

of, 141; opposition to, 27, 51, 52, 53, 161, 162, 167, 202–3n153, 232n82; purpose of legalizing, 47; second queer wave and views on, 136
Gay Pride: charges against, 101, 103, 107–8; counter-demonstrations to, 13, 78, 101, 104, 105, 107–8; in Germany, 115, 118–19; history of, 104; and Inter-LGBT, 116, 162; pinkwashing and, 132–33; renaming of, 104–5, 108; in Toulouse, 82
Gay Shame, 103
gay squats, 82
gay stereotypes, 48, 93–94
gay weddings: avoiding officiating at, clause permitting, 17; disruption of, lack of, reason behind, 6; economic argument for, slogan on, 72; first performances of, 3, 72, 158, 176; media coverage of, 72; mobilizing to petition mayors to perform, 3, 176
gender: as a critical tool, 78–79; criticism of, 75; fear of, conferences broadening, 23; focus in the marriage debate extending from sexual orientation to, 3–6; grammatical, 98, 166; as an interpretive grid of race, 135; and intersectionality, 130; pathologizing, 135; in the Pontifical Council's *Lexicon*, 23; and the pronoun "I," 96; "queer" perceived as symbol of teeming discourse on, 86; removal of term, from school material, 18; and sex, notions of, 22, 78–79; widespread use of the term, and drift, 78
gender categories, performative power of, deconstructing, 80
gender equality: law favoring, reactionary movement hijacking aspects of, 42–43; monitoring international authorities and programs of, 22, 23, 24
gender identity: criterion of, failure to introduce, to fight transphobia, 160; United Nation's declaration on, 24
gender marker, change of, court rulings on, 5, 160
gender-monitoring projects, 21, 22, 23–24
gender parity, 42
gender performance, 84
gender privilege, 121
gender roles: reversal of, 11, 152, 235n126; stereotyping and, addressing, in school,

18; traditional division of, 21, 49, 52, 53, 161, 235n126
gender segregation, 120
gender studies: emergence of, 75; essentialization in, 78; exposure to queer theory in, 109; integral part of, 20; new perspectives on, promoting, 80; origin of, claim to, 111; process ascribed to, by Francis, 22; program of, at Sciences Po, 111; rhetorical issues involving, 18, 19–20
gender theory: as a catch-all concept, 75–76; centrality of religion in opposition to, 37, 38; compared to totalitarianism, 23; debunking the premises of, but not abandoning the idea of, 112; denunciation of, fantasy underpinning, 78; fantasies over, 56–59; heterotopic readings extended to the polemic over, 101; idea of parity and opposition to, 43; as an imported ideology from the United States, 1, 57, 58, 75, 111; opposition to, 57, 58–59, 62, 67–68, 75, 76, 111, 159–60, 196n44, 205n186, 206n203; origin of the Taubira Act attributed to, 1–2, 4, 57; perceived as a threat, 2, 11, 76; political links of groups in opposition to, 40; as queer theory in general, 1; rhetorical issues surrounding, 19–20, 207n228; roots of opposition to, 11, 20–26; teaching of, opposition to, 11, 17, 20, 22, 25–26, 63, 64, 65, 66–67, 69, 70, 71, 73, 76; in the United States, 75–76
gender trouble, 160
genealogical analysis, 9
genealogy, play on, 118
Genet, Jean, 130, 236n145; Our Lady of Flowers, 169
gentrification, 168
Germany: arrival of queer theory in, 98–99; and Berlin Pride, 115, 118–19; and immigration, 116; liberation from occupation by, 33; opposition to gender theory in, 57
Gervais, Pierre, 230n38
Ghachem, Malick W., 192n13
ghetto homophobia, 126
ghettoization, 87, 125, 130, 162
ghetto youth, 125
Gide, André, Corydon, 150

Gilligan, Carol, 78
Girard, Gabriel, 211n43, 238n171
Girard, Quentin, 218n155
Giudicelli, Colette, 205n195
Glaser, Linda B., 210n25
Glissant, Édouard, 192n23
global culture, 172
globalization: of categories, rejection of, 183; dimensions to, and effects, 114; of queer theory, relativizing, 98–99; of sexuality, 13, 14, 114–15, 125–34, 224n94
globally gay, 114, 125–34, 187
Glucksmann, André, 85, 228n9
Goldstone, Jack A., 201n132
Golebiowska, Ewa, 220n35
Gopinath, Gayatri, 224n95
Gosselin, Philippe, 44
Gouines Rouges (Red Dykes), 73, 96, 97
Grabowska, Magdalena, 204n172
grammatical gender, 98, 166
grammatical sex, 166
Greater Paris Lesbian & Pride. See Inter-LGBT
Greco, Luca, 92, 110, 213n93
Green Party, 56
Gremetz, Maxime, 88
Grosjean, Blandine, 235n127
Groupe de Libération Homosexuelle (Homosexual Liberation Group), 82
Groupement de Recherche et d'Études pour la Civilisation Européenne (Research and Study Group for European Civilization, GRECE), 75
Groupe Union Défense (Union Defense Group), 34, 36
Guattari, Félix, 138, 226nn125–26, 227n145
Guedj, Jérémy, 152, 230n40
Guéhénno, Jean, 230n43
Guénif-Souilamas, Nacira, 97, 130, 223nn83–85
Guérin-Pace, France, 133, 224n97
Guibert, Hervé, 172
Guigou, Élisabeth, 159
Gunther, Scott, 233n94

Habed, Adriano José, 222n63
Halberstam, Jack, 168, 192n16, 210n28, 235n133; Female Masculinity, 80
Halley, Janet, 122, 222n51

Halperin, David, 12, 209nn21–22, 222n71; on Foucault, 79; *How to Be Gay*, 92; *One Hundred Years of Homosexuality and Other Essays on Greek Love*, 91; *Saint Foucault*, 91; seminar attended by, 88; "Why Is Diotima a Woman?," 91

Hammarberg, Thomas, 160, 233n87

Hamon, Benoit, 18

Haraway, Donna, 216n133; *Cyborg Manifesto*, 101

Haritaworn, Jin, 120

Hark, Sabine, 204n172

Harvey, David, 214n98

Hauchecorne, Mathieu, 215n119

Hawley, Charles, 219n18

Hazan, Adeline, 162

Heidegger, Martin, 92

Heinich, Nathalie, 232n82

Hennessy, Rosemary, 214n105

Herbrand, Cathy, 98

Héritier, Françoise, 159, 232n79

hermaphrodism, 75, 78

Herring, Scott, 216n127

Herzog, Dagmar, 230n39

He-Say, Vincent, 110

heterodox approach, 9

heterogeneous temporalities, inability to conceptualize, 121

heterosexism, 79

heterosexuality: deconstruction of, 24, 76; Duras on, 175; early definition of, 127; equivalency between homosexuality and, opposition to, 7, 22, 23; homosexuality being of interest when it restores, 94, 95; no longer defining homosexuality against, 141; perceived as a second chance, 172. *See also* homosexual/ heterosexual dichotomy

heterosexual roles, traditional, 147

heterotopia, 100, 149, 168

heterotopic initiatives, 100, 101–12

Hidalgo, Anne, 18

hierarchical systems: deliberate lack of, 99; and the notion of difference, 79

Hirschman, Albert, 235n129

Hitchcock, Peter, 225n103

Hitler, Adolf, 197n54

HIV/AIDS, 91, 146, 168, 237n159; counter-community created by, 238n166; fantasized expression of, 238n165; fight against,

5, 72, 79, 84, 163, 172; Foucault and, 72, 163, 234n104; mourning death from, 180–81; prevention of, 193n4; psychoanalytical views of, 15, 171–72; sexual practices and prevalence of, 238n170; spread of, paradox involving, 238n166; summer seminars ceasing during height of, 82

Hocquenghem, Guy, 229n29

Hoggart, Richard, 240n209

Hollande, François, 28, 30, 202n153; controversial appointment by, 65; criticism of, 71, 155; on dividing the country, 14, 46; on medically assisted procreation, 18, 158; and the Taubira Act, 17, 29, 38, 197n54

Hollinghurst, Alan, 237n155

home, idea of, 169

Homel, David, 226n129

Hommage National (National Tribute), 34, 36

Hommen (anti-feminist group), 11, 32–33, 34, 35, 40, 59

homocolonialism, 114

homoeroticism: Arab, 127–30, 131; literary forms marked by, 153, 154; pronounced, among Hommen and Manif pour Tous, 34

Homoland, 82

homonationalism, 108, 143; context leading to the spread of, 115–17; deconstruction of, 115, 187–88; defined, 13–14; Eribon's response to, 121; intention behind, human rights and, 224n99; and intersectionality, 134; and opposition to gay marriage, 124–25; protesting participation in symposium and, 120–21; Puar on, 14, 121–25; spread of, 118–19

homonormativity, 121, 124, 187–88

homophobia, 3, 23, 40, 41, 79; and anti-Semitism, linking, 58, 59, 152; and class, 177, 178–79; and gay imperialism, 14; ghetto, 126; and nationalism, 116, 117, 118, 119, 120–21; as a personal aversion, diminishing of, 149; responsibility for, accusations involving, 116, 119, 125–26; school curriculum addressing, opposition to, 20, 69; transferring rejection in response to, 117; zaps in opposition to, 103

homosexual cabal. *See* secret societies

homosexual/heterosexual dichotomy, 80, 127, 128, 131, 135, 146

Homosexualité et Socialisme (Homosexuality and Socialism), 73, 117, 158, 161, 162

homosexuality: being of interest when it restores heterosexuality, 94, 95; Catholic Church/Vatican on, 22, 24, 38; criminalization of, 24, 127, 131, 132, 150–52, 217n151, 229n29; decriminalization of, 10, 122; drawing a parallel between Judaism and, 11, 230n39; equivalency between heterosexuality and, opposition to, 7, 22, 23; ghettoization of, 87, 162; international recognition of, perceived Trojan horse leading to, 23; legal recognition of, effect of, 7, 115–16, 168; as a lifestyle, focus on, 10, 69, 150, 159; link between the word "queer" and, 214n98; monitoring of, 149–50, 152, 171; no longer defining, against heterosexuality, 141; propagation of, fear of, 2, 10, 15, 20, 36, 40, 54, 66, 73, 100, 149, 172, 185, 191n3; repression of, 175, 239n195; research on, dismissing, 12; stigmatization of, 15, 48, 54, 162, 178

Houzelot, Pascal, 94

Huchon, Jean-Paul, 70

Hugo, Victor, Les Misérables, 51–52, 203n161

Huisman-Perrin, Emmanuelle, 217n154

Hullot-Guiot, Kim, 197n56

human agency, 128

human body: and basis for reproduction, 164; Catholic Church/Vatican on, 22, 23, 56; commodification of, 54, 55, 56; individual relationships to, cultural influences on, seminar dissecting, 88; instrumentalization of, 106; sacredness of, childhood and, 52–56

human ecology, 11, 20–26, 157, 173, 205n192

humanism, 21, 113, 179

human nature, view of, 21

human rights: based on natural law, 21–22; convention on, 55, 56, 125; and intention behind homonationalism, 224n99; mechanisms of, effectiveness of, 114; trans identities and, 160

Huret, Romain, 230n38

hybrid cultures, 10, 14, 92, 114, 122, 123. See also multiple identities

hybridization effects, 127, 133

"I," positing, as a preliminary to analysis, 135, 209n18

Iacub, Marcela, 85

identification: and deidentification, 145; double deconstruction of, 79; multiple forms of, challenge represented by, to the model of national belonging, 170; multiple systems/processes of, 134, 146; oscillation in, 9; retrospective, problem of, 8; unstable mechanism of, issue of, 7

identities: confusion of, belief in, and resulting effect, 66; cultural, conceiving fantasy echo in the formation of, 8; desire to describe roles and, classification system arising from, 78; growth of critical analysis of, emergence of queer theory and, 79–80; impact of gendered language on, attempt to address, 98; multiple, 9, 24, 79, 80, 81, 142, 145, 147, 166–70, 186; nature of, queer theory noting, 145; oscillation in, 9; refusal to critically reexamine, 2, 15; rethinking norms and, initiatives involving, 87, 88–92; use of categories as, queer theory on, 142, 145; variety of sexual practices and, 133

identity: assigned, rejection of, as part of defining "queer," 83; confusion of, belief in, 66; considerations of, in gay and lesbian studies, 12; critiques of, in other national contexts, effect of, 140; gay, 131, 133, 136, 139; gender, 24, 160; institutional LGBT culture and, 12; at the locus of power relationships, 140–41; need to assert, 47; queer theory and analysis of, 77, 145, 184; reactionary, 40; sexuality and, 9; side-stepping, 80; transhistorical, illusory relationship to, 7

identity documents, change of, 116–17

identity politics, post-identitarian, 135

Idier, Antoine, 236n143, 240n203

Ignatius of Loyola, 22

immigration, 136; Eribon on, 121; and ghettoization, 125, 130; hardening of policies on, 146; homonationalism and, 116, 120, 121, 125; increase in, 114; and integration, 130; marginalization of, 158; opposition to, 59; schools and, 68; in the United States, 210n29

individualism, 159, 160, 176, 177

indivisibility, 14, 46, 116–17, 241n222
infantilism, 66, 76
infertility, 4, 161, 171, 172, 202n153
initiation: Queer Week labeled as, 111; role
    of, spaces for, 100
Institut de Recherche Interdisciplinaire sur
    les Enjeux Sociaux, 120
Institut de Sociologie in the Université
    Libre de Bruxelles, 98
Institut d'Études Politiques. *See* Sciences Po
Institute for Advanced Study in Princeton,
    209n18
Institute of French Studies, 85
institutionalization, strategies to counter,
    105–7, 109
Institut National de la Propriété Industrielle
    (National Institute of Industrial
    Property), 94
integration, 126, 130, 169, 176
interchangeable and unique roles, 188
Inter-LGBT (Greater Paris Lesbian &
    Pride), 73, 116–17; *Livre blanc*, 162
International Conference on Population, in
    Cairo, 23
internationalism, 108, 114
International Queer Liberation Tour, 81
International Theological Commission, 21
Internet campaigns: to oppose male/female
    equality in school curricula, 11, 66–67;
    for recruiting new members, 36; target-
    ing opponents of gay marriage, 70. *See
    also* blogs; social media
interpretation, authenticity and, 113
interracial marriage, 122
intersectionality: lack of, 130; limits of, 9, 14,
    134–38, 188
intersexuality, 75
Intifada, first, view of sexual minorities
    during, 134
invariants, 159, 232n80
invisibility, 119, 128, 168, 236n140
Iran, criminalization of homosexuality in,
    132
Iranian Queer Association, 132
Irigaray, Luce, 213n89
Islam: and capability for change, 221n42;
    criminalization of homosexuality in,
    131; and homophobia, 119, 120, 125–26;
    immigrants associated with, profiling,

116; and opposition to gay marriage,
    38–39; viewed as competition, 37; and
    wearing of headscarves, 15, 46, 52, 68,
    97, 146, 185
Islamophobia, 65, 119
Israel, pinkwashing by, 119
Israeli-Palestinian conflict, 108, 119
Italy, opposition to gender theory in, 57

Jablonski, Olivier, 85, 229n26
Jackson, Julian, 230nn35–36
Jacob, Christian, 44
Jagose, Annamarie, 227n137
Jaquet, Chantal, 178, 240n208, 240n212
Jaunait, Alexandre, 194n14, 221n43,
    221nn45–46
Jean Jaurès Foundation, 154
Jean-Jean (fanzine author/activist), 82
Jérôme Lejeune Foundation, 25–26, 27
Jeunesse Action Chrétienté, 44
Jeunesses Nationalistes (Nationalist Youth),
    34, 36, 62–63
Jivraj, Suhraiya, 120
John Paul II, 39, 69, 194n19; "Letter to
    Women," 21; *Theology of the Body*, 21
Johnson, David, 149, 228n16
John XXIII, 21
joint adoption by same-sex couples. *See* gay
    adoption
"Jolly Roger" symbol, 102
Jospin, Lionel, 42, 160, 162
Jouhandeau, Marcel, 154, 220n30
Journiac, Michel, 235n126
Jouve, Christiane, 163
Jouvet, Emilie, 100
Judaism: and citizenship, 156; drawing a
    parallel between homosexuality and,
    11, 230n39; and fear of betrayal, 147, 156;
    and opposition to gay marriage, 38, 39.
    See also anti-Semitism
Jung, Cy, 83
Juppé, Alain, 186, 242n9

Kail, Michèle, 97
Kandel, Liliane, 97
Kaplan, Alice, 231n46
Kashnik (artist), 110
Kauffmann, Grégoire, 66
Kefi, Ramsès, 200n105

Kergoat, Danièle, 226n117
Kestel, Laurent, 231n59
Khirouni, Chaynesse, 233n91
Killmister, Suzy, 241n225
King, Martin Luther, 41, 42
King, Rodney, 135
kinship, 146; and adoption, 167; alternative, 168; and civil unions, 30, 40, 158–59; and gay marriage, 4, 47–48, 54; laws of, fictional nature of, 141; legal, establishing, increasingly biological basis for, 52–53; limited, model of, bioethical laws reinforcing, 167; and multiple identities, 168, 169; propagation of homosexuality by means of, 54; queer theory and, 183; relationships of, in gay communities, 169–70; relations of, nurturing, parental and maternal roles in, 203n153
Kipling, Rudyard, 71
kiss-ins, 72, 119
Klumpke, Anna, 169
Knapp, Andrew, 232n69
Koksal, Mehmet, 130
Kollias, Hector, 90
Kollman, Kelly, 208n234
Koskovich, Gerard, 89
Kraus, Cynthia, 85
Krehely, Jeff, 203n159
Kringelbach, Hélène Neveu, 228n6
Kristeva, Julia, 8
Kuhar, Roman, 207n228
Kulpa, Robert, 125, 215n122, 222n64
Kumsieh, Ramzy, 119
Kunert, Stéphanie (Wendy Delorme), 100, 105–6, 214n104; *Insurrections! En territoire sexuel*, 106

La Barbare (The Female Barbarian), 73, 105
La Barbe, 110
Labarrère, André, 118
Lacan, Jacques, 8, 164, 213n86, 213n89
Lacanian School of Psychoanalysis (École lacanienne de psychanalyse), 91, 92, 213n86
Lacoin, Clément, 109
La Coordination Lesbienne en France (Lesbian Coordination in France), 105
Lacorne, Denis, 192n22
Lacoue-Labarthe, Philippe, 239n195

La Croisière (The Cruise), 82
Lacroix, Xavier, 25, 196n48
Ladenson, Elizabeth, 88
La Diagonale (UMP support group), 161
La Dispute (publishing house), 12
La Droite Forte (A Strong Right), 44
La Fabrique (publishing house), 125
Lafont, Samuel, 45
Lagasnerie, Geoffroy, 222n59
La Gauche pour le Mariage Républicain (Liberals for Republican Marriage), 28
Lajeunie, Arnaud, 217–18n155
La Maison des Femmes, 97
Lamont, Michèle, 193n27
La Mutinerie (queer venue), 100, 110, 163
Langlois, Anthony J., 219n10
language: Arabic, 133–34, 225n100; and Arabic expression of sexual difference, 133–34; Berber, 225n100; individual relationships to, cultural influences on, seminar dissecting, 88; micro-resistance through, 102; social norms in, deconstructing, 8. *See also* English language; French language; translation
Lannes, Christopher, 199n87
Lanquetin, Marie-Thérèse, 203n160
Laplanche, Jean, 192n21
Laplantine, François, 240n217
Laporte, Roger, 239n186
Laprade, Bruno, 98, 215n118
Lascoumes, Pierre, 208n233
Laufer, Laurie, 213n99
Launet, Édouard, 214n101
law: as an analytical structure, 6; associating, with privilege, as a stereotype, 137; contemporary expertise on, emerging critique of, 85; destiny and, 164; fenced in by, 170; as an identitarian archive, 210n29; individual relationship to, cultural influences on, seminar dissecting, 88; international, 138, 160; natural, 20, 21–22, 33, 39, 52–53
Lawrence, John, 122, 123
Lawrence and Garner v. Texas, 121–22, 123
laws: banning guilds (Loi Le Chapelier), 156; bioethics, 4, 161, 167; biologicalization of, 156; civil, 76; civil union, 176, 191n17; colonial, 129; of kinship, fictional nature of, 141; national, influences on,

72; nationality, 54, 55, 56; obscenity, 151; parity, 42, 89; slavery, 11, 47, 56; sodomy, 121–22, 149. *See also* marriage laws; Taubira Act

Lebanon, colonial law in, 129

Le Bitoux, Jean, 83, 150, 229n28

Le Blevennec, Nolwenn, 200n109

Lebovici, Elisabeth, 12, 89, 101, 216n132

Leclerc, Gérard, 26

Leclère, Anne-Sophie, 63–64

Lefebvre, Rémi, 161, 232n72, 233n93

left-wing movements, groups borrowing approach associated with, 11, 17, 41, 50

left-wing republicanism, 14, 15, 51, 156–57

left-wing thought, rhetoric of, deconstruction of, 85

Le Fur, Marc, 44

Le Gall, Anne, 42, 89, 201n124

le Gallou, Jean-Yves, 200–201n118

legal status, 1, 5, 18, 121, 170

legal system, 148, 170, 189

Legendre, Pierre, 159, 164, 234n111, 237n163

Lejeune, Jérôme, 27

Lemaître, Éric, 41–42

Le Mené, Karine, 27

Lenormand, Xavier, 45

Leon, Monica, 3–4

Le Pen, Jean-Marie, 44, 117–18, 154, 220nn33–34

Le Pen, Marine, 44, 117, 118

Lerch, Arnaud, 89, 214n106

Le Renard, Amélie, 92, 221n43

Leroyer, Anne-Marie, 232n78

Les Antigones (anti-feminist group), 32–33, 40

"lesbian," as overly essentialist, seeking alternative to, 106

lesbian activism, 142

lesbian and gay studies. *See* gay and lesbian studies

lesbian group, women-only, 73, 105

lesbophobia, 126

Les Camelots du Roi, 37, 199n85

Les Éditions Amsterdam (publishing house), 12, 90, 212n75

Le Séminaire gai (online archive), 85

Les Furieuses Fallopes (Furious Fallopians), 102, 103, 105

Les Gavroches (ad-hoc group), 51, 52

Les Indivisibles, 119, 221n39

Les Juristes pour l'Enfance (Jurists for Childhood), 54–55

Les Mots Sont Importants, 119, 221n40

Les Panthères Roses (Pink Panthers), 73, 102–3, 119, 210–11n39, 216–17n145

Les Républicains. *See* Union pour un Mouvement Populaire (UMP)

Lesselier, Claudie, 85

Les Sissies (gay squat), 82

Les Sœurs de la Perpétuelle Indulgence (Sisters of Perpetual Indulgence), 12, 77, 81

Les Tordu(e)s (Bent), 13, 78, 97, 101–7, 108, 165, 216–17n145

Lestrade, Didier, 84, 130, 163, 220n27, 233n103; *Why Gays Have Moved to the Right*, 117

Les Tumultueuses, 97, 110, 119

Les Veilleurs (Watchers), 31–32, 40, 41, 44, 45, 57

Letablier, Marie-Thérèse, 203n160

Le Talec, Jean-Yves, 81

Levet, Bérénice, 75, 76, 208n3, 209n6

Levinas, Emmanuel, 135

Lévi-Strauss, Claude, 87

Lévy, Bernard-Henri, 85

Lévy, Elisabeth, 110, 218n157

Lewis, Nathaniel M., 235n137

"LGBT," vs. "queer," 81, 139

LGBT archive, 86

LGBT associations, 70, 72–73, 109, 116, 161–63

LGBT cultures: assimilation of "queer" into, 142; and equality in South Africa, 236n140; existence of, in time, 6; institutional vs. radical, term used to distinguish, 12, 78; moral relativism applied to, conservative criticism of, 6; ongoing critique needed by, as a minority, 187; urban culture and, 168

LGBT movements: arguments stressed in, 125; and borders, 99; borrowing tactics from, 32; broadening, goal of, 78; connection between queer movements and, 81–82; conservative drift of, 117; demonstrations by, in defense of the Taubira Act, 70–72; early use of "queer" among, 81; fragmented, 72–73; groups forming to address issues with, 101, 104, 105, 107; and immigration, 116; institutionalization of, strategies to counter, 105–7; nationalist drift of, 143; racist drift of, 126. *See also specific people and groups*

LGBT propaganda, perceived, 66

LGBT rights: crediting the idea of, as the product of "theory," reasoning behind, 7; demand for, as situational, 136; key figures in, marginalization of, 158; in other countries, opposition to, 57

Liberté pour Tous (Freedom for All), 41

"liberty of conscience" clause, 17, 29

Lichterman, Paul, 201n133, 227n1

Ligue Communiste Révolutionnaire, 211n39

Lilienfeld, Jean-Paul, *La Journée de la jupe* (Skirt Day), 68

Lindell, Henrik, 198n72, 198n74, 200n113, 201n122

Lippert, Leopold, 209n9, 237n152

Lipton, Eunice, 101, 216n134

literary works/criticism. *See specific authors*

Liu, Petrus, 224n94

local/global polarity, 114, 115, 143–44

logos, 101–2

Lorde, Audre, *Zami*, 134

Lorne, Anne, 45

Loud and Proud Festival, 101

Louis, Édouard, 240n205, 240n214; *En finir avec Eddy Bellegueule* (The End of Eddy), 177–79

Loving v. Virginia, 122

Lucey, Michael, 12, 88; *The Misfits of the Family*, 89

Lune (artist), 100

Lutz, Amy, 222n58

Macé, Éric, 97, 223n85

Macedo, Stephen, 242n16

Madame H (cabaret performer), 83

Mad Kate (artist), 100

magazines: *Androzine* (gay alternative magazine), 81; *Causeur* (monthly news), 110; censorship of *Inversions* and *Futur*, 150; *Commentaires*, 231n60; *Esprit* (literary review), 85, 159, 231n60; *French Cultural Studies* (academic journal), special issue, 91; *L'Assiette au beurre*, stereotypical caricatures in, 152; *Le Débat* (review), 159, 231n60; *Le Fléau Social* (Scourge of Society), FHAR publication, 217n151; *Les Temps Modernes* (Sartrean review), 97; *L'Imparfaite* (erotic student publication), 109; *Minorités* (online), 130; *Paragraph* (academic journal), special issue, 90–91; *Politiqueer* (online site for queer and feminist analyses), 98; *Raisons Politiques*, special issue, 221n43; rejection of feminization developed in, 69; *Têtu* (gay magazine), 110; *Valeurs Actuelles* (Catholic magazine), 65; *Vive la révolution*, special issue, 188; *Zone Books*, and Feher's publishing house, 85

Maghreb region, homoeroticism in, 131

Magliani-Belkacem, Stella, 186–87, 222nn65–67, 222n70; *White Feminists and Empire*, 125–27

Magnan, Nathalie, 101

Maikey, Haneen, 119

majority: as an accumulation of minority experiences, 187; minority defined in relation to, 143

majority voice, 181

Malabou, Catherine, 89

male bonding, 153, 154, 171, 229n33

male/female dissymmetry, romantic relationships based on, threat to, 68–69, 165

male/female equality: Catholic Church/Vatican on, 21–22; in school curricula, opposition to, 1, 2, 11, 17–18, 20, 65, 66–67, 193n6, 207n219; teaching, history of, in the schools, 18, 193n6; and the wearing of skirts, 68

male/female roles, construction of, as mutually exclusive, challenge to, 167, 235n126

male/masculinity/knowledge, linkage of, attack on, 76

Mamère, Noël, 3

Mandel, Georges, 152

Manet, Édouard, 101

Mangeot, Philippe, 83, 163, 210n30, 211n40, 233n102, 234n106

Manif pour Tous (Demo for All), 93, 194n10; ad hoc groups joining, 27–28, 31–34, 54–55, 202n141; and anti-Semitism, 59; attacks targeting, in defense of the Taubira Act, 70–71, 72; and

Constructing or Deconstructing Man: Upbringing in the Age of "Gender," 41; development of, 28–29; far-right groups joining, 34, 36; film targeted by, 65–66; formation of, 27; and homoeroticism, 34; implicit goals of, 65; obsession of, 164; opposition to gender theory, 57, 63, 67–68, 69, 159; paradoxes involving, 34, 45; personal attacks against Christiane Taubira, 59–60, *61*; politicization of, 43–44, 45–46; posters of, *29*, 40, 50, 53, *54*, *55*, *60*, *61*, *62*, *63*, *64*; religious conviction in, 28, 37, 39; spread of, to other countries, 31, 57; street demonstrations by, 27, 29–30, 31, 34, 36, 38, 39, 40, 41, 44, 49, 51, 52, *54*, *67*, 197n58; and surrogate pregnancy, 54, *55*, 56; symbolic tactics of movements emerging alongside, 31–37, *51*, 52, 59; united front of, 72; use of mass media by, 19

Marcus, Sharon, 236n148

Maréchal-Le Pen, Marion, 30, 44

Margalit, Avishai, 224n94, 237n154

marginalization, 158, 168

Margueritte, Victor, *La Garçonne*, 150

Marianne (national symbol), 49, 116

Marik, Nadia, 111

Mariton, Hervé, 44

marketing/advertising strategy: gay, 94–95, 103; in Israel, pinkwashing and, 119

Maroh, Julie, *Le Bleu est une couleur chaude*, 110

marriage: approach to rights based on, 242n16; Catholic Church/Vatican on, 11, 21, 167; of contrivance (*mariage gris*) vs. convenience (*mariage blanc*), 146; court rulings on, 3, 4, 5; early campaigns for reform of, 72; eccentric forms of, objection to, 62–63, 205n195; as an economic issue, 48–49; faithfulness in, 153, 167; focus in the debate on, extended from sexual orientation to gender, 3–6; institution of, hegemonic nature of, deconstruction of, 188–89; interracial, 122; politics of, 136, 164; and the principle of exclusiveness, 13, 166–67, 186; propagation of homosexuality through, fear of, 2; reform of, as a locus of change, 137. *See also* gay marriage

marriage laws: additional debate sparked by reform of, 56; and bilateral conventions with other countries, 4–5, 73; debate over reform of, comparison of, to other European countries, 48, 56–57; reformation of, in Europe, 3, 47, 72, 185, 191n6. *See also* Taubira Act

Martel, Frédéric, 88, 212nn63–64; *Le Rose et le Noir*, 87, 162

Marteu, Élisabeth, 221n43

Martin, Biddy, 140, 141, 226n131, 227n134

Martinet, Stéphane, 162

martyr ethic, 41

Marxism, 23, 174

masculinity: attack on, 76; and the basis for domination, 96; dominance of, femininity confirming, notion of, 58; forms of, expressed outside the framework of the male body, 80; restoration of, calls for, 33, 34

Massad, Joseph, 114, 128–29, 130, 219n8, 223nn77–78; *Desiring Arabs*, 125, 127, 131

mass media: anti-Semitism in far-right, 152; conservatism in, 6, 58; coverage of Queer Week, 110; and coverage of the "first" gay wedding, 72; criticism of, 41, 155; designated as an enemy, 37; foreign cultures perceived as a threat covered by, 146; indigenous party attracting the attention of, 223n86; as an interface between social movements and institutions, 202n145; Les Tordu(e)s' approach to, 105; mainstream, access to, by opponents of gay marriage, 19; manner of presenting the Taubira Act to, 47; marketing/advertising strategy in, 93, 94–95; and pinkwashing, 119; politician outed by, 117; rejection of feminization developed in, 165; response of, to demonstrations against gay marriage, 1, 72; strategy to catch the attention of, 41; on threat to heterosexual romantic relationships, 68–69, 165; universalist image in, retaining, 95; use of the word "queer" in, 12, 77–78, 84, 93–96. *See also* magazines; newspapers; television

Massumi, Brian, 226nn125–26

masturbation, teaching, claim about, 66

materialist feminist theory: conflict between queer theory and, 96–97; effect of, 100; relating to both queer theory and, 97–98

materiality, 79, 137, 138, 179, 241n222

maternalist philosophy, 78

Mathieu, Bénédicte, 207n221

Mathieu, Nicole-Claude, 96, 214n109

Mathy, Jean-Philippe, 233n96

Mauger, Gérard, 240n207

Maurras, Charles, 36, 154, 199n85, 199n90

Mazières, François de, 43

McCarthy, John D., 198n70

McCarthy, Paul, 6

McCarthyism, 149

McElwee, Joshua J., 195n29

Mécary, Caroline, 3, 89

media. See mass media; social media

media events, creating, 32

medically assisted procreation (MAP): adoption and, 4, 73, 155; condition for access to, 52, 167; extension of, opposition to, 5, 18–19, 30, 37, 54, 73, 155, 158, 161, 202n153; focus of anti-gay-marriage movement shifting to, 17, 31; forestalling on reform of, 47, 159; protesting absence of legal clauses on extending, 71–72

Mehl, Dominique, 237n161

Meier, Petra, 207n230

Mélenchon, Jean-Luc, 158

Mendès-France, Pierre, 152

Mennucci, Patrick, 46, 202n148

meritocracy, 130, 178, 217n152

Mesnil, Marie, 109, 217n153

Metzgerei, DJ, 100

Meunier, Philippe, 48

Meurent, Victorine, 101

Meyers, Mark, 230n39

Michel, Jean-Pierre, 158, 162

Michels, David, 210n34

Migliore, Celestino, 24

migratory stages, 133

Milewski, Françoise, 111

militantism, 97

military enlistment, 124

Millière, Guy, 218n158

Ministry for Women's Rights, 18

Ministry of Education, 18, 25, 193n4

Ministry of Health and Social Affairs, 41

minority claims vs. local claims, 14

minority cultures, 13; and achieving autonomy, 106; anticommunitarian discourse directed at, 15; continued critique needed by, 187; defined in relation to the majority, 143; designated as an enemy, 37; efforts to "immunize" against, 2; emergence of, fear triggered by, 170–71; marginalization of, 158; and the notion of community, 15; as a perceived threat, 14, 58; as a political minority, meaning of, 143; portraying, as monsters and freaks, 59–61, 62–64, 65; radical foreignness of, notion of, invoking, 59, 65; reactionary claim about, 40, 41; repentance and debt toward, fear of, 60, 61; Socialist Party's view of, 157; transferring rejection onto other, 117; using English as a vernacular for, 107

minority democracy, plea for, 186–89

minority evolution (le devenir minoritaire), 138, 141–42, 143, 226n125

minority experiences: critical, conceptualizing norms based on, 187; essentialization of, 188; idealization of, 187–88

minority/majority polarity, 115, 143, 144, 187

minority practice, 120–21

minority principle: incarnate, 102; universalized, 140

minority voice, 181–82

Minx, Judy, 100

Mirguet, Paul, 151–52, 217n151

Mirkovic, Aude, 194n9

Mitterrand, François, 157, 158

Mitterrand, Frédéric, 94

Mizielinska, Joanna, 215n122

modulating approach, 9

Molinier, Pascale, 86, 92, 217n148

monarchist movement, 36

Money, John, 75–76, 78, 209n13

monotheistic religions: challenge to, 69; positions of, on gay marriage, 38–39, 124

Montfort, Élisabeth, 27, 111, 194n9, 218n163

Moore, Michael Scott, 219n20

moral corruption, 40, 110–11, 118

moral relativism, 6, 7, 21

Morocco: criminalization of homosexuality in, 131; cultural hybridity in literature of, 92; gay identity in, 131; marriage laws involving, and bilateral conventions, 4–5, 73

Möser, Cornelia, 215n121, 218–19n4

Mosse, George, 10, 120, 193n32, 230n43

Mossuz-Lavau, Janine, 228n4

Mouillard, Sylvain, 197n56

Moulin, Jean, 34

mourning, 135, 180, 181

Moussaoui, Mohammed, 38

Mouvement pour la France, 44

Movement for World Unity, 27

multiculturalism, 68, 85, 122, 138

multiple identities, 9, 24, 79, 80, 81, 142, 145, 147, 166–70, 186. See also hybrid cultures

multipositionality, 169, 170, 188–89, 236n140

Muñoz, José Esteban, 238n175

Murat, Laure, 89, 150, 229n21

Musulmans pour l'Enfance (Muslims for Childhood), 39

Myard, Jacques, 44

Nancy, Jean-Luc, 15, 174, 186, 238–39nn180–81, 239n186, 239n193

Naquet, Alfred, 152

Nash, Catherine J., 216n127

nation: betrayal of, fear of, 10, 14; destruction of, as a perceived threat, 2; image of, drawn by reactionaries, 40; interwoven with sexuality and community, 9, 13, 145–46; as a republican value, 14, 46, 157

National Association for Research and Therapy of Homosexuality, 23

national belonging, model of, challenge of, 170

national boundaries, crossing of, attentiveness to, 80

national identity: adopting sexual categories in the name of, 132; base of, 60; demolition of, laws equated with, 60; evolution of, 120; exploiting the issue of, opposition to gay marriage and, 125; "French theory" label in the United States and, 8; immunological based conception of, 2, 15, 147, 186; intellectual crucible of, challenge to, 111; linking, to sexual difference, 164, 165; perceived threat to, 7, 13; sense of, growth of, 179; separation of Church and State as part of, 37; and

sexual identity, 221n43; sexual stereotypes and discourse on, 152

nationalism: class and, 124; community free from, 186; and essentialization, 124; as a form of subordination, 187; radical critiques of, 115; rise of, in Europe, during the interwar period, 10; and sexuality, connection between, 14, 115–21, 220n29, 221n43; social construction of, 120; trend in, 183; undertones of, in public demonstrations, 20; in the United States, 123. See also homonationalism

nationality law, 54, 55, 56

national laws, influences on, 72

National Organization for Marriage (US-based), 59

natural law, 20, 21–22, 33, 39, 52–53

natural order, favoring, 160

nature, destiny and, 164

Naudier, Delphine, 92

Nazism, 23, 33, 59, 64, 237n163

Nazi Sturmabteilung (SA), 175

neoliberalism, 8, 80

Nesme, Jean-Marc, 39–40

Netherlands, citizenship and, 116

Newsom, Gavin, 3

newspapers: access to, 19; censorship of, and Arcadie news bulletin, 151; Figaro (conservative paper), 196n52; front-page article on Eribon's symposium, 87; Gringoire, articles by Drieu la Rochelle, 152; Je suis partout, anti-Semitic articles in, 153; La Croix (Catholic paper), interview with Balmand, 206n203; Le Monde, 3, 87, 88; Minute (far-right paper), 48, 63, 65; opposition to gay marriage in, 48; petition for gay marriage in, 3; racism in, 63; use of the word "queer" in, 12

New York University, 85

New Zealand, debate over gay marriage in, 48

Nicolet, Claude, 231n61

Nikita (speaker from STRASS), 110

Ninja, Lassein, 110

Ni Putes ni Soumises (Neither Whores nor Doormats), 68, 126

Nobles, Melissa, 61–62, 205n194

nonassimilation, 86, 90, 141

nonconformism, advocating, 86
nonessentialism, 86
non-identity, 79
nonnormativity, 103, 113, 121, 124, 139–41, 221–22n50, 225n112
normative conflicts, object of, 6
norms: conceptualizing, based on critical minority experiences, 187; deconstruction of, 8, 189; ongoing critique of, 2, 187; transcending, 139; transforming, way of, 15–16
"no-school-today" movement, 67
Noureddine, Juliette, 110
Noyé, Sophie, 98, 215n117
nudity in public, 17, 34, 92, 116, 198n79
Nunokawa, Jeff, 171, 237n160

Oakley, Ann, 78
obscenity laws, 151
Observatoire des Transidentités, 85, 110
Occidentalism, 132, 224n94
Oedipal principles, 159
O'Leary, Dale, 195n33; *The Gender Agenda*, 23
Olivier, Cyril, 229n32
Ollier, Patrick, 4
Ollion, Etienne, 89, 193n28
Onfray, Michel, 66, 192n18, 206n205
open-mindedness: media flaunting, 93, 94, 95; model of, purported duty to preserve, 146
Opus Dei, 11, 21, 23, 25
order, attachment to, 7, 14, 149, 160, 184
Ordre des Arts et des Lettres, 76
Orientalism, 114, 123, 126–27, 128, 129, 132, 224n94
Orlan (artist), 70
O'Rourke, Kevin H., 219n12
orphans, 4, 167
Orthodox Christian organizations, and opposition to gay marriage, 38
Osez le Féminisme! (Dare to Be Feminist!), 68
OUTrans! 107
Ozouf, Mona, 234n116; *Women's Words*, 164–65

Pacte Civil de Solidarité (PACS), 176, 191n7. *See also* civil unions

Pagès, Bernard, 4
Palestinian Queers for Boycott, Divestment and Sanctions (PQBDS), 119
Panik Qulture, 89–90
parental tie, 4. *See also* kinship
parenthood: according, through adoption, as a stated purpose, 47; and certifying candidates for adoption, 167; condition of, sexual difference as, notion of, 52; desire for, 170; presumption of, lack of, 4, 47–48, 71–72, 73; propagation of homosexuality through, fear of, 2, 15; traditional, perceived threat to, 202–3n153, 237–38n163. *See also* gay parenthood
parent-teacher associations (Catholic), 11, 66
parity law, 42–43, 89
Parti Chrétien Démocrate (Christian Democratic Party), 45
Parti des Indigènes de la République (Party of the Indigenous of the Republic), 131, 223n86
Parti Radical de Gauche (Radical Party of the Left), 47, 56, 145
Parti Républicain, 200n118
Parti Socialiste (PS). *See* Socialist Party/government
partisan system, 148
paternal and maternal roles, 52, 161, 203n153
paternity, presumption of, 47
Paternotte, David, 57, 98, 191n6, 196n44, 204nn173–74, 207n228, 207n230, 208nn234–35, 223n76
pathological categorization, 75
pathologizing gender, 135
pathologizing sexuality, 10, 75, 90, 141, 145, 171
Patriarchate in Moscow (Russian Orthodox Church), 57
patriarchy, 60, 69, 106, 118
patriotism, appeal to, 49
Paul VI, 39; *Humanae Vitae*, 21
Payne, Robert, 226n130
"Peanut Butler" parties, 101
pédé (fag) identity, 82, 83
Pédérama, 162
pederasty, 150, 153, 154, 229n23
pedophilia, 24, 53, 54
Peeters, Marguerite A., 24, 76, 173, 196nn38–41, 208n4, 238nn176–79

Peillon, Vincent, 19
Peltier, Guillaume, 44
Pentecostal groups, 39
Peppy, Guillaume, 111
Peretz, Pauline, 230n38
performance: Bourcier on, 88, 140; drag, 83, 92, 105, 110; gender, focus on, 84; phallocentric academic, 86; presentation on, Borghi appearing naked during, 92; queer, 81, 165–66; and theatricality, 165–66; transformation through, fantasy of, 140, 141; and translation, 165–66
performance art: *Drag King Fem Show*, 105; initiatory role of, 100; *Kisses Cause Trouble*, 105; at Queer Week, 110; *Queer X Show*, 100, 105; and translation, 165–66
performative chains, 135, 145
performativity: anti-identitarian agenda and, 140; emphasis on, 96–97, 98; and homonationalism, 124; of the law, materiality and, 137; queer studies of, and availability of translations, 100; rethinking, 79–80; traditional street demonstrations and, critical gaze on, 105
Périvier, Hélène, 111, 203n160
Perreau, Bruno, 203n155, 203n163, 208n242, 212n70, 225n114, 229n30, 231n66, 234n111, 235n131, 238n164; *The Politics of Adoption*, 52, 156; at Sciences Po, 217n154; seminar influencing, 89
Perrin, Marine, 109
Peter Damian, Saint, 195n26
Peterson, Christopher, 206n196
Petzen, Jennifer, 120
Peuportier, Bruno, 81
phallocentric academic performance, opposition to, 86
Pham-Lê, Jérémy, 194n8
Philbert, Delphine, 233n88
Philippot, Florian, 44, 117, 118, 154
Philippot, Jean-Claude, 40
physical difference, 22
pinkwashing, 108, 119, 132–33, 187–88, 224n99
Piore, Michael, 210n26
Pisier, Evelyne, 241n4
Pius, 199n85
Place Vendôme, artwork at, attack on, 6–7

Plato, 91
Plug'n Play, 109
Plus Gay sans Mariage (Gayer without Marriage), 28
point of reference, examining, 8, 9
Poirot, Richard, 206n197
Poisson, Jean-Frédéric, 44
Poland, opposition to gender theory in, 57
political category, 124
political affiliation, sexual orientation and, 117, 121
political campaign financing, 45–46
political community, membership in, 62, 164
political correctness: criticism of Gay Pride event and, 103; rhetoric of, deconstruction of, 85; of the United States, 57
political establishment, as a designated enemy, 33, 37
political history, as an operation of categorization, 148–49
political networks, 29
political parties: legitimacy of, contested, 73; misconception about, 43
political rights, 23
politicized movement, 43–46
Pollard, Miranda, 229n31
Pollet, Camille, 199n88
polygamy, 189, 242n16
Pompidou Center: Les Tordu(e)s march ending next to, 104; symposiums at, 77, 87, 90, 101
Pontifical Academy for Life, 21
Pontifical Council for the Family, 11, 21, 22, 23, 25
Popular Front government, 37
Porcher, Francis, 230n45
pornography: homosexual, 129–30; post-, presentation from the analytical perspective of, 92
Portier, Philippe, 232n75
Portugal, and marriage laws, 57
postcolonial history, situated in, effect of, on concerns, 227n143
posters (signs/banners): in alternative Gay Pride events, 108; against gay parenthood, 53; of Inter-LGBT, objections to, 116; by opponents of gay marriage, 29, 32, 34, 36, 40, 42, 50, 54; to oppose gen-

der theory in schools, *60, 61, 62, 63, 64, 71*; by proponents of gay marriage and adoption, 70, 71–72; against surrogate pregnancy, 55

postmodernism, criticism of, 6, 24, 66

Poujol, René, 204n178

Poulin-Deltour, William, 218n1, 233n101

Pouliquen, Jan-Paul, 83, 158

Pouzol, Valérie, 133

poverty: impact of marriage on, 48–49; symbol of, 51

Povinelli, Elizabeth, 227nn143–44, 236n151, 240n215

Powell, Leanne, 235n137

power relationships: appeal to a group rigidified by, 173; archaeological approach to considering, 9; caught up in, 138; critiquing, threat perceived from, 87; in defining a minority, 143; and globalization, 114; identity at the locus of, 140–41; inverting real, strategy of, used by opponents of gay marriage, 41; and the mechanism of representation, 181; redistribution of, 76; use of English language and the question of, 99

Pratt, Murray, 208n237, 237n159

prayer: community, sessions of, 39; street, *27, 28*; during vigils, 32

Prearo, Massimo, 233n100

Preciado, Paul B., 76, 97, 211n54; *Le Manifeste contra-sexuel*, 86; pioneering role of, 12, 77

Prémare, Alix de, 31

Prémare, Guillaume de, 19, 31

Pride de Nuit ("night pride" march), 107, 108

Pride parades. *See* Gay Pride

Prieur, Charlotte, 92, 98, 100, 215n118, 216nn127–28

primer on equality (*Les ABCD de l'Égalité*), opposition to, 17–18, 66–67, 207n219

Printemps Français (French Spring), 11, 31, 40, 41, 65, 67, 111

Programme de Recherche et d'Enseignement des SAvoirs sur le GEnre (PRESAGE), 111

Prokhoris, Sabine, 211n60, 232n81

prostitution: and colonial law, 129; debate over, 46; and gay identity in Thailand, 133; police investigations of, in port zones, 149, 150

Protestant organizations, and opposition to gay marriage, 38

Proust, Marcel, 214n99; *Contre Sainte Beuve*, 58

Provencher, Denis, 214n100

provisional representation, 189

Pruvost, Geneviève, 92

psychoanalysis, 15, 85, 91, 92, 135, 159, 171, 241n223

Puar, Jasbir, 14, 120, 221n49, 222n53, 222nn55–57, 226nn121–24; on homonationalism, 121–25; on intersectionality, 137–38

publishers, strategy of, 12

Pugh, Daniel, 235n137

purity, paradox involving, 65

Quebec, queer theory initiatives undertaken in, 98

"queer": associating, with LGBT culture, 12; avoiding defining, 86; Butler on, 142; changeability of, 142; depoliticization of, 84; distortion in meaning of, 8; as either utopian or dystopian, 95; first usages of, 79; vs. "gay," 77, 139; increasing use of, 12, 77, 81, 93, 134, 185; interchanging "gay" with, 81; lack of suitable translation for, 83; vs. "LGBT," 81, 139; link between homosexuality and, 214n98; meaning of, in English, 95, 214n98; more abrasive term used instead of, 105; partially circumscribing, 82, 83, 84; reappropriation of, as an epithet, 80; reiterated use of, effects of, analysis of, 78, 112; trademarking, 94; unclear meaning of, 95; used as an euphemism, 93–96; used in activism, 101, 108, 142

queer child, figure of, 65–66

queer children, generation of, defining, 100. *See also* Les Tordu(e)s (Bent); Queer Week

queer community, global, desire for, 107

queer culture, drawing a distinction between gay and, 85–86

queer database, 81

Queer Days, 92

Queer Factory, 83

queer festivals, 99
Queer Food for Love, 73, 163
Queeristan festival, 99
queer movements: connection between
    LGBT movements and, 81–82; contro-
    versial debate among, 13; criticism of,
    and the response to HIV/AIDS, 84; rise
    of, 78, 97. *See also* Les Tordu(e)s (Bent);
    Queer Week
Queermunard, 82
Queer Nation, 81, 142
queer politics, Foucault on, 79
queer propaganda, perceived, 2
queer squats, 82
queer studies: avoiding defining, 86; ex-
    amining, in relation to gay and lesbian
    studies, 12, 86, 139–40, 141–42; fear of
    the ordinary in, 14; and feminist stud-
    ies, 140; more recent, and availability
    of translations, 100; Vatican reports
    condemning, 11
queer subject, agenda of, 140
Queers United in Support of Political
    Prisoners, 81
queer theatricality, specter of, 147, 164,
    165–66
queer theory, 209n18; approach to, 9; appro-
    priation of, 114; arrival of, in France, 2,
    12, 77, 81, 87, 143, 185; contextual meaning
    of, continually redefining, 13; as a decon-
    struction, 2, 183–84; disinformation on,
    22, 24; examining, in relation to gay and
    lesbian studies, 139, 141–42; and femi-
    nism, as threat to heterosexual romantic
    relationships, 69, 165; in general, 1;
    globalization of, relativizing, 98–99; het-
    erotopic use of, 100, 101–11; initial spread
    of, in France, 81; intellectual cleavages in,
    84–92; link between ACT UP's methods
    and, 83–84; mapping, reason for avoid-
    ing, 76; origins of, 1–2, 13, 75, 77, 78–80,
    81, 87, 134, 143, 210n23; as a point of refer-
    ence, 8; reaction to, basis of, 10; simulta-
    neously feared and desired, 171; spread
    of, to other countries, 98–99; use of the
    term, clarifying, 8; waves of, idea of, 134
queertopias, 96–101
Queeruption, 99
queer venues and activities, fleeting nature
    of, 100

queer waves, 134-136
Queer Week (La Semaine des Genres et
    Sexualités), 13, 78, 101, 108–12, 217n154
Quintana, Nico Sifra, 203n159

race: essentialist understanding of, by in-
    digenous party, 223n86; interpretive
    grid of, 135; and intersectionality, 130,
    136, 137; sexualization of, 134
Rachilde (novelist), 235n126
racial boundaries: crossing of, attentiveness
    to, 80; upholding, of the nation, 157
racialized minorities: and economic is-
    sues, 122, 123; and establishing a private
    sphere, 122; and homonormativity, 121;
    Inter-LGBT poster and, 116
racializing sexuality, 60–61, 121, 122–23,
    134–36, 137
racial purity, 65
racial stereotypes, 59
racism, 202n141; in Berlin Pride, Butler in
    protest of, 115, 118–19; and categorizing
    sexual minorities, 11; class, 79; directed
    at Christiane Taubira, 11, 59–60, 63–64;
    and homonationalism, 14, 119, 124; in
    homophobia and anti-Semitism, 58; im-
    brication of, and sexual stereotypes, 129;
    in the media, 63; multiple identities and,
    79; organization fighting, 221n39; and
    performativity, 98; and stigmatization,
    126; zaps in opposition to, 103
racist drift, 126
Radical-Socialist Party, 151
Radicaux de Gauche. *See* Parti Radical de
    Gauche
radio: access to, 19; *Pédérama* program,
    126, 222n69; Radio Libertaire, 102, 126;
    Radio Notre-Dame, 38
Rahman, Momin, 114
Rainbow Attitude (trade show), 103–4
Rassemblement pour la République (RPR),
    157
Ratzinger, Joseph. *See* Benedict XVI
Rault, Wilfried, 241n6
Rawls, John, 189
Raynaud, Philippe, 242n10
reactionary movements, 1, 40–43, 137, 155,
    157. *See also* far-right movements
Reboul, Marcel, 153
Reddy, Chandan, 210n29

reeducation, 65, 70, 73

relations between the sexes, deconstruction of, perceived as a threat, 76

religious conviction: centrality of, in opposition to gay marriage and gender theory, 37–40; in Manif pour Tous, 28

religious minorities, stigmatization of, 119

religious networks, 27, 40, 197n58, 232n75

religious purity, 65

Rémès, Erik, 83, 84, 172

Renaissance (Catholic group), 103

Renard, Antoine, 27

Renon, Alain, 199n95

reparation, forms of, collective memory and, 61, 170

repentance and debt: fear of, 60, 61; going beyond, purpose of, 61–62

representation, 144, 146, 148, 179–80, 181–82, 186, 189

reproduction: human, basis for, 164; self-, idea of, fear over, 2, 172; sexual, psychoanalysis involving, misuse of, 171, 172; social, 177

reproductive rights, 23

reproductive techniques: artificial, model of, 185; rhetorical issues involving, 19, 21. *See also* medically assisted procreation

Restauration Nationale, 36

Rétif, Sophie, 28, 197n55

retour sur soi (turning back on oneself), 175

Reucher, Tom, 233n89

Révenin, Régis, 90, 212n80, 228n20

Rifkin, Adrian, 90, 212n81

right-wing rhetoric, deconstruction of, 85. *See also* far-right movements

Riley, Denise, 78–79, 112, 209n18, 218n165

Robcis, Camille, 85, 194n18, 211n48, 231–32nn67–68, 232n71; *The Law of Kinship*, 156

Robichon, Suzette, 96, 226n132, 236n147

Rodrigue, Aron, 228n13

Roger, Philippe, 218n2

Rokvan, Axel, 31

role reversal, 11, 152, 235n126

roles: desire to describe identities and, classification system arising from, 78; interchangeable and unique, 188; male/female, construction of, as mutually exclusive, challenge to, 167, 235n126. *See also* gender roles

Rosenthal, Josh, 203n159

Ross, Susan A., 21, 194n16

Rossignol, Laurence, 18–19

Roucher, Jean, 45

Roux, Sébastien, 133, 224n98

Royal, Ségolène, 46, 161

royalist movement, 36

Rubin, Gayle, 76, 79, 91, 135; "Marché au sexe" ("Sexual Traffic"), 91; "Thinking Sex," 92

RuPaul, 101

Rupnik, Jacques, 192n22

Russia, spread of Manif pour Tous to, 57

Sachs, Maurice, 152

Sadie (artist), 100

Saghiyeh, Nizar, 129, 223n79

Saïd, Edward, 219n4

Salamon, Gayle, 235n125

Salins, Ghislain de, 109

same-sex couples, key issues involving. *See* gay adoption; gay marriage; gay parenthood

Sanos, Sandrine, 89, 154, 230n44, 231n51, 231n52, 239n186

Sarah, Robert, 24

Sarajevo party, 85

Sarkozy, Nicolas, 126; on civil unions, 40, 162; on the family and marriage for all, 200n111; and immigration, 146; opposition to gay adoption, 161; and opposition to gay marriage, 40, 72, 161, 194n10; reelection loss of, effect of, on the UMP party, 43–44

Sartre, Jean-Paul, 230n42, 231n48; "Qu'est-ce qu'un collaborateur?" (What Is a Collaborator?), 153, 154

Sassen, Saskia, 219n13

Sawicki, Frédéric, 161, 232n72, 233n93

Schaffauser, Thierry, 110

Schiappa, Edward, 191n9

Schneebaum, Alyssa, 203n159

scholarly/academic events. *See* seminars; symposiums

schools: Catholic, state supervision of, 1; curricula/textbooks in, content of, 1, 2, 11, 17–18, 20, 25–26, 57, 63, 64, 66–67, 69, 71, 76, 193n4, 193n6, 207n219; focus on, by opponents of gender theory, 66–70; and immigrant cultures, 68; perceived purpose of, 69, 70; propagation of homosexuality through, fear of, 2; public, education bills establishing, 179; secular, mistrust of, history of, 66; skirt day in, 11, 67–68; wearing of headscarves in, controversy over, 68

Schooyans, Michel, 23–24, 195n36; *The Gospel Confronting World Disorder*, 24; *The Hidden Face of the United Nations*, 24

Schuck, Peter H., 193n31

Schulteis, Franz, 237n162

Sciamma, Céline, 76; *Tomboy*, 11, 65–66, 110

Sciences Po: described, 217n152; gender-studies program at, 111; Queer Week at, 13, 78, 101, 108–12, 217n154; "Sexual Identity in Question" course at, 217n153

scopic, defining, 241n223

Scott, Joan W., 7, 8, 76, 78–79, 192n24, 201n125, 209n17, 209n18, 241n8, 242n13

Scout movement, 32, 202n141

Seckinelgin, Hakan, 223n76

second queer wave, 134–36

secret societies, 10, 145, 149

secularism, 21, 24, 27, 37, 66, 69, 116, 120, 146, 162

Sedgwick, Eve Kosofsky, 12, 80, 143, 145, 176, 198n82, 209nn11–12, 209n23, 214n99, 228n2, 228nn7–8, 237n156, 239n198; *Billy Budd*, 134, 170–71; "Making Queer Meanings," 77; *The Weather in Proust*, 77

Seidman, Steven, 232n70

self-definition, language of, coming out and, 225n100

self-determination, 24, 73, 97, 117, 160–61

self-identification: modes of, complex weave of, 133–34; as queer, 105, 108

self-reproduction, idea of, fear over, 2, 172

seminars: awarding credit for attending, 99; boycotting of, 14; "Current Sexual Affairs" organized by Fassin, Feher and Tort, 84, 85, 89, 90; focus of, in terms of network of guests, 98; "Fuck My Brain" launched by Bourcier, 90; on "Geography of Sexualities," 216n127; organized by Zoo working group, 85–86; purpose of, 12; Queer Week as a break from traditional, 110; role of,

in the emergence of queer theory as a movement, 77, 82–83; run by Cixous, 213n89; run by Scott on gender, 209n18; "The Sociology of Homosexualities" organized by Gaspard and Eribon, 3, 88–89, 90, 101, 105–6, 212n67; "The Uses of Queer Theories: Norms, Sexualities, Power," 92. *See also* symposiums; workshops

Sénat, 28, 30, 39, 41, 46, 197n64, 205n195

Sens Commun (Common Sense), 45

serial collectives, 236n139

Serrano, Andres, *Piss Christ*, 27

Serres, Michel, 84

Servan-Schreiber, Claude, 42, 201n124

Sève, Bernard, 192n25

several personal statuses, simultaneously holding, 189

sex: and gender, notions of, 22, 78–79; human reproduction and, 164; notion of difference as crucial to, fixation on, 164. *See also* biological sex; grammatical sex

sex change, 5, 160

sex education, 25, 146, 193n4

sexism, 106, 118; in homophobia and anti-Semitism, 58, 59; multiple identities and, 79; protest against, 11, 67–68; school curriculum addressing, opposition to, 17–18, 20, 207n219

sex objects, play on, 165

Sextoy (queer squat), 82

sexual boundaries, upholding, of the nation, 157

sexual categories: adopting, in the name of national identity, 132; critique of dominant, reflection of, 113; de facto, questioning, 131; essentialization of, 14, 106, 124, 137, 185; performative power of, deconstructing, 80; queer studies of, and availability of translations, 100; reessentialization of, 14

sexual citizenship, 123

sexual concord, linking, to social concord, 14

sexual cultures: and contamination, 171; multiple, 81

sexual democracy, 115–16

sexual development, halted, 66, 76, 238n165

sexual difference: absence of, specter of,

157–63; acknowledging, relationship informed by, 94, 235n125; arguments pinned on, 42–43, 54, 159, 164–65, 184, 202–3n153; Catholic theologian on gender theory and, 23; citizenship moored in, 156, 164; as a condition of parenthood, notion of, bioethical reforms and, 52; denial/rejection of, 161, 171–72, 175, 202n153; distinct, loss of, opposition to, 65–66, 69, 110, 160, 164, 165; excess of, fear of secession through, 164; indifference to, 164; and language, 166; language and Arabic expression of, 133–34; linking national identity to, 164, 165; queer theatricality and, 164–66; queer theory criticized for school curricula's approach to, 69; reification of, mode of thought based on, 6; relativization of, 20, 184; seminar questioning, 88; Socialist Party and beliefs about, 147–48; transfiguration of, 15
sexual dissymmetry, model of seductiveness based on, 164–65
sexual freedom: and Arab homoerotic practices, 127; Eribon on, 121; unbridled, idea of, 84; zone of, establishing, and yet denying, 122
sexual harassment, 185
sexual identities, 227n143; disparities in production of, analysis of, absence of, 126; as fixed political categories, notion of, challenge to, 145; and national identities, 221n43; and nationalism, 124; in school curricula, 25. *See also* multiple identities
sexual imperialism, 131
sexualist international, betrayal by, fear of, 14, 58–59
sexuality, 192n21; assigning, to either private or public spheres, 25, 122; capitalist accumulation and its effects on, 98; Catholic Church/Vatican on, 20, 21, 22; as a challenge to national order, 14; as comedy, 165; conservatism and, 6–7; culturalist views of, deconstructing, 14; fascination with, 7; globalization of, 13, 14, 114–15, 125–34, 224n94; hierarchy of, reproducing, 48; and identity, 9; as an important vector of anticommunitari-

anism, 146, 148; interwoven with nation and community, 9, 13, 145–46; legal statutes on, convergence of, 114; links between sense of belonging and, 115; and nationalism, connection between, 14, 115–21, 220n29, 221n43; organizing, according to a principle of difference, issue with, 164; pathologizing, 10, 75, 90, 141, 145, 171; political stakes of, seminar contextualizing, 85; presentation of, in school curricula, 25, 70, 193n4; racialization of, 60–61, 121, 122–23, 134–36, 137; reprivatization of, 136; research on, opposition to, 20; using "queer" to acknowledge, without a more explicit reference, 95; Western and non-Western, paradox involving construction of, 224n94
sexual markers, lack of, condemnation of, 164
sexual nationalism, 220n29
sexual networks, 169
sexual orientation: Arab homoerotic practices previously not linked to, 127; as a basis for marginalization, 158; focus in the marriage debate extending from, to gender, 3–6; official education bulletin's mention of, opposition to, 25; and political affiliation, 117, 121; United Nation's declaration on, 24
sexual pleasure, 147, 165, 166, 171
sexual-political roots, function of, 140
sexual practices: multiple, 81; and nationalism, 124; and prevalence of AIDS, 238n170; racialization of, 123
sexual purity, 12, 65
sexual reproduction, psychoanalysis involving, misuse of, 171, 172
sexual stereotypes, 25, 93–94, 129, 152
sexual venues, pinkwashing and, 133
sexual violence, 120
Sherry, Michael S., 149, 228n17
Sidéris, Georges, 85
silent and neglected majority, claim as, 40, 41
silent interraciality, 122
skinheads, 30
"skirt day" event, 11, 67–68
Slama, Serge, 228n6
slavery, threat of, 56

slavery law, 11, 47, 60, 61

"slippery slope" idea, 19, 43

slogans: in alternative Gay Pride events, 105, 107, 108; in defense of gay marriage and adoption, 71–72; of Inter-LGBT, objections to, 116; to oppose gay marriage, 17, 30, 31, 40–41, 42, 50, 54, 61; to protest against gender theory in schools, 63; and usage of "queer," 95

Social Catholicism, effect of, 156

social concord, linking, to sexual concord, 14

socialism, 23

Socialist Party/government, 228n12; accelerating passage of the Taubira Act, 30, 46; advisory group close to, 154; and anticommunitarianism, 15, 156, 157–59, 162; backtracking by, to appease anti-gay-marriage forces, 1, 17, 18, 29, 108, 158; and beliefs about sexual difference, 147–48; and civil unions, 3, 158; committing to gay marriage, 3, 72, 158; conservative drift within, 117, 161; feminist groups close to, 68; and Gay Pride events, 108; on homosexual parenthood, 3; indecision over the Taubira Act, attacks targeting, 71–72; on individualism, 177; on medically assisted procreation, 18, 158; racist drift of LGBT movements close to, 126; and reliance on family experts for consultation, 158–61; strategy of, in electoral accession to power, 14–15, 155–56, 157; universalist rhetoric of, 46, 47, 48

social media: internationalization of, 114; queer venues and activities sustained by, 100; Queer Week and, 111; racist imagery posted on, 64; use of, by opponents of gay marriage, 14, 19; use of, by opponents of gender theory, 58

social movements: fragmented, 73; and institutions, media as an interface between, 202n145; mass, common problem for, 31; misconception about, 43; monitoring of, 156; new, view of, 187; sex-based, emergence of, in postcolonial nations, 227n143

social networks, 31, 32, 36, 67, 73, 92, 92–93, 103, 154

social norms, deconstructing, in language, 8

social order, perceived threat to, 24

social reproduction, 177

social rights, 23

social-welfare issues, failing to present the Taubira Act in terms of economic and, effect of, 11, 48–52

Sociovision Institute, 37

sodomy, 121–22, 123, 131, 134, 149, 195n26

songs: *Let My People Go*, 42; "Monocle et col dur" and "Monsieur Vénus," 110; satirical, in the early 1900s, 152

Soral, Alain, 68–69

SOS Racisme, 41

Soukaz, Lionel, 88

South Africa, equality in, LGBT cultures and, 236n140

sovereignty, 9–10, 147, 149, 173, 174, 179, 180, 181

Spain: and marriage laws, 3, 56–57, 72; presence of queer theory in, 99

"spectacle of the closet," 94

Spivak, Gayatri Chakravorty, 241n1, 241nn220–21

Stainville, Raphaël, 196n52, 199n96

Stalinist politics, 33

Stasiska, Agata, 215n122

Stavisky Affair, 37

Stein, Gertrude, 154

stepparents, legal status of, 1, 18

stereotypes: in anti-Semitism and homophobia, 58, 152; of Arab boys, 130; class, 79, 93–94; gay, 48, 93–94; gender, deconstruction of, objections to, 160; and gender roles, addressing, in school, 18; Orientalist, 128; racial, 59; sexual, 25, 93–94, 129, 152; shedding light on, 221n40; that associates the law with privilege, 137

Stevens, Jacqueline, 164, 234nn113–14

stigmatization, 15, 28, 48, 54, 119, 126, 127, 132, 162, 164, 168, 178

Stille, Alexander, 191n1

Stockton, Katherine Bond, 65–66, 206n202

Stolk, Robert, 240n213

Stoller, Robert, 78, 209n15

Stonewall riot, allusions to, 108

straight mind: defined, 6; persistence of, 6, 184

STRASS (sex worker's union), 110

street art, 110

student and youth movements: participation of, in opposing gay marriage, 29, 31–37; at Sciences Po, related to gender and sexuality, 13, 78, 217n154
subjectification, conceptualizing, 69, 80–81, 87, 124, 133, 143, 155, 163, 168, 176, 180
subjectivity, 75, 79–80, 97, 127, 138, 176, 227n143, 235n125
Surkis, Judith, 228n6, 229n34
surrogate citizenship, 123
surrogate pregnancy: opposition to, 5, 17, 18, 19, 30, 43, 54–56, 73, 161, 185; support for, demonstrating, 72
Switzerland, gay anarchist event in, 82
Symond, John Addington, 229n24
symposiums: attack on gender theory at, using anti-Semitic rhetoric, 205n186; boycotting of, 14; on Eribon's work, 91; first of major, called/organized by Eribon, 77, 87, 90; and homonationalism, 120–21; on "Homosexualities in the Plural," 141; international, organized by Bourcier and Robichon, 96; on "Let's Queer Art History," 101; on *Mapping Desire* (Bell & Valentine), 216n127; organized following Eribon & Gaspard's final 2004 seminar, 89; on "Sexual Nationalisms," 14, 120; on "Transgenders: New Identities and Visibilities," 90. *See also* seminars; workshops

Tackett, Timothy, 228n14
Taïa, Abdellah, 131, 224n88
Tamagne, Florence, 10, 89, 193n33, 204n182, 229n24, 230n37
Tartakowsky, Danielle, 193n1, 196n50, 199n89
Taubira, Christiane: directive signed by, on nationality, 54; objectionable poster presented to, 116; racism directed at, 11, 59–60, 63–64, 65; resignation of, 202n151; and the slavery law, 11, 47, 60; sponsorship of the Taubira Act by, 1, 47
Taubira Act ("marriage for all"), 173, 184, 196n44, 196n52, 197n54, 197n58, 198n83, 200n111; bilateral conventions with other countries and, 5; Christianity vs. Islam and capability for change, 221n42; claim about the origin of, 1–2, 4, 57;

constitutionality of, 2–3; consultation on, prior to passage, 46, 158–61; continued debate following passage of, 1, 6, 19, 43, 101, 159, 188; contrast in arguments for and against, 73, 125; failing to employ economic arguments for, effect of, 11, 48, 49, 50, 72, 146; and homonationalism, 124–25; impact of, on LGBT individuals, 6; indecision over clauses of, demonstrators attacking, 71–72; inequalities maintained and created by, 4, 5, 47–48; legal recognition through, effects of, 168, 176, 179, 185; limiting the scope of, 17, 29; and the majority's universalist aspirations, 46–48; opposition to, 1, 6, 10, 14, 19, 20, 25, 27–36, 37, 38–45, 47, 49–51, 52, 54, 59, 60–62, 70, 72, 73, 92, 93, 124–25, 155, 158, 167, 176, 186, 194n10; passage of, 1, 2, 30, 46, 47, 48, 179, 197n64; political economy of, 48–52; political emotions surrounding, 70–73; and the principle of equality, 47; promotion of, 70–71, 72, 125, 176–77, 192n14; real stakes behind, 61–62; and the slavery law, linkage between, 60, 61; stated purpose of, 47; temporal perspective of, 6; viewed as a "slippery slope," 19, 54
taxation, 37, 189
Taylor, Alex, 94
Tcheng, Laurence, 28
Tea Party, 37
television (TV): access to, 19; Arte TV channel, 217n154; Butler's work included in documentary on, 217n154; Canal+ channel, 93; coming out on, 214n100; Delarue's shows, 103; diversity on, approach to, 94–95; Jimmy channel, 214n96; *Le Set*, 94; *Loft Story* (reality show), 214n100; *The L Word*, 94; M6 channel, 214n100; marketing strategy on, 94, 95; Pink TV channel, 94, 110; *Queer as Folk*, 93, 108, 214n96; *Queer Eye for the Straight Guy* adapted as *Queer, cinq experts dans le vent*, 12, 93–94, 214n96; and Queer Week, 110; rejection of feminization developed on, 69; satirical, targeting opponents of gay marriage, 70; use of the word "queer" on, 12, 77–78, 93–95

temporality, 121
Terrenoir, Vincent, 27
territorial relationships, normal, displacing, 104
Tessier, Gilles, 214n102
Tevanian, Pierre, 221n40
textual pleasure, 165, 166
Thailand, gay identity in, 133
theatricality, queer, specter of, 147, 164, 165–66
theatrical play, *Les Yeux bleus, Cheveux noirs* (Blue Eyes, Black Hair), 174
theatrical workshop, 83
theory: fantasies over, influence of, 74; use of the term, clarifying, 8. *See also* French theory; gender theory; queer theory
Théry, Irène, 158, 159, 160, 176, 232n74, 232nn77–78, 240n199, 240n201
Thévenin, Patrick, 218n159
Thévenot, Laurent, 193n27
Third Republic, 150–51, 156, 231n65
Thollot, Marie-José, 27
Thomas, Clarence, 85
Thomas, Maud-Yeuse, 85, 110; *Transyclopédie*, 92
Thomas Aquinas, Saint, 22, 195n26
Thoreson, Ryan, 219n7
Timmerman, Claude, 205n186
Tiphaine (speaker from STRASS), 110
Tissot, Sylvie, 169, 221n40, 236n141
Toinet, Marie-France, 192n22
tolerance, issue of, 22, 123
Tort, Michel, 213n85, 234n112; seminar run by Fassin, Feher, and, 84, 85, 89, 90
totalitarianism, gender theory compared to, 23
tourism, 114, 119, 132, 133
Trachman, Mathieu, 110, 241n7
tradition, construction of, 7
traditional family: Catholic Church/Vatican on, 22; marker of, 52; perceived threat to, 13, 19, 20, 22, 23–24, 36, 38, 40, 57, 60, 149, 171–72, 200n111, 202–3n153, 237n162, 237–38n163; symbolic meaning of, 184
transcultural flows, historical, 114–15
transgender identity, 73, 80, 90, 98, 116, 160–61, 176
trans identities, 66, 92, 98, 103, 116–17, 160, 164

translated works: promotion of, 12, 86; queer, sufficiency of content in, addressing, 184. *See also specific authors*
translation: authenticity and, 113; cultural, insistence on, 143, 227n142; decisions in, over using the term "gay" and "queer," 77; direct interaction with American queer theory without, 100; of *dispositif*, assemblage and, issue with, 226n124; meaning lost in, example of, 226n129; overcoming the problem of, linguistic strategy for, 107; performing and, 165–66; "propagation" as choice of, reason for, 191n3; queer echoes in, 166; suitable, lack of, for "queer," 83; tensions arising over, 89–90
trans movement, 90
transpédégouine/transpdgouine (transfagdyke), preference for using, 105, 106–7, 216–17n145
transphobia, 103, 121, 126, 160
transsexuality, 3–4, 5, 10, 20, 24, 40, 66, 75, 142, 164, 165, 188
Traub, Valérie, 129, 222n72, 223n80
Treat, John, 224n99
Trémolet de Villers, Vincent, 196n52, 199n96
Tribunal de Grande Instance (civil county court), 3, 4, 160, 229n23
Tricou, Josselin, 194n11
"Trojan horse" metaphor, 23, 96. *See also* enemy within
Tsvetaeva, Marina, 236n146; *Mon Frère féminin* (My Feminine Brother), 169
Tucker, Andrew, 216n127, 236n140
Tufft, Ben, 195n28
Turcotte, Louise, 97, 215n112

Ukraine, Femen feminist group from, 11
unification, 69, 158, 159, 179
uniform equality, 12
Union des Bouddhistes de France, 39
Union des Organisations Islamiques de France (Union of French Islamic Organizations; UOIF), 38–39
Union Nationale Inter-Universitaire (UNI), 29, 31
Union pour un Mouvement Populaire (UMP), 26, 31, 43–44, 45, 71, 72, 117, 161, 200n111

United Kingdom: and marriage laws, 56–57; and openly gay politicians, 147; research project in, 90
United Nations (UN), 21, 24
United Russia, 57
United States, 192n14; community model in, view of, 14, 77, 87; comparative sociology in, impact of, 9; court rulings in, 121–22, 123; culture of, critical analysis of, fueling, 8; emergence of queer theory in, 77, 78–80, 81, 83, 87, 97, 98, 99, 134; and expansionism, 123; vs. France, 14, 37, 57–58, 87, 164–65, 183; gay community in, 169; gay identity in, 131; gay weddings in, performance of, 3; gender theory in, 75–76; and gentrification, 168; ideologies from, 1, 12, 13, 57, 58, 75, 110, 111, 143, 163, 185; immigration in, 210n29; label attached to French intellectuals in, 8; McCarthyism in, 149; and national identity, 2, 8, 37; and nationalism, 123; neoliberalism in, 8, 80; opposition to gay marriage in, 37, 59; queer academic life remaining oriented toward, 98, 99; United Nation's declaration signed by, 24; views toward/conceptualizations of, 2, 7, 10, 13, 14, 20, 57, 87, 96, 113, 143, 147, 149, 162, 165, 184, 205n195
universalism, 46–48, 95, 162, 186
Université de Lausanne, 141
Université de Paris I (Panthéon-Sorbonne), 84, 92, 99, 216n127
Université de Paris IV (Paris-Sorbonne), 92
Université de Paris VIII (Saint-Denis), 111
Universités d'Été Euroméditerranéennes sur les Homosexualités (Euromediterranean Summer University on Homosexualities, UEEH), 82–83, 163
University of Amsterdam, 14, 120
University of California, Berkeley, 87
University of California, Santa Cruz, 134, 209n18
University of Edinburgh, 90
University of Michigan at Ann Arbor, 39
urban culture, 168
US Supreme Court, 121–22, 123
utopia, 65, 95, 96, 100, 168

Valensise, Cecilia, 218n155
Vallaud-Belkacem, Najat, 18, 40, 64–65
Valls, Manuel, 18, 37, 52, 56, 160, 202n151
Vanneste, Christian, 40
Vatican. See Catholic Church/Vatican
Veyne, Paul, 3
Vichy regime, 118, 127, 129, 149, 150, 151, 197n54, 229n31
victimization, appropriating, as a strategy, 7, 41
Vidal, Jérôme, 212n75
Vigi Gender, 67
vigils, 31–32, 44
Villa, Paula-Irene, 204n172
Villepin, Dominique de, 3
Villers-Cotterêts decree, 179
Villiers, Philippe de, 27, 44
Vingt-Trois, André, 38
Virgili, Fabrice, 229n33
visibility, 80, 81, 82, 100, 103, 107, 109, 128, 133
voguing workshop, 110

Wahnich, Stéphane, 220n32
Warner, Michael, 122, 222n52, 227n146; Fear of a Queer Planet, 143
Wauquiez, Laurent, 44
Weston, Kath, 168, 236n144
Wideman, John Edgar, 222n54, 240n211
Wiesnerová, Vendula (Esteban), 215n123
Wilde, Oscar, 230–31n45
Williamson, Jeffrey G., 219n12
Wilson, James Q., 193n31
Winter, Jean-Pierre, 159
Wittig, Monique, 79, 87, 135, 192n17, 214n107; La Pensée straight, 86; "The Mark of Gender," 96
Wojtyla, Karol. See John Paul II
women-only groups: feminist, 102, 103, 105; lesbian, 73, 105
women's liberation movement: French (Mouvement de Libération des Femmes), 96, 97; wearing pants identified with, 68. See also feminism
women's rights, Vatican's perception of, 23
women's studies, 75
Wood, Andrea, 219n9
workshops: on "Gender(s) and Sexuality(ies)" in Belgium, 98; introductory, on notion

of queer titled "Screw Your Gender,"
83; pansexual, idea of, issues raised by,
83; during Queer Week, 110, 111; role of,
in the emergence of queer theory as a
movement, 77; theatrical, titled "Queer
Academy," 83; unofficial, by Zoo, 99. *See
also* seminars; symposiums
World Conference on Women: fourth, in
Beijing, 11, 20, 21, 23; third, in Nairobi,
23
World Wide Web, language of, 165, 166
World Youth Days, 32, 39
Wouters, Cas, 240n213
Wright, Vincent, 232n69
Wurst, Conchita, 70

xenophobia, 146, 154–55

Yacine, Tassadit, 224n89
Young, Madison, 100
youth corruption: fantasy of betrayal and,
58; fear of, 19; gay parenthood and,

54; gender theory and, 62, 65, 66; as a
perceived threat, 2, 40; protection from,
postwar period marked by, 151; queer
theory and, 69
youth movements. *See* student and youth
movements

Zabus, Chantal, 90
Zaganiaris, Jean, 92, 213n94
Zald, Mayer N., 198n70
zaps (direct action), 31–33, 83, 89–90, 103
Zay, Jean, 152
Zemmour, Éric, 68–69, 165, 234n117
Zéro, Karl, 31, 197n66
Zivi, Karen, 208n240
Zobel, Clemens, 223n86
Zoberman, Pierre, 216n131
Zone Books (publishing house), 85
Zoo (working group), 85–86, 88, 99, 105–6,
106, 139
Zralos, Samuel, 211n57
Zucker-Rouvillois, Élisabeth, 208n232